D0844818

OMAHA
TRIBAL MYTHS
AND
TRICKSTER TALES

OMAHA
TRIBAL MYTHS
AND
TRICKSTER TALES

Roger L. Welsch

SAGE BOOKS

SWALLOW PRESS
CHICAGO

Library of Congress Cataloging in Publication Data

Welsch, Roger L.
  Omaha Tribal myths and trickster tales.

  Bibliography: p.
  Includes index.
  1. Omaha Indians—Legends. 2. Indians of North
America—Nebraska—Legends. 3. Trickster.
I. Title.
E99.04W44   398.2'08997   80-22636
ISBN 0-8040-0700-4

Sage/Swallow Press Books are published by
Ohio University Press
Athens, Ohio

For my Omaha friends and relatives—

CONTENTS

INTRODUCTION

Life in the eighteenth-century Omaha-Ponca village was good. The lush Missouri River bottomlands provided fine harvests and ample game. The annual winter buffalo hunts, when hunting parties left the comforts of the earth-lodge village in the valley for the skin tipi encampments on the harsh, open plains, were certainly a time of difficult conditions. But here again the harvest was rich, and the weeks of hard work and discomfort were rewarded with the increased comfort brought to the permanent lodges with the bundles of dried meat and the warm buffalo hides.

A system of paths and trails connected the scores of villages strung along the Missouri Valley, and the strength of the tribe offered security from the Dakota to the north and Pawnee to the west.

In short, the Omaha and Ponca—the two are very closely related and speak virtually the same language—enjoyed the best of both worlds: the woodland and the plains.

The Omaha had come to their country about 1650, having migrated across present-day Missouri and Iowa. They occupied what is now the northeastern quarter of the state of Nebraska (from Omaha words meaning "broad water," after the Platte River which bisects the state). The Omaha are related linguistically and culturally with the Quapaw, Osage, and Kansas to the south, and it was from this geographical relationship that they derive their name "Omaha," originally Maha, "the people upstream."

The Ponca, as stated, are more closely related to the Omaha, and can be treated as members of the same cultural unit. Estimates of when the two tribes separated range from "1390 to the middle of the seventeenth century to 'rather late.' "[1] But the histories of the two coincide until the last century, and the tales and language of the two tribes can be viewed as parts of a single culture. Therefore, while a few of the stories in this collection are from Ponca sources, they can be regarded as closely related to or identical to Omaha tales.

Omaha accounts of their first encounter with the white invader vary, but then so did the nature of the first encounters. Alice Fletcher provides the following account:

"One day the people discovered white objects on the waters, and they knew not what to make of them. The white objects floated toward the shores. The people were frightened. They abandoned their canoes, ran to the woods, climbed the trees, and watched. The white objects reached the shore, and men were seen getting out of them. The Indians watched the strange men, but did not speak or go near them. For several days they watched; then the strangers entered into the white objects and floated off. They left, however, a man—a leader, the Indians thought. He was in a starving condition. Seeing this, the Indians approached him, extending toward him a stalk of maize having ears on it, and bade him eat and live. He did eat, and expressed gratitude by signs. The Indians kept this man, treating him kindly, until his companions returned. Thus the white people became acquainted with the Omaha by means of one whom the latter had befriended. In return the white people gave the Indians implements of iron. It was in this way that we gained iron among us.

"From the story of this encounter and the fact that the Omaha are known historically to have traded at a fort near Lake Winnipeg, it is probable that the incident cited in the legend refers to some reconnoitering party of white adventurers, possibly of the Hudson Bay Company, one of whose number remained behind, and was later picked up or joined by the rest of the party."[2]

The Omaha not only met trappers exploring from the Winnipeg area but even, it appears, ventured to the northern outpost themselves:

"De l'Isles's map (1703) places the Omaha near the mouth of the Big Sioux. About 1737 a trading post was established near the southern end of Lake Winnipeg, where the Omaha are said to have traded; they have a tradition that 'long ago they visited a great lake to the far north and traded there with white men.' This post may have been Fort La Reine. It appears on Jeffery's map of 1762. Carver, who travelled in 1766, says that 'to this place the Mahahs, who inhabit a country 250 miles southwest, come also to trade with them; and bring great quantities of Indian corn, to exchange for knives, tomahawks, and other articles.' "[3]

French traders and trappers were certainly the Omaha's first white contacts. There is some speculation that Coronado's band ventured into southern Nebraska, but it is unlikely they encountered any Omaha or Ponca.

The French came to the Plains as visitors to a strange land. They honored Indian ways and frequently adopted them, at least while they were living among the Indians. They were therefore called *wache ukethi*, *ukethi* meaning "not strange," "one of us."

Another Omaha legend of the first encounter also provides a possible etymology for *wache*:

"The Omaha were camped in the timber, and one day a man heard pounding in the woods. He went to see what caused the strange noise and returned to camp in great fright. He said he had seen some sort of beast, his face covered with hair and his skin the color of the inner layer of the corn husk. This inner husk is called *wachoha*, and the Omaha name for white man, *wache*, is probably a corruption of this term."[4]

In short, these unlearned French wanderers deported themselves with sufficient diplomacy and sensitivity to be considered by the Omaha as one of their own people. Further evidence of this civility are the many French names left among the Omaha as a result of marriages between trapper-traders and Omaha' women: La Flesche, Sanssouci, Fontenelle, Cayou, Peppin, for example.

The Anglo-Americans, however, who came primarily as conquering soldiers and missionaries, were branded as *monki tonga* (*monki*—"knife"; *tonga*—"big"), "big knives," obviously because of the soldiers' sabers. Fletcher reports that old Omaha men told her this term did not originate among them but had been borrowed from some other tribe,[5] which of course does not detract from the accuracy or infamy of the label.

In 1804 Lewis and Clark met with the Omaha. In 1820 Fort Atkinson (now Fort Calhoun) was established on the western bank of the Missouri, well within Omaha lands and about ten miles north of the present site of the city of Omaha. The soldiers occupied themselves primarily with farming, but their liaison with Omaha women was considerably less honorable than those of the French had been. The fort was abandoned after only seven years of occupation, however.

The population of the Omaha tribe had fallen from 1,800 in 1650 to 300 after the smallpox epidemic of the late eighteenth century, then climbed slowly again to 600 in 1804 and 1,900 in 1829, but fell to 1,600 in 1843.[6]

In 1836 the Omaha saw their first steamship coming up the Missouri, the first of many thousands of such boats to carry supplies to northern forts and gold fields. Since the little boat, the *Antelope*, appeared to move by no visible means, the Omaha called it *mondewachube*, "mystery boat," a term Fletcher reports the Omaha were still using for steamboats sixty years later.[7]

The Mormons were forced from their homes in Illinois in 1846, and they settled in a camp just north of the present site of Omaha city. They had to prepare for the terror of a northern Plains winter with the few supplies they had managed to bring with them on their flight across Iowa and with whatever they could forage along the river or trade from the Omaha. The Mormons built the Plains' first sod houses, perhaps borrowing the idea from the great Omaha earth lodges.

Death's harvest during that winter among the Mormon camp was bountiful, as is still evidenced today by the Mormon cemetery in the Omaha suburb of Florence.

The Mormon camp, however, posed a problem for the Omaha, for a heavy and concentrated demand was being put on the timber and game, to the Omahas' distress. Although the problem was alleviated to some degree when the bulk of the Mormon camp moved on to the New Zion, Salt Lake City, more Mormons moved in to replace those who left. Then the Oregon Trail began to cause the same sorts of problems. Now, too, the city of Omaha was developing, and covetous eyes were being cast on Omaha lands.

The cultural integrity of the tribe was also under assault. As official governmental contacts were formalized with the tribe, "paper chiefs" were appointed arbitrarily by government agents. These chiefs were seldom the true spiritual or political leaders respected by the people; therefore, these chiefs, the government that dealt with them, and the decisions that came from their intercourse were viewed with contempt and derision, later, with fear.

The Omaha, like so many other Indian nations, were trapped by cultural misunderstandings. They simply had no concept of "ownership" of the land. Morton said of them that "they had no idea of exclusive possession of the soil on which they lived."[8] And Dorsey, normally the detached ethnographer, wrote with passion:

"Each tribe claimed a certain extent of territory as its own, for purposes of occupancy, cultivation, hunting, and fishing. But the right of a tribe to sell its land was something unheard of. Portions of the Omaha territory were sold because the people feared to refuse the white men. They consented just as a man would 'consent' to hand his purse to a highway robber who demanded his money or his life. Land is enduring, even after the death of all of a generation of Omahas; for the men of the next generation succeed and dwell on the land. Land is like water and wind, *wethiawathe*, 'what cannot be sold.' But horses, clothing, lodges, etc., soon perish, and these were the only things that they could give away, being personal property."[9]

So, in March of 1854, when the Omaha ceded their lands for a reservation (the kind of deal which could be summarized as "I'll give you your dime for your dollar"), they really could not grasp the implication of the arrangement. Even if it had been carefully explained, which it most assuredly was not, the Omaha could not have been considered to be understanding parties to the treaty.

The Omaha, like the Winnebago, were not altogether pleased with their reserved lands. Although the area around Macy ("*Ma*ha Agen*cy*") had always been a part of tribal land, it lay in the northernmost limits of their area, and they feared it was too close to the increasingly hostile Sioux country.

And with good reason. In 1854, just after the Omaha moved onto their new reservation, the Sioux attacked an Omaha buffalo-hunt party and killed a number, including Chief Fontenelle. At that time they removed to Bellevue to the south of the present site of Omaha until the next spring, when they were returned to the reservation.[10] The Sioux continued hostilities, of course, until the 1890s.

In 1857 Joseph La Flesche built the first Plains Indian frame house,[11] but earth lodges remained on the reservation until about the time of the First World War.

The Omaha ceded a large part of their reservation to the Winnebago tribe in 1865. The Winnebago are not native to the Plains but had fled to the Omaha down the Missouri after military harassment and resettlement on what the Winnebago found to be uninhabitable lands in the Dakota territory. Additional cessions were concluded in 1874 and twice in 1882, narrowing even further the geographical wealth of the Omaha tribe.

The concern of the tribe for its security was heightened in the 1870s when the Ponca were forced from their land into less desirable Indian Territory, Oklahoma. At that time the situation was so outrageously immoral that even a segment of the white population and press was outraged. The Ponca had been forced to march to the Indian Territory, but some walked back to bury a chief's dead son in Ponca soil. The government forced them to walk back again but only after the case had been taken to federal court and Judge Elmer Dundy had ruled that Indians are indeed persons,[12] doubtlessly to the outrage of some civilized whites!

Then the Omaha were the only remaining native Nebraska tribe with a reservation constituting a fragment of their original tribal holdings. One of the few positive results of this concentration has been the artificially high degree of cultural maintenance in the tribe.

Missionary schools, which had been initiated in 1846 at Bellevue by the Board of Foreign Missions of the Presbyterian Church and moved to the Macy vicinity in 1857, contributed to the cultural attack on the Omaha. Francis La Flesche, who suffered as much as any from the insensitivity of the white school staff, gives an example of the callous atmosphere:

"All the boys in our school were given English names, because their Indian names were difficult for the teachers to pronounce. Besides, the aboriginal names were considered by the missionaries as heathenish, and therefore should be obliterated. No less heathenish in their origin were the English substitutes, but the loss of their original meaning and significance through long usage had rendered them fit to continue as appellations for civilized folk. And so, in the place of Tae-noo-ga-wa-zhe, came Philip Sheridan; in that of Wa-pah-dae, Ulysses S. Grant; . . . and so on."[13] Imagine what cruel and mindless people these teachers must have been to substitute the names of Indian-murdering generals for the gentle Indian names! And La Flesche's later narrative indicates that while the missionaries were not ashamed to admit they could not pronounce the Indian names, they nonetheless demanded perfect elocution from their young wards.

Even though tribal hunting and warring did not completely stop until 1876, the principal assault on the Plains Indians' life had reduced that rich culture to a shambles of tantalizing remnants, cancerous innovations, and degrading oppression. It is to the immense credit of the Omaha people that in the face of their ruthless destruction they have maintained an astonishing amount of their cultural treasures and have in large degree accepted only with discrimination those segments of the surrounding, dominant society which are necessary or useful.

*   *   *

The tales of this collection were taken primarily from the massive collection of James Owen Dorsey, a missionary-ethnologist who worked among the Omaha late in the nineteenth century, one of the first scholars to have any contact whatever with the tribe. He collected from the Ponca from 1871 to 1873 and from the Omaha from 1878 to 1880. His work was published in a massive book entitled *The Çegiha Language* (1890). On the 800 folio-size pages were the stories retold here, as well as all manner of letters and notes in Ponca and Omaha. The texts of the tales appeared in the original, in an interlinear, literal translation, and then in an English translation, along with notes, particularly on grammatical anomalies.

The book has its problems. Alice Fletcher attacks Dorsey's use of the word *Çegiha* contending that it was never used to designate the tribe but was used only as a team title during games, and that Dorsey's translations can only be described as execrable. But Dorsey must be commended for the heroic task he undertook. Without him there would be no tales to retranslate.

Dorsey worked with several other tribes, too, and published books dealing with this field work. Further, I have used for annotation purposes his important 1885 book, *Omaha Sociology*.

In 1911 there appeared another ambitious study of the Omaha people, *The Omaha Tribe*, by Alice C. Fletcher and Francis La Flesche. It was published as a Bureau of American Ethnology study and consisted of 650 pages of precise and knowledgeable descriptions, along with photographs and drawings. I have drawn freely from this work in annotating and translating Dorsey's tales.

Alice Fletcher was born in 1838, and in 1881 went to work among the Omaha. She published many works on them and other tribes and gained special respect among the Omaha because of her sincerity and sympathy for the Indian way and the Indian plight. She was with the tribe during the decade when it underwent the most profound changes, and she was entrusted with many sacred Omaha materials, including medicine bundles and tales and songs.

Her coauthor was actually her principal informant. Francis La Flesche later went on to occupy many important federal positions and proved to be a real scholar, publishing books of his own on Indian culture. He earned a law degree from the National University in 1893, and was awarded an honorary doctorate by the University of Nebraska in 1926. He was, for Alice Fletcher, a remarkable and fortuitous combination of the Anglo-American scholar and the Plains Indian. He knew and remembered the ancient customs and concepts of his people and was at the same time capable of interpreting them suitably for academic investigation. La Flesche was also one of Dorsey's primary informants.

These collectors must be complimented on their difficult work. We are all grateful that they took on the demanding tasks of collecting the tales. They had to live and work under very difficult conditions, and yet their publications are quite sound.

However, the problems that inevitably arise from such field conditions must also be recognized. Alice Fletcher certainly encountered difficulty in obtaining sexually sensitive materials because she was woman working primarily with male informants. Dorsey, as a white man, certainly did not have total access to native concepts and materials, and his ecclesiastical position also diminished the amount of mythic and obscene materials imparted by his informants. La Flesche obviously was best equipped to elicit a broad range of materials, since he was both a social scientist and an Omaha, but his education and traffic with white scholars and politicians probably cast a suspicious light on him too.

Even for La Flesche the conditions for ethnographic documentation were difficult. Today's anthropologist uses the tape recorder and camera to record data more completely and less obtrusively, but Dorsey, Fletcher, and La Flesche had to transcribe laboriously by hand and describe in words whatever they heard and saw. Necessarily, then, their materials were sometimes incomplete. In addition to the inaccuracies incurred from the ethnologists' part in the recording process, it must be noted that informants frequently abbreviate texts or make mistakes in narrative when they must recite slowly or repeat items for purposes of transcription. It can be seen clearly in a few texts, where the informant refused to repeat, how little material could be transcribed on the first recitation.

In addition to her principal informant, La Flesche, Fletcher also quotes other materials and gives general references, like "as heard from the old men." I have passed on such citations whenever they are available. Dorsey mentioned his informants more specifically, but still little information is given about them: ·

1. Joseph La Fleche [sic, after Dorsey] is a gentleman to whom I am
indebted, not only for myths in Çegiha and Tsiwere, but also for a
knowledge of the latter tongue . . . . I regard him as my best authority. By
birth he is a Ponka, but he has spent most of his life among the Pawnees,
Otos, and Omahas. He has acquired a knowledge of several Indian
languages, and he also speaks Canadian French. While Frank, his younger
brother, has remained with the Ponkas, and is now reckoned as a chief in
that tribe, Mr. La Fleche has been counted as an Omaha for many years.
Though debarred by Indian law from membership in any gens [one must
be a full-blood Omaha to belong to an Omaha clan: Welsch], that did not
prevent him receiving the highest place in the Omaha governmental system.
He has some influence among the Pawnees, and when the Yankton
Dakotas wished to make peace with the former tribe, it was effected
through the instrumentality of Mr. La Fleche, who accompanied Struck-
by-the-Ree to the Pawnee village. Mr. La Fleche is the leader of the
'Citizens' party among the Omahas. The names of two of his children,
Susette (Bright Eyes) and Frank (Woodworker, or Carpenter), are familiar
to all who have read of the Ponka case.

2. Mrs. Mary La Fleche is of white descent on the father's side. She
learned Oto by a residence among her mother's people. She was known in
former years as 'the beautiful Omaha girl,' having been adopted by the
latter tribe.

3. Frank La Fleche is the eldest surviving son of Joseph. He has a fair
knowledge of English, writes a good hand, and is devoted to reading. I have
had many opportunities of testing his skill as interpreter, and I did not find
him wanting. He is the only Omaha who can write his native dialect.

4. Susanne [sic, after Dorsey] La Fleche is Frank's younger sister. She
is still a child and was not over thirteen when she gave me an abstract of a
myth told her in Omaha by her Oto grandmother.

5. Pathinanpaji (He-who-fears-not-a-Pawnee-when-he-sees-him) is a
full-blood Omaha, who has passed middle age. He belongs to the 'Citizens'
party, and is one of my best informants. His articulation is rapid; but after
he repeated a sentence I had no difficulty writing it.

6. Hupetha is a full Omaha, one who refuses to join either political
party in the tribe. He has not given me much information.

7. Mantsunanba (Two Grizzly Bears) is the aged ex-chief of the Hanga
gens of the Omahas, which keeps the two sacred tents and regulates the
buffalo hunt. He has been a medicine-man, and is the head of the old men's
or chiefs' party. He was always friendly to me and was the first Omaha to
pay me a visit. Owing to his rapid articulation, common to Omaha orators,
I was obliged to revise his myth, with the assistance of Mr. La Fleche, who
gave me the corresponding Oto version.

8. Mawadanthi (Mandan) is a full Omaha. He is short, and of a
nervous temperament (the opposite of Hupetha), his utterance being thick at

times. While he means well, his information is not equal in any respect to that given by Pathinanpaji. He belongs to the 'Citizens' party.

9.   Te-ukaha[14] (Sentinel-Buffalo-apart-from-the-Herd) is head of a subgens of the Thunder and Reptile[15] gens of the Omahas, being keeper of the sacred pipe of his gens. He is full of fire as a speaker; and his enjoyment of the burlesque was shown when he told me the myth of the turtle who led a war party. He declared that he had added a little to it, but only such parts as he thought were needed to make the myth complete. The songs in the myth point to an Oto derivation. Te-ukaha is one of the 'Citizens' party and a good farmer.

10.   Can-ge-ska (White Horse) is head of the Wolf gens of the Omahas and a member of the chief's party. He understands the Kansas (Kaw) dialect of the Çegiha as well as his own.

11.   Anpantanga (John Big Elk), an Omaha, is one whom I regard as a dear friend, a good example to his tribe. He is the authority for several myths and most of the Omaha historical papers. The Indians call him 'The man who is always thinking about the Great Spirit.' He is a full Indian, a nephew of the Big Elk mentioned by Long and others. He is an adherent of the 'Citizens' party.

12.   De-da-uthikaga (Dried Buffalo Skull) is head of the Singers, a section of the Black Bear subgens of the Omahas. He is half brother to Pathinanpaji, but he is so far advanced in life, and his articulation is so rapid, that it was impossible to record all his words, which he would not repeat.

13.   Nudanacha (Cried-to-go-on-the-War-path) is a Ponka chief. He is head of a part of the Thunder-bird gens. I have known him since 1871, whereas I did not become acquainted with the Omahas until 1878. Nudanacha has furnished me with eleven myths, three historical papers, and some valuable ethnologic notes. He is a very patient man, and is deserving of sympathy and encouragement in his efforts to become self-supporting.

Informants for whom Dorsey gives no information are Mikasinazi, John Springer, George Miller, One Horn, and Yellow Buffalo.

Today these myths are lost of the Omaha. Several of my Omaha friends and relatives have told me that they remember hearing there were stories about Rabbit, but not the slightest fragment remains.

Margaret Mead, in *The Changing Culture of an Indian Tribe*, deals with the Omaha of the 1930s, but she also comments on the earlier role of the myth in Omaha culture: "To the grandfather was reserved the duty of telling the children myths with appropriate morals attached and generally training them in manners and morals.

And: "During the winter season, the villages broke up and the people went to live in tipis in small camp groups in the sheltered ravines to escape the ravages of the winds. This was the least popular season. The people were split up into small kin groups; there was little festivity; the men were away all day hunting; the women were busy from morning till night grinding corn and dressing skins; the grandmother sat in the far corner mending the mocassins, and the grandfather spent his time admonishing the children in long homilies and legends."[16]

Alice Fletcher, who was of course closer to the situation, said of the storytelling tradition: "Story telling was the delight of everyone during the winter evenings. It was then that the old folk drew on their store of memories, and myths, fables, the adventures of the pygmies and of the *gajazhe* (the little people who play about the woods and prairies and lead people astray)—all these and also actual occurrences were recited with varying intonation and illustrative gestures, sometimes interspersed with song, which added to the effect and heightened the spell of the story or myth over the listeners clustered about the blazing fire. The uncle (the mother's brother), who was always a privileged character and at whose practical jokes no nephew or niece must ever take offense, often made the evening merry with pranks of all sorts, from the casting of shadow pictures on the wall with his fingers to improvising dances and various rompings with the little ones."[17]

While the narration of myths apparently played an important role in tribal life, there was apparently no dramatic representation of the myths: "there was no ceremony in the tribe that corresponded to the drama, the acting out of a myth, a legend, or a story. There were dances and movements which were dramatic in character, as when at the meetings of the Hethushka society a man acted out his warlike experience; also during the closing scenes at the ceremony of Anointing the Sacred Pole."[18]

Thus, the individual items of this collection have come from a wide variety of sources. Any folklorist knows that it is a dangerous thing to take someone else's word for the accuracy of a transcription or to mix texts (and therefore standards of accuracy) from various sources. But my first excuse is that we must use what we have, and early sources of Omaha folktale texts are not so common that I could be exclusively selective. Moreover, the writers included here, especially Dorsey, show signs of a determined effort to remain faithful to the nature of the Omaha text and, therefore, these works can be treated as scientifically gathered data.

The vast majority of these texts are from Dorsey's book, *The Ȼegiha Language*, which was actually intended to be a broad sampler of Omaha texts for linguistic analysis and language instruction. From the letters, notes, agreements, reports, reminiscences, and folk narratives, I have tried to select the traditional items and in this book make them available for the folklorist and general reader now that the nineteenth-century wave of enthusiasm for Indian language analysis has passed.

I have mentioned the work of Alice Fletcher and Francis La Flesche, and I have also extracted narrative elements from their *The Omaha Tribe*, an ethnography describing a wide range of Omaha cultural features, from children's games to rituals, from hair styles to foodways. As a part of this ethnography the authors included an occasional folktale, legend, or myth, and those tales too have been included here.

A curious story is that of Francis La Flesche himself. For Dorsey he was only an informant, if an extraordinary one. La Flesche very quickly, however, became an ethnologist in his own right, working with Alice Fletcher on *The Omaha Tribe* (an allegorical relationship indeed, since the word *fletcher* in English means "arrow maker" and *la fleche* in French means "the arrow"!).

La Flesche then produced ethnographic materials on his own, apart from Alice Fletcher, also writing *The Middle Five*, a fine book describing the life of a young Indian child in the missionary schools at the transition of the Omaha tribe from a "nation" to a minority.

La Flesche corresponded with other noted ethnologists and anthropologists throughout the world, including the giant, Franz Boaz, to whom he sent seven transcriptions of Omaha tales, also included in this collection. The La Flesche-Boaz tales appear here in print for the first time to my knowledge; I found them buried in the manuscript files of the American Philosophical Society library in Philadelphia. All of the other tales in this collection have been printed before but now are difficult to find or interpret.

My contribution to the materials has been threefold. First, I have assembled them as texts from remote and diverse bibliographic nooks and crannies where they might not easily be detected as Omaha folktales or might be difficult to find because of the limited availability of the books in which they originally appeared.

Secondly, I have annotated the tales, using the ethnographic research of others in the field during the past hundred years, from James Owen Dorsey to Margaret Mead, from Francis La Flesche to Larry Evers. Perhaps most important in this regard has been the information I have drawn on and included here from my own decade of extensive experience among the Omahas (and to a much lesser degree the Sioux) from 1964 to 1974. Enough Omaha culture persists in today's culture to provide valuable background for tales collected nearly a hundred years ago.

Third, I have made an effort to improve on the early translations of the tales by rewording them and correcting errors. This was accomplished with the help of contemporary informants and by referring to the original Omaha transcriptions and the interlinear renderings provided in the publications of the Bureau of American Ethnology.

I must stress that this has not at all been an effort to romanticize Indian narratives but rather an effort to restore the native eloquence that has been lost in the clumsy English renderings. Knowing the brilliant rhetoric customary with Omaha speakers, I have always been embarrassed to see in print the inarticulate translations published as Omaha texts, especially considering the fact that eloquence is a major factor in social prestige among the Omaha. Note, for example, this text from Dorsey's *The Çegiha Language*:

There was a Hill that drew (people) into its mouth. And the Rabbit was with his grandmother. "A Hill is there, but it is bad. Beware lest you go thither. Go not thither," said she. And he said, "Grandmother, wherefore?" She said, "Whenever people go thither, it draws them into its mouth." And the Rabbit thought, "Let me see! Why is this? I will go thither." And he went thither. When the Rabbit arrived there, the Hill knew him. As he knew him when he arrived there, the Rabbit said, "ɟahe-wacahuni, draw me into your mouth. ɟahe-wacahuni, you who, as they say, are used to devouring, devour me." And ɟahe-wacahuni knew the Rabbit, so he did not devour him. And it came to pass that a great many people belonging to a hunting party were coming to that place. And they arrived there. And ɟahe-wacahuni opened his mouth, and the people entered the mouth of the Hill. And the Rabbit entered too. The Rabbit pressed onward. And when he reached the stomach of the Hill within, ɟahe-wacahuni was not pleased by it. And ɟahe-wacahuni vomited up the Rabbit. Again some members of a hunting-party were approaching. When the party reached there, ɟahe-wacahuni opened his mouth again, and the people entered the mouth. And the Rabbit entered again (as a man, this time). And then ɟahe-wacahuni did not vomit him up. And there were lying in the distance the whitened bones of the people who had entered first and had died, the dried flesh next to the bones adhering to them; also those who had been dead but a little while, with the flesh (on the bones); and those, too, who had just died and the living ones too. And the Rabbit said as follows: "Why do you not eat? You should have eaten that very fat heart. Were I (in your place), I would eat it," he said. And the Rabbit seized his knife. When he seized his knife, he cut the heart. And ɟahe-wacahumi said, "Ha^n! ha^n! ha^n!" And the Rabbit said, "Do not say 'Ha^n! ha^n! ha^n!' " And the Rabbit gathered together the heart and the scattered pieces of fat. And the Hill split open of its own accord. All the people went out again. When they went homeward all the people assembled themselves. Said they, "Let us make the Rabbit chief." And he said as follows: "It is said 'You shall make the Rabbit chief.' As if *I*, for my part, had been desiring to be chief!! (Or, Have I been behaving as if I wished to be chief?) From whatever places ye may have come, begone ye (to them). I too have come hither to get some of the fat belonging to me, as my grandmother had none." And the Rabbit went homeward, carrying the fat on his back. Having brought it home on his back, he put it outside. "O grandmother! I have killed ₫ahe-wacahuni," he said. "Oh! You very bad big-foot! you very bad split-mouth! Have you killed him who only should have been killed in the past?" "Grandmother, I say that because I have killed him. See the pile farther away," he said. The old woman having gone out of doors, said, "Oh! my grandchild told (nothing but) the truth (though I *did* doubt him at first)." And she took the (pile of) fat (meat).

I believe that my retranslations are an improvement on Dorsey's, but I must also confess that they still fall far short of the brilliance of the Omaha original.

The storytelling tradition among the Omaha has faded and changed during the past hundred years, just as it has in non-Indian American and European cultures. The fairytale, for example, has almost completely died away as an oral tradition but, in return, the legend and jest have reached previously unattained popularity. So it is also among the Omaha. As I have stated, the purpose of this book is to make available in more accurate form and with the context of annotation Omaha tales collected in the nineteenth century and now generally unavailable to the public. But this is not to suggest that these tales are all there are. Omahas rarely tell these stories any more, but other tales have developed, other forms have become prominent, myths have died, and legends arisen.[19] This book is not at all an effort to revive the old tales, for they are no longer relevant to contemporary Indian life, as is best evidenced by their own natural death. My hope is that the tales will provide easier, more cogent access to the background and historical materials that can help us understand modern tales and help non-Indians appreciate the fact that the Omaha had a rich culture well before white soldiers and missionaries brought "civilization" to them.

The Trickster

The Trickster is the most common, and most interesting, figure of the North American Indian tale tradition. From tribe to tribe he may appear as a demigod, a spider, a coyote, or a rabbit. Even among the Omaha, within a single culture, he might appear in any number of different guises: as a rabbit, a turtle, or just a nondescript creature.

Stith Thompson, the dean of American folktale scholars says, "Undoubtedly the most characteristic feature of the tales of the North American Indians is the popularity of trickster stories. We cannot speak of a definite, all-inclusive trickster tale, or even with any strictness of a trickster cycle. Nevertheless, there does exist over the western two-thirds of the continent a considerable body of widely known anecdotes told in various areas as the adventures of different tricksters. Best known of all of these is Coyote, familiar to the tribes of California, the Southwest, the Plateau, and the Plains."[1]

But even more intriguing than his multiple forms in different tales is his ambiguous character. Even though we may be told or see *what* the Trickster is—Rabbit, Ictinike, or Coyote, among the Omaha—we still can never know *who* he is. He is simultaneously the creator and the destroyer, savior and corruptor. In one episode he saves a tribe from the ravages of some terrible, evil, supernatural force, and then he goes through an equally strenuous exercise of his powers to seduce a chief's virgin daughter. He is divine and brute, powerful and degenerate, brilliant and stupid: in one tale, by his wit alone, he triumphs over more powerful adversaries, but in another he is so ingenuous that he attacks his own anus with a firebrand.

Thompson says of the trickster's dual character, "The adventures of the Trickster, even when considered by themselves, are inconsistent. Part are the result of his stupidity, and about an equal number show him overcoming his enemies through cleverness. Such a trickster as Coyote, therefore, may appear in any one of three roles: the beneficent culture hero, the clever deceiver, or the numskull."[2]

John Greenway concurs, with an additional observation regarding motive. "It is inaccurate to call him a 'trickster,' for this implies intelligence and cleverness; Trickster usually does not play wilful tricks, but blunders into situations that often result in his being rudely discomfited. He is cunning, but that is different from being clever; and he has other bad qualities as well."[3]

Paul Radin devoted a full volume to an examination of the Winnebago Trickster cycle, which shares many episodes with the Omaha-Ponca series. His observations are, like mine, still in the form of questions: "This, of course, raises an old question, namely, whether Trickster was originally a deity. Are we dealing here with a disintegration of his creative activities or with a merging of two entirely distinct figures; one a deity, the other a hero, represented either as human or animal? Has a hero here been elevated to the rank of a god or was Trickster originally a deity with two sides to his nature, one constructive, one destructive, one spiritual, the other material? Or, again, does Trickster antedate the divine, the animal and the human?"[4]

Probing the Trickster's psyche or attempting to provide parallels of the Trickster for Anglo-American audiences is a difficult task because the ambiguity of the Trickster is not resolvable, and there are so few valid analogues in American culture.

Greenway, as is his custom, presents an interesting and provocative comparison. "It would be easier to understand the roles of Culture Hero and Trickster if literatures, primitive and sophisticated, kept them separate, but more often than not the Culture Hero is also the Trickster. Even Christ, the least ambiguous of all Culture Heroes, is worrisome in the apocryphal legends that have persisted for two thousand years, in spite of the penalties that were visited upon heretics and blasphemers whenever the Church was strong enough to keep the thinking of its communicants pure. The orthodox mythology of Christianity retains only one clear vestige of a Trickster nature: the disobedience in the temple; but European folklore and folksong tell of Christ as a Trickster from before his birth ("The Cherry Tree Carol") to just before his death (the legend of the Wandering Jew). His tricks were not merely disobedience and mischief, but fatal ones for his human playmates, just like those of the North American Indian Trickster. This ambiguity of Trickster and Culture Hero has worried everyone who has dealt with this area of mythology and folklore."[5]

Thus, many, many efforts have been made to explain the nature and the role of the Trickster, not only in Indian culture but within non-Indian cultures too. Why was the court jester alone given the right to ridicule the court and court figures? Why today can a comedian stand at a microphone with the President of the United States present and say things just short of cruel, barely short of the truth, and be immune from the punishment that would be meted out to a sincere petitioner who would say the same words? Why is wisdom so often associated with its antithesis, stupidity? Til Eulenspiegel, the German trickster, is in one tale exceedingly clever, heroically brave, and in the next he is abominably stupid, cruel, or obscene.

This is also the nature of the Omaha Trickster. He is a man, a rabbit, a coyote, a god of lower nature, an unknown kind of spirit. This particular ambiguity is not so confusing to the Omaha mind because man is seen as a part of the flow from the very earth through creatures of the earth, merging indistinctly into man, on through the spirits, and into the heavens and gods.

But where does the Trickster fit into this spectrum? Analysts have tried to find his spot at every convenient blending point. C. G. Jung saw the Trickster as a primeval concept only thinly veiled with modern thought, an original concept of man and god and nature. Others have seen the Trickster as a composite of man, in all his extremes of stupidity and cleverness, obscenity and heroics, victory and defeat. This interpretation, moreover, notes the fact that these Indian tales, like early European fairytales (usually designated in folklore studies as *Märchen* since such stories never have fairies in them), display the same arbitrariness of triumph. The clever Trickster sometimes fails despite his wile and the stupid Trickster sometimes succeeds despite his slow-wittedness—a view of the ways of the world far more in keeping with reality, I believe, than the banal and naive view held by most non-Indians that there is a logic and justice in the ways of fate.

An extension of this view is the Trickster as a god, totally unpredictable, capable of great transformations, divinely mad, the bringer of fire, and the maker of things. Again, non-Indians find this theory hard to accept because, the thinking goes, if our wisdom is divinely inspired, then truly divine wisdom must be an extension, a refinement of that same kind of logic. To my mind, and most Indian minds, that is hopelessly arrogant. If the premise were correct, then divine logic would, perforce, be so much more refined than our own, it would transcend our understanding and might be as inexplicable, as apparently confused and confusing, as the nature of the Trickster.

But there is yet another possibility. Non-Indians, especially Americans, have come to think that every problem has a solution and almost every problem has only one solution. Both of these suggestions are nonsense of course. Taking the second error first, we can see that most problems actually have several solutions, many often absolutely equivalent.

This may be the case of the divine logic of the god-Trickster. His logic is not an extension or a denial of our own but actually an alternative, neither better nor worse, simply equivalent. How can his madness, contradiction, cruelty, kindness, random behavior, his uncertain nature, and erratic identity possibly reflect the nature of god or of divine intent? Look about you, White Man, and you will find that there is no better description of the ways of the gods! Ask Job. Ask Jesus.

Another answer rests on the first of the pair of logical fallacies stemming from cultural misdirection that there *is* an answer. Perhaps that was the lesson of the Trickster for the eighteenth-century Omaha audience. Sometimes there are no answers; there is no logic. Sometimes the corn grows and sometimes it does not, despite the finest tribal piety, the hardest of work, the best of medicine, the purest of intentions. Sometimes the buffalo come and sometimes they do not, and there is nothing the Omaha can do about that. Death strikes the young and good and spares the old and miserable. The buffalo are mighty and many and yet they fall to man. The rattlesnake is small and lowly, but kills.

I would therefore argue that the explanation for the nature and social function of the Trickster is that he is an accurate reflection of the perversity, ambiguity, and contradiction of life, needing no further explanation or analysis because he is an explanation and analysis. The truth of the statement is only clouded by the non-Indians' hopelessly mythic view of a romanticized cosmography.

Rabbit

The Trickster appears throughout the world folklore and literature in a thousand forms, from a god to a ghost, from a spider to a spirit. In Omaha culture the Trickster appears as a rabbit, as a coyote, and as Ictinike, a strange spirit-man, and in one lone tale as a raccoon.

It would be a real delight if I could clearly delineate the character of the Trickster in these different guises, but just as nature blends with the supernatural in Omaha life, just as animals and man are blended into the one concept of life, the Trickster, too, does not present us with such a clear and obvious set of categories. Rabbit, Ictinike, and Coyote merge at their edges. Bewilderingly, these alternate masks of the same mysterious character even encounter each other in some of these tales and try to outdo each other in roguery. In some cases the same story is told about Rabbit and Coyote, about Coyote and Ictinike. They change forms at will and yet remain always the Trickster.

And yet there are some concentrations of characteristics about the identities of the three major Omaha Trickster figures. I will discuss Ictinike and Coyote later, where I tell their tales, Ictinike being the most prominent of the taboo violators and Coyote, the fool, the victim of his own perversity.

Rabbit is ever the Trickster, deceptive and naive, clever and stupid, showing all the contradictions that so encourage comparisons with man and god, with the environment of the Omaha tribe. But Rabbit more than the other forms of the Trickster in Omaha tales is two things, the culture hero and a surprise source of courage.

To me this is a powerful and vivid statement of the Omaha sense of irony. The Plains Indian was painfully aware of the contradictions of life. Rabbit, the most timid of Plains animals—"split mouth," "big eyes," "big foot," as he is cursed in the tales, assumed coward even by his grandmother—is the Omaha Prometheus, Odysseus, and Ictharus. This terrified little trembler, we are told in these stories, is a killer of ogres, a capturer of the sun, gives turkeys red eyes, and can be a clever and courageous fighter.

The lesson cannot have been lost on the young Omaha listening to these stories 150 years ago. The Omaha were a small tribe of farmers, faced with the awesome fury of the Plains climate and neighbors like the Cheyenne, Arapaho, Pawnee, and Sioux.

And in retrospect we might ask if this was a vain comparison, a pathetic optimism. Well, the Plains still teem with rabbits, the Nebraska night still trembles with the coyote's aria, and the Omaha are the only Nebraska Indians who remain on their native soil.

How Rabbit Killed Hill-That-Swallows
Told by Joseph La Flesche

Once there was a hill that ate people. Rabbit was at his grandmother's house and she told him, "There is a very bad hill over there. Stay away from it. Don't go there."

"Why not?" he asked.

She said, "Because whenever anyone goes past it, the hill eats him."

Rabbit thought to himself, "Well now, what's this all about? I think I'll just go over there and have a look for myself." And he did and when he got there the hill recognized him.

Rabbit knew that he couldn't fool the hill, so he said, "Hill-That-Swallows, swallow me."

Well, the hill knew Rabbit, so he did not swallow him.

A little later a hunting party came along. Hill-That-Swallows opened up its mouth and swallowed them. Rabbit sneaked in along with them and went down, down into the hill. When he reached the hill's stomach, it got upset and the hill vomited up Rabbit.

Later another hunting party appeared. When they arrived, Hill-That-Swallows opened its mouth again and swallowed the people. And Rabbit sneaked in with them again—this time disguised as a man—and Hill-That-Swallows did not vomit him up.

Deep down in the hill he saw the whitened bones of the people who had been swallowed a long time before, and only a little bit of flesh was left on the bones. Then there were those who had been dead just a little while, and there was still quite a bit of flesh on their bones. And finally there were those who had just recently been swallowed, and some of them were still living.

Rabbit said to them, "Why don't you eat something? You should eat that big, fat heart. If I had been you I would have eaten it." And Rabbit took out his knife and cut into the heart.

Hill-That-Swallows said, "Ha ha ha!" [Omaha equivalent to "Ow ow ow!"]

Rabbit said, "Don't say 'Ha ha ha.'"

So Rabbit gathered up the cut-up heart and scattered the pieces of fat, and the hill split open. All of the people went out. As they walked home they decided to make Rabbit a chief. But he said, "You say, 'Let Rabbit be chief,' as if I wanted at all to be chief. Go back to your homes. I came to get some of the heart fat because my grandmother had none and that was my only reason."

So Rabbit went on home carrying the fat on his back. When he got home with it, he set it down outside the lodge and said, "Grandmother, I have killed Hill-That-Swallows."

"Oh you big Bad-foot! You bad Split-mouth! Have you truly done this thing that should have been done long ago?"

"Grandmother, I am only telling you this because I really did kill it. See that pile over there?"

The old woman went out of the lodge and said, "Oh, Grandchild, you were indeed telling me the truth though I really did doubt you at first."

And she accepted the gift of the pile of fat meat.

COMMENTARY

The fact that the hill could not stomach Rabbit is certainly a comment on his physical offensiveness, a feature he retains even when he is acting as a culture hero.

The conclusion should be noted, for it is a scene repeated with variations in several other Rabbit tales. Although the grandmother's words seem to a rebuke of skepticism, she is actually proud of Rabbit's accomplishment.

How Rabbit Captured the Turkeys
Told by Susette La Flesche

Once there was a young man named Rabbit, who lived with his grandmother. And she told him to get something to eat.

"Well, I will get some food, Grandmother," he said, "if you will have the fire ready." So he took his bow and arrows, and also a bag filled with grass. By and by he saw some turkeys.

"Ho! Rabbit, what do you have in your bag?" they asked.

"I have songs."

"Sing us some," the turkeys said.

"Come dance for me and I will sing for you," he said. "But while you are dancing, you must keep your eyes closed, for if any of you open your eyes, all of you will have red eyes."

And he started to sing:

Hé! wa-daⁿ'-be ¢iñ-ké ¢aⁿ, I-ctcá-ji-de! I-ctcá-ji-de! Iⁿ'-be ¢i-aⁿ.

dje! Iⁿ'-be ¢i-aⁿ'-dje!

Alas for him who opens his eyes!
His eyes will be red!
Spread your tails!
Spread your tails!

The turkeys danced while he sang this over and over, and as they danced he grabbed first one and then another, putting them into his game bag. But one turkey, suspecting something wrong, opened one eye and cried out, "He is killing us all." Then the surviving turkeys flew away.

Rabbit took the sack home and said, "Grandmother, now I have something. Keep the bag while I go out and get some water." But the grandmother's curiosity was too great; she opened the bag and all the turkeys but one got away. The old woman, who was blind, held the turkey by both legs.

When the young man returned, she called out, "Come quickly and help me, I have two of them." The young man was angry, and he scolded her, not letting her eat any of the turkey.

And from that time on, turkeys have had red eyes.

COMMENTARY

Here is the only mention that Rabbit's grandmother is blind.

This etiological tale explains another animal characteristic and, like the following tale, is very popular among North American Indians. Indeed, Stith Thompson states that this tale (although his text has ducks rather than turkeys) is the most popular of the Trickster cycle.[6] Here is only a sample of Rabbit's capacity for deception, however.

Dorsey gives another version of this same tale (informant: George Miller) which provides a fragmentary etiological account of menstruation.

How Rabbit Snared the Sun
Told by Francis La Flesche

Once upon a time Rabbit lived in a lodge with no one but his grand-mother. And it was his custom to go hunting very early in the morning. No matter how early he went, someone with a long foot followed him leaving a trail, and Rabbit wanted to know who it was.

"Now," he thought. "I will get up before him." So he got up very, very early and went out. But again it turned out that someone followed him and left a trail.

When he got home, he said, "Grandmother, I am going to make a trap and catch him."

"Why do you want to do that?"

"I hate him," Rabbit said, and went out again. And again he found that the footprints had gone along behind him. So he lay in wait for the night. He made a snare out of a bowstring and put it in the path of the footprints.

He returned early in the morning to check his trap, and it turned out that he had caught the sun. He ran home quckly to tell his grandmother about it.

"Grandmother, I caught something peculiar and it scares me. I wanted to get my bowstring back, but I was too frightened," he said.

He went back with his knife. He went very close to this thing in his trap.

"You have done wrong. Why did you do this? Come here and let me loose," the sun said.

Rabbit tried to do what the sun wanted but he was so frightened that he could only pass around his side. Finally he dashed in, holding his head down and his arm out in front of him, and he cut the bowstring with his knife. The sun rose up into the sky.

The hair between Rabbit's shoulders was scorched yellow by the great heat he suffered when he stopped to cut the bowstring.

Rabbit went home. "I am burned, Grandmother. I am almost burned up," he said.

She said, "Oh, Grandchild, I believe you *are* almost burned up."

From that time on, the rabbit has had a singed spot on his back between his shoulders.

COMMENTARY

The tale of the sun snarer is one of the most broadly distributed folktales of the world. This Rabbit tale is a classic example of that narrative. The sun, its passage, and its annual variations were of profound importance and interest to Indians; so when Rabbit interferes with it, he has taken on an important opponent, indeed, in the Omaha's eye.

The tale is etiological; that is, it explains an origin, in this case the origin of the coloration of the rabbit's pelt. The initial statement about Rabbit's living alone with his grandmother is a formulaic opening, frequently used to introduce Rabbit stories.

Dorsey comments that some of the statements in his transcription seem illogical, perhaps a result of an impatient informant.

Rabbit and the Grizzly Bear
Told by Nudanacha

Grizzly Bear came home, having been scouting for Rabbit. Rabbit went to attack the buffalo herd Grizzly Bear had found. Rabbit killed a very fat buffalo. "Go tell everyone about what I have done, so they can come for the meat," said Grizzly Bear.

"Go to red-eyed Grizzly Bear and help him pack the meat," said Rabbit.

"O My Husband's Brother, in which direction?" said the Grizzly wife, and they left. They brought home all the buffalo meat. And there were four young grizzly bears. The youngest pitied Rabbit and secretly brought him bits of food.

The next day Grizzly Bear said to him once more, "Rabbit, your hunting ground is full of game."

"O Elder Brother!" said Rabbit, "I'll put on my mocassins." And he went to attack the herd, and again he killed a fine, fat buffalo.

Grizzly Bear went there and said, "Go tell everyone about what I have done, so they can come for the meat."

Rabbit went home and said to the Grizzly Bear's wife, "Go to red-eyed Grizzly Bear and help him pack the meat."

"O My Husband's Brother, in which direction?" said the Grizzly woman. They went to pack the meat, and they brought home all the meat on their backs; again the young grizzly sneaked a bit to Rabbit.

Grizzly Bear said, "I think that you took a piece to someone."

The next day he returned from scouting. "Rabbit, your hunting ground is full," said Grizzly Bear.

"O Elder Brother! I'll put on my mocassins," said Rabbit. He attacked the herd and again killed a fine, fat buffalo.

The bear came. "Go tell everyone about me so they can come after the meat," said Grizzly Bear.

"O Elder Brother, I will carry my own piece," said Rabbit.

"What?! He wants to carry his own meat," he said. "Go tell everyone about me so they can come after the meat." And he got angry with Rabbit because Rabbit insisted on carrying his own piece of meat. So Rabbit cut at the meat several times with a knife, causing several pieces to tear off. He picked up a piece of blood about the size of two fingers and put it in his belt.

"What did you take?" asked Grizzly Bear.

"O Elder Brother, I took nothing at all," answered Rabbit.

Grizzly Bear picked up Rabbit by the nape of his neck and pushed him repeatedly into the blood. Rabbit cried out, and finally he went to tell them about the meat, as Grizzly Bear had told him to do.

After they went for the meat they returned to the lodge, and Rabbit put the piece of blood he had taken beside the lodge.

Night came. Rabbit said, "I hope, my child, that you will be like some children who talk quite early, saying a word now and then." And when he had said this, the blood said yes like a child.

Then he said, "I hope, my child, you will be like some children who speak plainly without missing a word." And that was the way it turned out to be.

Grizzly Bear said, "Who were you talking to, sitting out there?"

"Why Elder Brother, I wasn't talking with anyone at all. I was just sitting out here talking to myself," said Rabbit. Then he said to the blood-child, "I hope, my child, you will be like boys who pull the bow so very well and run now and then for a short distance." And that is the way it was.

"I hope, my child, that you will be like the young men I have seen carrying the quiver." And it was so.

Then came daybreak.

"Come, Rabbit. Your hunting ground is full," said Grizzly Bear.

"Wait, Elder Brother, I am putting on my mocassins," said Rabbit.

"Hurry, you-who-have-not-put-on-any-mocassins. You bigfoot. Stinky one. Big eyeballs! Split mouth!!" said Grizzly Bear.

"Oh, what a scoundrel! he treats my relation like that!" said Rabbit's new son.

"Yes, my child, he treats me like this all the time. He keeps me in misery," said Rabbit.

Rabbit's son said, "When he goes, I will be just over the hill where they occasionally surround the herd. You must tell him you want to carry a piece."

Then Rabbit attacked the herd, and he killed a buffalo. Grizzly Bear came there. "Go tell them about me so they can come for the meat," he said.

"No, Elder Brother, not at all," said Rabbit. "I want to carry a piece of my own, Elder Brother."

"What?! He actually wants to carry some! Go tell them about me so they can come for the meat."

"But, Elder Brother, I want to carry my own piece," said Rabbit.

"Why Rabbit, you usually don't talk so tough, but you are now," said Bear.

"No, Elder Brother, that isn't it at all. I am used to being hungry; I just want to carry my own share," said Rabbit.

"Why Rabbit, I actually think you have an ally somewhere or you would not talk to me like that," said Grizzly Bear. He told him again and again and knocked Rabbit over time and time again. He knocked him over very suddenly. The Rabbit's son came up, pulling several arrows from his quiver. Rabbit's son strung his bow.

"All right, Younger Brother, carry your own meat, that which is over there by you," said Grizzly Bear.

He suddenly threw away the fresh piece of meat. "I don't want to carry it now," said Rabbit.

And his son came up and said, "Oh, what a cruel thing. I think that you have been treating my relation like this all along."

"Why, my child, your father can carry this. I gave it to him," said Grizzly Bear.

"Nonsense! Carry it yourself," said Rabbit's son to Grizzly Bear. He knocked Grizzly Bear over on his back time and time again, and then shot at him wounding him with two arrows. And finally he killed him.

"What do you usually tell his wife when you tell her to go and carry the meat?" asked Rabbit's son of his father.

" 'Go to the red-eyed Grizzly Bear and help him pack the meat,' is what I usually say." That is what Rabbit told him.

Then he went to the lodge. When he came in sight of it, he stretched out on his stomach at the front of the lodge and crept in at the door. Ka! And Rabbit's son killed the old woman Grizzly Bear. "Who of you pitied my father, Rabbit?" he demanded of the Grizzly children.

"I! I! I!" they all shouted loudly. And the youngest said, "Only I did not join them in abusing him."

So Rabbit's son killed the three and said to the youngest, "Go in peace as you get water for your father."

"Thank you, Elder Brother," said the young Grizzly, who was left alive.

Rabbit's son returned to his father with great rejoicing. "Father, make some arrows for me," he said.

So Rabbit made a great many arrows for him. He finished the arrows by fixing eagle feathers to all of them.

Then he sat awhile, and said, "Father, I would like some good clothes."

"Yes," said Rabbit, and he made him a hat out of a big owl. In fact, he made a whole suit of clothes for him out of birds sewn together. And he had mocassins, of which each had a great owl on them. When he walked, they said, "Hoo! Hoo! Hoo!" When he walked, he made the great owls hoot. In fact, all the birds called and made a great noise.

COMMENTARY

Rabbit is a relative of all other animals and frequently is found living in their lodges, playing the role of the stepchild in the Western fairytale model. As is also true in that tradition, the most abused member of the family becomes the ultimate victor.

The term "Brother" as used here by Bear and Rabbit does not imply blood relationship. Among the Omaha, all of the brothers of a person's father are called "Father" and all sisters of one's mother are called "Mother." In addition, the terms "Grandfather," "Grandmother," "Uncle," "Aunt," "Sister," or "Brother" are used as terms of respect.

Bear's insults toward Rabbit—"Big foot," "Stinky one," "Big Eyeballs," "Split mouth"—are standard curses for him and get a good deal of usage, for Rabbit all too frequently gets into situations where he excites understandable fury. Other than terms like these and "Waugh," the sound of an angry grizzly bear, there are no curses in the Omaha tongue.

Just as cycles and groups of three are traditional in Western folklore—three episodes, three tasks, three sisters—the Omahas' tales feature units of four, as do most other American Indian tales and customs. Here there are a sequence of four hunts and a group of four grizzly cubs.

The child springing from a blood clot is a common motif in woodland Indian tales,[7] as are the child's extraordinary powers.

How Rabbit Cured His Wound
Told by Nudanacha

Rabbit was living with his grandmother. He traveled to a certain place at the foot of a bluff where the prickly ash was very dense all the way around it. He said, "People have been on the trail, all of whom had very long feet."

And the next day he said, "Grandmother, I want to go out and scout around." And he went out that morning. After he left, the tracks reappeared all at once. He thought, "Those people who were moving about are back again."

He went ahead of their trail and lay concealed, lying in wait for them. When they reached the place where Rabbit was hidden, they could not find him. He had made so many tracks that the people did not know which way to turn to find Rabbit, and they went on past him.

Then again he went ahead of the trail and lay concealed, lying in wait for one of them.

"That one thing will come to you," shouted one to his companions. "Stand and head him off." They were milling around. Finally one walked off. "That which is hidden will come to you," he said to them again.

He told this to those who were a ways off, telling them to stand and head him off, and he went pushing through the undergrowth. And then after standing a while, he pretended that he had not found Rabbit, although he had. He stood off at the side of the thicket and took an arrow, and he fitted it to his bow. "Look out for this which is coming toward you," he said, tricking Rabbit by pointing in the opposite direction. But then he turned and let the arrow go and it went all the way through Rabbit.

Rabbit cried, "Nja nja nja."

"Friend, you have killed him," they said. "Friend, I will carry him on my back," said another.

But Rabbit jumped up, pulled out the arrow, and carried it off. They ran after him, and as they chased him they saw Rabbit's blood lying in a long line on the snow. They chased him into his burrow.

He grunted, "Grandmother, they have nearly killed me. Un, un."

His grandmother chided him, "You were disobedient. When I said they were after you, you should have stayed here without any fuss."

He said, "Grandmother, go for medicine."

She said, "My Grandchild, I doubt that I know the right medicine."

"Grandmother," he said, "bring me back one of the chokecherry bushes which was full of sap in the summer."

His grandmother brought one home. He ate it, and it made him well again.

COMMENTARY

It is a frequent occurrence in these stories that Rabbit does not obey the more rational admonitions of his grandmother, but as often as not he comes off all the better for his arrogance. In this case, however, the hunter is obviously aware of Rabbit's perversity and manages to shoot him by aiming his arrow first in precisely the opposite direction from Rabbit, thereby hitting him!

How Rabbit Killed a Giant
Told by George Miller

Once when Rabbit was traveling, he reached a certain village. The people said, "Rabbit has come visiting, hey!" On meeting him they said, "Who did you come to see?"

"Why, I'll go to anyone's lodge," answered Rabbit.

"Well, no one has anything to eat," they said. "He-for-Whom-They-Shoot-the-Deer is the only one that has plenty of food. You ought to go to his lodge." But Rabbit went on to the last lodge and went into it.

The host said, "Friend, we don't have a thing to eat."

"Well, my Friend, when there is nothing, people usually eat whatever they can get," said Rabbit.

Finally He-for-Whom-They-Shoot-the-Deer invited Rabbit to a feast.

"Oho! Friend, you are invited to come. Hurry up," said the man whose lodge Rabbit had entered.

Now all the people were afraid of the giant. No matter who killed what animal, Giant kept all of the meat. Rabbit arrived at Giant's lodge, and as he entered his host said, "Oho! Go around to that side."

But Rabbit jumped over and took a seat. When food was given to him, he ate it very fast, and the little that was left he tucked under his robe. Then he pushed the bowl aside.

"Friend," he said to the giant, "here is your bowl." Then he said, "Friend, I must go."

He jumped past the fireplace with one leap, at the second leap his feet touched the giant's servant on the chest, and with yet another leap he was gone.

When he got back to the first lodge, he gave his host the food which he had not eaten. The man and his wife were very glad to eat it, for they had been without food.

The next morning the crier passed through the village commanding the people to get up. They all said, "We just kill game for He-for-Whom-They-Shoot-the-Deer." But they went out hunting. They scared some animals out of a dense forest and shot at them. Rabbit ran there very quickly, but he found that the giant had beaten him there and had taken the game.

When Rabbit heard shots in another direction, he ran there immediately, but again he found the giant had beaten him.

"This is annoying," thought Rabbit. And when he heard someone shooting game in another direction, he went there right away, this time arriving before the giant.

"Friend," he said to the man who had killed the deer, "Let's cut it up!" But the man didn't want to. "No, Friend, He-for-Whom-They Shoot-the-Deer will be coming soon."

"No, Friend. When someone kills game, he usually cuts it up and then makes an equal distribution of the meat to his people," said Rabbit. But still the man refused, for he was afraid of the giant. So Rabbit ran up and grabbed the deer by its feet.

Just as he slit the deer's skin, the giant came along. "What do you think you're doing?! Leave that alone!" he said.

"What did I do wrong?" asked Rabbit. "When someone kills game, he usually cuts it up and distributes it equally among his people."

"Leave it alone, I say," said the giant. But Rabbit continued cutting the meat. "I will blow you right up into the sky," said Giant.

"Blow me into the air! Blow me into the air!" said Rabbit.

So Giant came close to him and when he blew on him, Rabbit went flying into the air with his fur fluffed well out. Giant walked on, grabbed the deer, put it in his belt, and walked off. This was the way he always did it: he would hang the deer that were slain in his belt and take them to his lodge. You can see from that that he was a very big person.

At night Rabbit wandered around and finally went all around Giant's lodge. He took a louse and said to it, "O Insect, go and bite him right in the side."

When morning came, Giant was said to be ill. His side itched. He scratched there and scratched there. He made a hole in his skin and eventually died.

The people said, "Make a village for Rabbit!"

But Rabbit said, "I don't want to be a chief. I left my poor old woman all by herself, so I want to get back to her."

COMMENTARY

"How Rabbit Killed a Giant" underscores the Omaha's contempt for those who are stingy, especially with food. Even Rabbit, who is perfectly capable of being a fool, knows this and makes it clear. "When someone kills game, he usually cuts it up and distributes it equally among his people." This was the only way a tribal unit could be sustained, by fully sharing wealth as well as poverty. In the face of such meanness, Rabbit is the hero, saving a people and being offered their greatest honor.

The next tale is a variant, from Dorsey's collection. While it is essentially the same story, it is worth noting that Rabbit comes upon the hunters first when he hears their shots—a clear influence of the introduction of firearms to the Omaha.

How Rabbit Killed a Giant
Told by Francis La Flesche

There was a giant called He-for-Whom-They-Shoot-the-Deer. No matter what animals the people killed, they always gave them to him, because they were afraid to keep game from him. And when the snow was on the ground, they went out to drive some animals from their lairs. Rabbit went along. He thought, "At last they will have a chance to kill He-for-Whom-They-Shoot-the-Deer."

He-for-Whom-They-Shoot-the-Deer went out hunting. Eventually Rabbit heard the sounds of shooting, so he went in that direction too. It seems that two men had shot and killed a deer and were standing around; they had not even begun to cut it up.

"Friends, cut it up. Why are you standing around?" he asked and started to cut it up himself.

"Friend, that is true, but we are afraid of He-for-Whom-They-Shoot-the-Deer."

"For shame!" Rabbit said. "Are you afraid of him because he is immortal? Cut it up. You can carry it on your backs."

So they cut it up and made pack loads. When they had finished, He-for-Whom-They-Shoot-the-Deer came along. He was carrying four deer in his belt. As he walked, he carried a huge oak tree for a bow. "Aren't you all afraid of me? What kind of people are you?" the giant asked.

"Rabbit—that one over there—made us cut the meat up, so we did," said the two men.

"Why don't you even hesitate to take this away from me?" he asked. "Rabbit, you are very bad. You have evil eyes. You have a foul, split mouth."

"What has upset you that you talk to me like this?"

"Stand still or I will squash you," said the giant.

"Shame on you. Go ahead and squash me, Giant."

He-for-Whom-They-Shoot-the-Deer jumped up and squashed him. Rabbit got up, bleeding all over. He said, "Shame on you." And the giant jumped on him again.

"These men here are afraid of you and won't attack you, but I'm not afraid of you, so I will," said Rabbit.

"Stand still or I will blow you right up into the sky," said the giant.

"Hurry up then, Giant. Blow me into the sky."

The giant seized Rabbit and blew him up into the sky with great force. As he fell toward earth, he kicked with his legs. When he got very close to the earth, the giant blew him back up again with great force. So He-for-Whom-They-Shoot-the-Deer stood there for a long time, blowing him into the sky with great force again and again.

"When I walk on the ground again I will kill you," said Rabbit. By and by the giant grew tired and Rabbit fell to the earth. He took his bow and shot at He-for-Whom-They-Shoot-the-Deer. He wounded him in the eye, and the giant died. All nations rejoiced at this.

Then Rabbit went home. When he got there, he found his grandmother.

He said, "Grandmother, I killed He-for-Whom-They-Shoot-the-Deer."

"Look here, Bad-eyes. It would be very hard to kill him," said his grandmother.

"I tell you this because it is true," said Rabbit.

COMMENTARY

Dorsey comments: "This is but a fragment of the original myth, being all that Frank remembered. He said that more followed the killing of the giant."

How Rabbit Killed the Black Bear
Told by Joseph La Flesche

Rabbit lived in a lodge with his grandmother. She once said to him, "Do not go to the village of the black bears. Black bears hurt people. Do not go there. They will hurt you. The chief of the black bears has a lodge on the hill just over the horizon. Do not go there."

Rabbit took his bow and went there. He went to the lodge of the chief of the black bears. When he got there and was standing at the door, he pretended to cry.

"Rabbit, why are you crying?" said Black Bear.

"Yes, Uncle—the old woman—said—'Go to—your mother's brother—the black bear'—and she—scolded me—so I came here," he sobbed.

Finally Black Bear said, "Sit down over there on the other side of the fire." And Rabbit did this. That night Rabbit went out of the lodge. Outside, Rabbit dropped his dung all around the door.

"Well, Dung-of-Mine," said Rabbit, "Please give the scalp-yell as soon as it is day."

When day broke, there was the sound of not a few men giving the scalp-yell.

"Oh, Uncle, a great many men are here to drive us from the lodge," said Rabbit.

"Even if I stay here for a long time—for years—who could possibly move me?" said Black Bear.

But then everyone of a great number of men gave the scalp-yell many times. Thinking it was indeed a big group of men, Black Bear left his lodge. Rabbit killed Black Bear just as he came outside.

"Oh, Uncle, they have killed you," said Rabbit. Having killed the bear, he went home, and when he got there he said, "Grandmother, I have killed the black bears' chief."

"How could you possibly kill him? It would be hard to kill him," she said.

"Grandmother, I killed him. Let's go there," he said. And the old woman went there with him. [See Wajinska's version, following.]

"Here he is, Grandmother."

"Yes, my Grandchild, you are right."

They cut up the body and carried it home on their backs. When they got home, Rabbit left again with Black Bear's scrotum.

When he reached the black bears' village, they said, "Here is Rabbit! Here is Rabbit!" They made a great uproar.

"Yes, I have brought you news," said Rabbit.

"Aho, Rabbit has come, he says, to bring us news." All of the black bears went to him in great numbers. "Tell us the news," they said.

"Yes, I'll tell you the news," said Rabbit. "A great number of men, it is said, went to the chief of the black bears and killed him."

"Our chief has been killed," said the black bears, and they all cried.

"Your chief is dead, and here is his scrotum," he said and hit them with it.

"Rabbit is the guilty one! Chase him and kill him!" And they ran a very great distance and finally caught him and killed him. They tore his body into small pieces and threw them away.

After a long time, and Rabbit had not yet come home, the old woman decided to go out and look for him. She took her bag and went out to search for Rabbit.

She said, "I will go looking for him at the place where he was killed."

When she got there, she gathered the scattered pieces. As she walked along, she put them in the bag and said, "Yes, Rabbit, you were disobedient. I said, 'Those villagers are dangerous, so stay away from there,' but you went, and they have killed you." The old woman went home, carrying the bag on her back; when she got home, she dumped the contents of her bag on the ground, and Rabbit came alive.

"I'll go," thought Rabbit. He took his bow and went out.

When he arrived at the black bears' village, one black bear had had a dream. He was crying bitterly. They said, "Why are you doing that?"

He said, "I had a dream. I dreamed that I was killed too."

"That was a silly dream. How could we all be killed?"

Now the black bears ate only human beings, but Rabbit sided with mankind and wished to kill them all. At the black bears' village he scattered his dung all around it during the night.

"Well, Dung-of-Mine," he said, "At early dawn give the scalp-yell. Let's kill all the black bears. First I will give the signal for the attack. At the same time you give the scalp-yell." As soon as it was day Rabbit gave the signal for the attack. The whole party of dung-men gave the scalp-yell. All the black bears ran out, and all of them were killed. One male and one female were left alive. Rabbit took hold of them and said to them, "You were bad, so from now on you will eat nothing but insects. You will have no souls. The human race, my mothers and mother's brothers, will eat you. You will be called *wa-sabe*—black animals. Go."

COMMENTARY

Reading a series of Rabbit tales, one becomes very aware that the surest way Grandmother can send Rabbit off to do something is to tell him not to go there. His defiant character insures the results.

It is not at all unusual to encounter the obscene in Trickster tales, and this example is in reality quite decorous compared to some. The tale is etiological in that it explains the origin of the Black Bear's way and it is mystic in that the bears have a dream-warning of their impending fate.

The following fragment is also titled "How Rabbit Killed the Black Bear," but it is obviously a sequel which offers another etiology.

How Rabbit Killed the Black Bear
Told by Wajinska

Rabbit returned with his grandmother to the place where he had killed the chief of the black bears. And he said, "Grandmother, carry this thigh on your back."

"Oh, Grandchild, he has declared himself a god, so he is very dangerous, even when he is lying there on the ground. He might crush me with his leg. I don't want to," she said.

"Well, then, what part *will* you carry?" he asked. "Carry his head on your back."

"Oh, Grandchild, his teeth are sharp and they might crush me," she cried. "I am very much afraid of them."

"Come then, Grandmother. Carry his breast on your back."

"Oh, Grandchild, that would be all right."

So he loaded her with the bear's breast, to which was still attached his penis. The old woman was happy with that load.

Rabbit said, "Come on, Grandmother. Let's go. Take your load and go. I will hurry home in about two hours."

His grandmother started home, carrying the load on her back. She had to go down into a valley along the way, and she suddenly slipped and fell in such a way that the bear's penis penetrated her, well into her body. "Uh-u!" she cried repeatedly.

Meanwhile her grandchild was on his way home, and eventually he caught up with her. He sneaked around her and went home. "The old woman has done something very wrong," he thought as he went along.

Rabbit reached his lodge. Later his grandmother came home.

He said to her, "What was the matter with you?"

"Oh, Grandchild, some young Pawnees, your friends, met me and took me to their lodge. They offered me food, so I did not come home." She said that she was sick when she reached home.

Suddenly he threw some blood on her. Then he made a menstrual cloth for his grandmother.

"Grandmother, you have done great wrong. Go outside. Cook outside. Eat your own meal out-of-doors—that beast that you carried on your back."

"Oh, Grandchild, I have killed my own relation," she said. "So be it, Grandson," said Rabbit's grandmother.

COMMENTARY

Dorsey says that "in the myth of the Rabbit and the Black Bears, Mactcinge, the Rabbit, threw a piece of the Black Bear chief against his grandmother, who had offended him, thereby causing her to have the catamenia. From that time women have been so affected. Among the Omahas and Ponkas the woman makes a different fire for four days, dwelling in a small lodge, apart from the rest of the household, even in cold weather. She cooks and eats alone, telling no one of her sickness, not even her husband. Grown people do not fear her, but children are caused to fear the odor which she is said to give forth. If any eat with her they become sick in the chest, very lean, and their lips become parched in a circle about two inches in diameter. Their blood grows black. Children vomit."[8]

How Rabbit Killed Winter
Told by Francis La Flesche

Rabbit was walking along. He happened to reach the home of Winter and his wife.

"Well, you don't often come around here. Sit down over there. You must be traveling on some very important business indeed."

"Yes, my Mother's Brother and my Father's Sister. My grandmother has beaten me until I am very nearly dead. That is why I have come here in such a bad mood," Rabbit said, crying and hopping from one foot to the other. He just could not sit still.

"Please sit still," said Winter.

"But, Uncle, I am always this way."

Finally Winter mentioned that he was going hunting.

"Oh, Uncle, I want to go with you," said Rabbit.

"Why, you would probably die," said Winter.

"No, Uncle. How could I die? Whatever happens, I'll stay near you."

"All right. But see that you do," said Winter. And Winter went outside and began to blow, "Wh! Wh!" And he blew up a fine driving snow-storm. It grew very, very cold. And when he left, Rabbit went with him.

Rabbit was very jumpy. He kept moving and running far ahead of Winter, and then he would come back again and again. He ran around Winter as he moved along.

"He really is an active one," thought Winter.

By and by Rabbit scared up a deer.

"Oho, Uncle, a deer is coming toward you. Shoot it!" he said.

"No, that's not what I'm hunting for," said Winter.

And Rabbit thought, "What can he be hunting?"

After a while Rabbit, as he roamed around, spied some men. "Oho, Uncle, here come some men."

"Yes, that's exactly what I'm after," Winter said. And he killed them and carried them home on his back. When he got them there, he boiled them. Winter told his wife, "Hurry! Your nephew is very hungry. So she cooked them until they were done. They filled a dish with the human meat for Rabbit.

"I usually don't eat such food," Rabbit said, and he gave it back to them.

When the food was all gone, Winter suggested that they go hunting again. "Let's go, Rabbit," said Winter.

"No, Uncle. You go alone," said Rabbit.

Winter made another blizzard and went out. When he had gone, Rabbit asked Winter's wife, "Oh, Aunt, is my uncle afraid of anything?"

"Your uncle is not afraid of anything," the woman said.

"But, dear Aunt, even I am afraid of some things. How can it be that my uncle is not afraid of anything at all?"

"Well, actually he is afraid of the head of the Rocky Mountain sheep."

"I thought there must be something," said Rabbit. He found one and killed it. He cut off its head with a knife and carried it home on his back.

When Winter returned home he asked, "Where has Rabbit gone?"

"He just went outside," said the woman.

After a while, when it was dusk, Rabbit came home again. "Uncle, that round thing there by you is the head of a Rocky Mountain sheep," he said. When he threw it suddenly at Winter, he died, and only his wife remained. This is why, from that time, it has not been very cold as a rule.

COMMENTARY

Rabbit is frequently characterized as being hyperactive, as is indicated here by Winter's comments. There is no real purpose to calling attention to his constant fidgeting here except to validate that this is indeed Rabbit.

The Omaha must have had particularly strong feelings about Winter and felt that it was indeed hostile toward them. Winter would have been a hard condition, even if it had been spent in the warm and secure earth lodges, but it was during the winter that the buffalo pelts were heaviest, when the herds were most easily tracked, and when the big animals could be bogged down in snow drifts so that hunters could easily approach them on foot and kill them with lances with a minimum of danger for themselves. So it was during the winter that the Omaha hunters moved out onto the harsh, windy, snow-choked Plains. It is not surprising then that they would tell and hear about the death of Father Winter with particular relish. And it is the Father Winter, the harsher of the two members of the family, who dies; the Mother, a milder soul, lives with us yet today.

Winter's fear of the sheep head might seem peculiar to the non-Indian, but the situation is clear to the Omaha audience. The traditional Omaha clans have two taboos; each has a tactile and a dietary prohibition. The Wind Clan, of which I am a member, cannot, for example, touch verdigris or eat shellfish. Members of the Buffalo Clan cannot touch soot or eat the headparts of buffalo (now frequently extended to cattle). Members of the Deer Clan cannot touch fur or eat deer.

The word "cannot" (rather than "may not") is used here deliberately, for the prohibition is absolute and physical. Violations result in definite and serious consequences: paralysis, disease, other physical damage, or even death. The cause and its effect are as certain as putting one's hand into a blazing fire. One suspects from the phrasing of Dorsey's description above of the taboos surrounding menstruation that he, too, came to understand that the consequences were not just feared or suspected or predicted but simply came to pass upon violation.

Winter, therefore, clearly belongs to a clan in which the tactile prohibition is the sheep's head, and even an accidental touching of it could result in his death.

Dorsey comments further in his notes on Winter's ability to blow up storms. "Igacude [Winter] used to go each day to a lofty bluff, and gaze in all directions till he spied a party of hunters. When he discovered as many as he could carry on his back, he used to take up a ball of snow and blow off the particles till he made a snowstorm in which all the men were sure to perish. The Igacude gathered the bodies and carried them to his lodge."[9]

How Rabbit Went to the Sun
Told by Nudanacha

A long time ago Rabbit decided to go out. He said, "Grandmother, I am going out to hunt feathers."

"Oh," she cried in surprise, "where do you think you will be able to find feathers so easily?"

But he did go, and as he was crossing a level plain not far from his home, he cried, "Oooo, Mother's Brother! Oooo, Mother's Brother!" As he walked along he kept this up. The eagles he was looking for were circling round and round, pressing very close to the top of the sky. They flew along, wheeling and wheeling.

"They will catch me," he said.

The eagles shrieked, "T-t-t-t-t." Finally one dived down to attack Rabbit, and he seized him and carried him home. He took Rabbit to his home high above in the sky, where there was a lodge.

"My father brought home some very good prey," said the eaglet. "O Brother Rabbit, we love you very much."

"I do nothing but move around. Why should you love me?" asked Rabbit.

He sat up on his hind legs. The eaglets loved that, and one of them said, "Where did you come from?"

"When I was walking across the plain not far away, your father caught me," Rabbit said. "When does your father usually come home?"

"My father," he said, "usually comes home late in the afternoon, when water is falling one drop at a time from small round clouds of different sizes."

[It is clear that some text has been omitted at this point in the tale.]

One of the eaglets said, "Brother, how do you do that?"

"Yes," answered Rabbit. "As you see, they rest my head on one stone and strike it with another."

"O Brother, do that for us," the eaglet said.

"Sit over there," Rabbit said, and they did. And he did it to them. First he crushed one with a violent blow and then the other. He pulled out their feathers and threw the eaglets' bodies violently down to the earth below.

He bundled up the feathers and, just as the eaglets had told him, the father came back suddenly, late in the afternoon, with a snake. "Take this, children," he said, and Rabbit killed him with a violent blow as he pushed his way into the lodge.

After a while, precisely at the beginning of darkness, the mother eagle came home suddenly. She too had brought a snake home. "Take this, children," she said, and Rabbit also killed her with a violent blow. And again he sat pulling out feathers and tying them in a bundle. He was also crying.

He left with the feathers bundled on his back. And he was still crying. Finally he reached a lodge, and he stood there crying.

A woman spied him; it was his grandmother. She stood there a moment and then asked, "Mmm, what important business are you traveling on?"

He said, "I was hunting feathers, and I found quite a few, but I hesitate to start home because I don't know if I can make it, so I have been doing nothing but cry."

"Hmmm," said the woman. "I am with someone and he is very bad. You better go home quickly. Hurry," she said.

Rabbit sat in a woven-yarn bag the size of a hat. He tied the feathers to it.

The woman said, "You are on your way home now, but when you get there, put a red-oak acorn in the bag for me. When you are on the ground, give the rope a slight pull." And she lowered him down to the ground, quickly. When he reached the earth, he was hateful, and he was mean to the very one who had pitied him; he dunged in the bag. Then he took the rope and shook it a little, and she pulled it back up.

Rabbit started home with the feathers on his back. When he got there he shouted, "O Grandmother, I have come home!"

"What?!" she cried with surprise.

"Grandmother," he said, "I have brought home the feathers."

Then she said, "Have your mother's brothers make many arrows."

But he said, "Why?"

She replied, "There is a hill that has been swallowing people who pass by it."

He said, "I would like to see that."

"Now, now!" she said. "Sit still."

"No, I want to see that."

Although she was against it, he went to see it anyway. And eventually he reached the hill and said, "You are the swallowing hill. I have heard that you were here. Swallow me."

And he was swallowed for a long time. At length he reached the bottom. It happened that there were many dry bones of people who had been swallowed previously. Some had dried and hardened flesh sticking to them, and others were there who had died only a short time before and whose livers were still living. Finally Rabbit reached those who were still alive.

"Ci-ci-ci-ci! There aren't many of these," said Rabbit.

Fat was dangling down from the heart of the hill. "Why you should have eaten that," he said. He cut it off with his knife and sliced up the heart. The hill fell open at this. All of the men who were still alive became active when the hill split open and they said, "Let us elect Rabbit chief of the nation. He saved us."

But Rabbit said, "Go back to your own homes from where you came. Go."

Rabbit went home.

"Grandmother, I have come home to you," he said.

"Oh!" she said in surprise.

"Grandmother, I killed the hill that swallows people, which you told me about."

"Hmmm. It has been said that it would be good to kill it. But how could *you* have done it?" she asked.

"Why Grandmother, I did kill him. And of the people who were there, there were some who said, 'Let us make Rabbit the head of the nation,' but I didn't want this, so I ordered them all to go home."

COMMENTARY

Rabbit hunts for feathers because they are useful in costume, as tools (e.g., brushes), and in fashioning arrows.

This story shows a good deal of disintegration in the process of traditional transmission. There is an unfortunate omission in the first episode, in which Rabbit tricks the eaglets into letting him crush their heads. Then attached to the end is another independent, truncated story, "How Rabbit Killed Hill-That-Swallows," the more complete version of which was our first story.

In "How Rabbit Went to the Sun" Rabbit is both the rogue, befouling his benefactor's basket, and the culture hero, saving a whole tribe from the ravages of a supernatural power.

The opening and conclusion are formulaic, occurring in quite a number of the Rabbit tales.

How Rabbit Lost His Fat
Told by Francis La Flesche

At first the animals were all fat, and he who made them wanted to know which one looked best with the fat. So he called all of the animals together and they gathered. He grabbed by the head each animal that did not look good with his fat and scraped off the fat from the neck down, thus taking off the fat before he released the animal again.

Finally someone brought Rabbit to him. "I want to be the fat one. I'll look good fat," said Rabbit.

"Let's see. Come here." said the one who made the animals and had put fat on Rabbit. "You don't look any better with fat than any of the other animals," said the being. So he took Rabbit by the head and stripped the fat from the base of his neck. But he pulled too quickly at the flesh in the space between Rabbit's shoulders and since then there has been a depression in the space between his shoulders, and only in that place is there any fat on that animal.

In the end the being saw that the raccoon was the only animal that looked good fat, and so he made Raccoon's whole body fat.

Rabbit's Adventure as a Deer
Told by Pathinanpaji

Rabbit lived in a lodge with his grandmother. Once there were three women walking along. "O Rabbit," they said, "we are going to hoe our gardens."

"O First Daughter, Rabbit is very sick and is nearly dead," said his grandmother. "If you don't believe me, just look here how he is lying on the ground."

When they looked at him, he was lying on the ground, rolling at the edge of the ashes.

Rabbit lay groaning, "Han, han, han!"

The three women saw him. "O Husband's Sister, the old woman was really telling us the truth. He is very nearly dead," said one. And the three women left. They left him lying there.

When they had gone, Rabbit quickly got up. "Grandmother, hand me that spotted fawn-skin bag," he said, and she quickly threw it to him. Rabbit crawled into it and became a deer. He stuck an arrow into the middle of his side; he made his mouth bloody. Then he ran off.

He reached the women who were hoeing. The women continued to hoe their beans. "O Brother's Wife, here comes a badly wounded deer," said one. They ran along after it; all of the women chased it. While chasing it they hit at it and missed, the weapon striking only the air. So he led them a long distance away.

Then Rabbit circled around behind them and went back.

When he got home again, he stepped out of the sack, collected the women's beans, and put them into the sack. He promptly threw it over his shoulder and went home to his grandmother, not far away. He carried the sack home to his grandmother.

"Grandmother, hide this sack," he said. She took it and quickly hid it, sticking it under the grass at the side of the lodge.

And then the three women came back. "Why, Old Woman, your grandson came back this way carrying away all the beans we had been hoeing for ourselves," they said.

"O First Daughter, that isn't true at all. He is still dying sick, just as you saw him before," she said.

And when they saw him, they said, "O Brother's Wife, she told us the actual truth. He is nearly dead." And the women started home.

"Grandmother, come cook them," Rabbit said, and they ate the beans.

"Grandmother, I am going traveling," he said. And eventually he arrived at some good, deep grass. He rolled up and lay down in the grass. Then he hurried home. When he got there, he pretended to cry.

"Why are you crying?" asked his grandmother.

"Yes, Grandmother. I have been chosen to do a deed, but it is a very difficult one," he said.

"Even if it is difficult, you must tell about it," she said.

"Grandmother, I have been chosen for a dance. But, Grandmother, I must take you with me to sing in the chorus," he said.

"Let's go where this difficult task is to take place," the old woman said.

When they arrived there, he said, "Grandmother, this is the place, but they have finished dancing and have gone home." He snatched up his bow and danced. His grandmother sat singing the chorus. He had tricked his grandmother.

COMMENTARY

This tale provides a fine example of Rabbit's inveterate trickery. He is willing to cheat women out of their hard-earned food and his poor old grandmother into traveling a long distance to sing for him alone.

Rabbit, Umba, and Turtle
Told and published by Fannie Reed Griffin, probably collected originally from Susette La Flesche

There was an old woman who lived all alone. Rabbit was her son, and the old woman was Mother Earth. Rabbit had a magic skin, by which he exercised all his powers. It was a rabbit skin, the perfect image of himself. Rabbit lived with the old woman and brought her game. The old woman was the mother of all living creatures, feeding them on things which grew up out of herself.

Grandmother Mazhun (Earth) said to her grandson, "All the people are my children, all the men are your fathers, all the women your mothers, and all the children your uncles and aunts."

And Wakonda made a man and put him on the earth to take care of the people, but the man God sent hated the people and looked on them as his property. This man took all the buffalo and deer and put them in herds and made the people take care of them but did not allow them to kill any to eat, so the people were nearly starved.

Grandmother Mazhun said to Rabbit, "I thought I told you to be kind to your fathers and mothers." That was all she said; she spoke no more.

"I will see about this," said Rabbit. So Rabbit went on a journey to see this man and took his magic skin with him. He said nothing to Grandmother Mazhun about his project.

As he was going along, he passed a handsome man. "I have been waiting a long time," said the man. "You have been slow in coming."

"I hurried," replied Rabbit, "but I was slow after all." And in an instant he was transformed into a handsome young man himself.

This splendid young man whom Rabbit met was Umba. They traveled together and soon overtook another handsome man. He had a war club and a tobacco bag. This was Turtle.

"I have been waiting a long time," he said, "and you did not come."

The three walked on together until they came to where the herders were taking care of the buffalo and deer. A little fawn had been neglected by the herders or escaped by accident, and Rabbit said, "I will take this fawn with me."

The fawn followed, and the four went to the man whom God had placed on the earth to take care of the people.

"You have come to challenge me, have you?" he said to Rabbit. "What have you brought Turtle along with you for? He is always inventing tricks and devices to deceive."

"I have come to challenge you," said Rabbit. "Let us agree on a wager. What will you bet?"

"I will wager all the people over whom I rule," said the man, "for that seems to be what you want. If you win, you shall have them."

Then they sat down to gamble with reeds. Rabbit won every time. He won the buffalo and turned them out of the herds to roam at will. He won the deer and elk and all the people and told them to go where they pleased.

At last the man said, "Let's try something besides these reeds."

"What shall we try now?" asked Rabbit.

"Let's bet on walking in the same tracks," said the man.

"All right," said Rabbit.

"What animal do you want to use?" asked the man.

"My little fawn," said Rabbit. "And what animal will you use?"

"The wildcat," he replied.

There was a clump of wild gooseberry bushes nearby. It was agreed that the track should be made around the clump. Rabbit caused a snow to fall, and the trial began. The fawn made his track and the wildcat his, and they went around and around in their circles for a long time.

Turtle grew impatient and whispered to Umba, "That's enough."

"Wah! Let us do everything fair," said Umba.

Turtle wanted to win by a trick, but Umba would not listen to him. Finally, after the thing had gone on for a long time, each animal always stepping exactly in the former tracks, Turtle lost his patience altogether and said, "Come, let's end this."

The man, who was sitting nearby, gave a little puff. Turtle caught the puff and turned it into a great tornado. The wildcat fell over and put his foot out of the track.

"You did that," said the man to Turtle, and he struck him on the head. The blow mashed all the bones and the brains all ran out. That is the reason the turtle's head is full of little bones and no brains.

At the conclusion of the game Rabbit turned loose the bears and all the animals with fur and gave the man the name of *Cinidawagithe*, or Muskrat.

Rabbit thought he would go through the country a little and see how the people liked all this, so he took up his magic skin and said to Turtle, "You watch Muskrat while I am gone." As Rabbit took up the skin, it was so transformed that it looked exactly like him, so he put it down and left it there.

Rabbit noticed that Muskrat did not have his soul with him, and he said, "If we kill him, his soul will not be dead but will take some other form and live on."

Rabbit then went to the place where Muskrat's wife was to inquire of her where he had hidden his soul. The magic skin was still where the game had been played, and Muskrat, not knowing Rabbit was gone, said to Turtle, "Let's play another game."

"What?" asked Turtle.

"We will see who can keep his eyes open the longest without blinking. I will have the eagle play for me," said Muskrat.

"Rabbit will play on our side," said Turtle. Then he put two acorns in the place for eyes in the magic skin and the eagle sat down by the side of it with eyes wide open to play the contest, while he and Umba sat watching.

Meanwhile, Rabbit went to Muskrat's wife's tent, having on the way transformed himself to look exactly like her husband. "I have come, Wife," he said, "to rest awhile."

"No, no, Rabbit," she replied. "I know you."

"I am myself and I have come to rest. Give me some dinner."

Finally the woman was persuaded to believe Rabbit was her husband and gave him his dinner and supper, but being in such fear of her husband, she again insisted in great earnestness that he was Rabbit.

"Yes, it is I," said Rabbit. "Your husband is very bad. If he knew I was here, he would kill you. If you keep still, I will save you. Now tell me, where did your husband hide his soul?"

"There is a very large lake," said the woman. "By it there is a loon and this loon has my husband's soul in his charge."

The woman was very much afraid of both Muskrat and Rabbit, so she insisted that Rabbit must use all his power and trickery to kill the loon. "You can only kill it," she said, "by taking out its heart. No one has been able to get near it."

Rabbit started out to hunt the loon. He soon came across an old beaver woman. "I have been hunting," he said to her.

"What are you hunting?" she asked.

"I want to ask you something."

"What do I have that you want?" she asked, somewhat surprised.

"If you will lend me what I want, I will pay you well," Rabbit replied.

"Well, tell me what you want," she said.

Rabbit said without further ado, "I want your heart. Lend it to me."

The beaver woman took out her heart and gave it to Rabbit.

"To pay you for this," he said, "I will give you a tomahawk to cut down trees, and the work you do with it shall be better than man can do." And he gave her her teeth. This is how beavers got their sharp teeth.

All this time Muskrat did not know that Rabbit had gone. He thought the magic skin was the real Rabbit.

After a while Rabbit came near the lake and called the loon. It answered.

"Rabbit, I know you," the loon said, going further away.

Rabbit called again and again and at last said, "It is I. I have come to see how my soul is getting along."

The loon was finally deceived and gave Rabbit the soul of Muskrat. He kept it and then gave back to the loon the heart the beaver woman had given him.

"This does not look like the same thing I gave you," said the loon.

But Rabbit assured the loon that it was and then went straight to Muskrat's wife. "I have done it," he said. "It was a hard task but I succeeded." Then he sat down right in front of her and cut the soul into small pieces. "Now," he said, "You are safe. If Muskrat tries to kill you, he can't."

Rabbit went back where Umba, Turtle, and Muskrat were playing the game between the eagle and the magic skin with acorns for eyes. The eagle sat gazing, not having blinked even once.

Turtle had grown impatient again and as Rabbit came up said to Umba, "Let's finish this. I am tired."

"Let's wait," Umba quietly replied. "This is the last contest. We have nearly finished what we all came to do." But Turtle wouldn't wait any longer. His patience was all gone and he said, "Let's end this."

"All right," said Umba, and blew a breath in Turtle's mouth. Turtle blew it out again and then a great rain fell. The water ran down in the eagle's eyes and made him blink.

Turtle jumped up and shouted, "We have won! We have won! Wa! We have won!"

This made Muskrat very angry and he pounded Turtle's head until it was flat. That is how the turtles came to have flat heads.

Then Rabbit spoke in his proper person to Muskrat, saying, "Wakonda put you here to take care of the people but you had a bad heart and were selfish. I could kill you but I will turn you into a muskrat. You shall have no soul and must always live among the fishes."

COMMENTARY

This Rabbit tale is taken from Fannie Reed Griffen's book, *Oo-Mah-Ha Ta-Wa-Tha* (1894), and is a good deal more literary than Dorsey's texts, which were noted for scientific accuracy. It is therefore hard to know whether details unique to this narrative—for example, that Rabbit's mother (grandmother?) is actually Mother Earth—are traditional or innovations. At any rate, the general tale appears to be authentically Omaha and traditional.

A footnote in the original explains that a "game is played by throwing a small bundle of reeds on the ground and grasping as many as possible in the hands at once. He who grasps an even number wins."

Another note observes that "a belief of universal acceptance among Indians is that it is possible for the body to live without the soul."

Umba means "Light of the Sun," and this powerful, calm figure in the story may be in reality the sun.

The mention of the lake may be a reference to earlier Omaha situations in the area of the Great Lakes, or it may only refer to the ox-bow lakes along the Missouri near their present site or even the "Great Lakes" area in northwestern Iowa.

There can be little question that Omahas would watch the reaction of the white listener upon telling this story about the misuse of the animals which were meant for all mankind.

Ictinike

An Omaha proverb says, "He is like Ictinike; . . . He is very cunning, watch him closely." The following set of tales will show just how closely this rogue has to be watched. Like Rabbit, he is capable of any deception. Just when he seems to be a genuine hero, he displays some special stupidity or dishonesty that shatters all confidence.

Who is Ictinike? Who can say? We cannot even be sure *what* he is. If he is a man, he is a very powerful one. If he is an animal, we have no way of knowing what sort. He assumes various forms at will and yet sometimes appears to be helpless to alter his unfortunate lot in any way whatever. I prefer to think of Ictinike as the very essence of the Trickster, a non-corporeal essence. It is not really important to know exactly who or what he is. He is *the Trickster*, and whatever form he happens to have at one moment is never his real form, for he can never be trusted to be what he seems. Perhaps not even Ictinike himself knows any longer who he is; perhaps not even he is capable of unraveling his own perversity.

Dorsey notes that "the Iowas say that Ictinike was the son of Pi, the sun. Ictinike was guilty of the sin of Ham and was therefore expelled from the Upper World. He is usually the deceiver of the human race and once he was the benefactor of a few persons. The Iowas say he taught the Indians all the things which they know. According to an Omaha myth, he taught all the war customs. In the myth of Haxige, Ictinike assumes the form of Hega, the Buzzard."

The word Ictinike is used in the modern Omaha tongue for "monkey," and monkey stories are still told among the Omaha. The transformation of this spirit-creature into an actual animal being is, to my mind, a diminution of the power of the tales.

Young Rabbit and Ictinike
Told by Nudanacha

Once by chance Rabbit met Ictinike. "Hello, Grandchild," said Ictinike.

"Honored Elder, what do you say?" asked Rabbit.

"Grandchild, kill for me that bird that is resting there on its way home," he said.

So Rabbit shot it. He shot it through the body in such a way that the arrow stuck out the other side. It fell down and lodged in the tree.

"Oh, Grandchild, Grandchild, pity me, your own relation, again," he said.

"No, Old Man, I am going to let it go. You can get it."

"No, Grandchild, that arrow is very good, and if you don't get it, someone else will."

"Well, this old man really wants his own way," thought Rabbit. So he pulled off all his clothes and climbed into the tree.

"You can just stay there where you are," said Ictinike.

"What did you say, Old Man?" said Rabbit.

"Why, Grandchild, nothing at all. I said only, 'He has always done so much for me.' "

And as he was climbing up into the tree, the same thing happened. "You can just stay there where you are."

"What did you say, Old Man?"

"Why, Grandchild, nothing at all. I said only, 'He has always done so much for me.'"

So Rabbit climbed on.

"You can just stay there where you are!"

"What did you say, Old Man?"

"Why, Grandchild, nothing at all. First-born Son, I was only saying, 'He has nearly got it for me.' "

And again he climbed and climbed, and again it happened the same way: "You can just stay where you are."

"What did you say, Old Man?"

"I said, 'You can just stay where you are.' " And Rabbit stuck to the tree. Ictinike put on Rabbit's clothes and went to a village and married one of the chief's daughters.

The younger one left very angrily. Once she looked up and saw someone stuck up in a tree, so she cut it down. When it had fallen, she built a fire all along it, and she caused the sticky substance to melt, and Rabbit sat with her by the fire. "The man who abused me this way went to your people," said Rabbit.

"Yes," she said. "He did come, but my elder sister took him for her husband."

And they went to her village together. They said, ridiculing her, "Here is our daughter who was sulking about marrying. She went away, but now she has returned with the son of Rabbit."

"That thing, an eagle, goes to you. Let Rabbit's son come here," they said, speaking to Ictinike. They ordered someone to shoot at it. But when Rabbit's son came close, the birds on the clothing recognized him and cried out.

Ictinike said, "They are always this way. Be quiet."

"An eagle is coming toward you," the villagers said. "Tell Rabbit's son to appear." And Ictinike came. It passed directly over him. He shot and missed it. Then Rabbit's son came in sight. When he had been there some time, the eagle began circling around at the center of the tribal circle.

Rabbit's son shot at it with great force, and he killed it.

"See there! He killed it," they said. "He must be Rabbit's son." And when they reached the place where the eagle had died, there was a fine feather.

Rabbit took it. "Put that away," he said. The next day came.

"Look at the feather you put away," he said.

"This is the whole eagle," she said.

"Take it to the old men," he said. And she took it.

The next day they said, "An eagle is going toward you. Tell Rabbit's son to come out."

Ictinike came out. It passed right over him. He shot at it and missed. Another one came. When it had been there a long time, it circled around the very center of the tribal circle. When he shot at it with great force he killed it.

"Wuhu! He killed it. Why, that one is Rabbit's son," they said. When they reached the place where the eagle had been killed, a fine feather had fallen. He took it.

"Put that away."

The next day came. "Look at the feather which you put away," he said.

She looked at it. She said, "Oh!" She spoke with wonder. "This is the whole eagle."

"Take it to the Old Man," he said, and she took it to him.

And Rabbit's son said, "Well, let the Old Man have some people bring the drums here to me."

On that day Ictinike had put on a very bad, worn-out piece of old tent-skin. He had been wearing Rabbit's son's clothes.

"Wear your own things again," said Rabbit's son. And he gave them to him. Rabbit took up his own clothes and put them on again, even his own mocassins.

As Rabbit's son had them beat the drums, he threw Ictinike up high into the air. And when he had gone a long ways, he let him fall back down. And Ictinike died of the great fall.

COMMENTARY

There is clearly no honor between these two thieves. Dorsey comments on some variations in the tale between informants. "The first day that Nudanacha told this myth, he said as follows: 'The old men beat the drum once, and Ictinike jumped up. When they beat it the second time, Ictinike leaped higher. Then he leaped still higher when they struck it the third time. "Stop! stop!" said Ictinike to Rabbit's son. But Rabbit's son made the men beat the drum the fourth time, when Ictinike jumped so high that when he came down he struck the ground and the shock killed him.'"

Sanssouci never heard this of the Rabbit but of Orphan.

Rabbit and Ictinike
Told by Nudanacha

Ictinike was walking along, and so was Rabbit.

"Ho! Younger Brother! Aho!" said Ictinike. "I said I hoped to see my relative, and now I see him."

Rabbit said, "I just keep moving around. Who would love me?"

"Come," said Ictinike.

"Why?" asked Rabbit.

"Never mind. Just come," said Ictinike.

He reached a place, and Ictinike said, "Younger Brother, whatever I say, you must say yes."

"Yes," said Rabbit.

"O Younger Brother, I am going to mount you," said Ictinike.

"No," said Rabbit. "I am going to mount you first."

"Oh no, Younger Brother," said Ictinike. "When the elders talk about something, they generally have their way."

"Oh no! Not at all, Elder Brother. The younger ones, when they talk about something, do not stop talking, so they usually have their way," said Rabbit.

"All right. Do it, Younger Brother." Ictinike rolled over, and Rabbit mounted him. When he had finished, Rabbit jumped up and ran off.

"Come here, Younger Brother," said Ictinike over and over.

But even as he was saying it, Rabbit was running off, but he ran headlong into a dense thicket.

"Waho!" said Ictinike. "Whenever I cheat someone, I at least keep quiet about it. You miserable Rabbit! You foul Big-foot! You miserable Big-eyeballs! You rotten Stink! You hurt me!"

But Rabbit ran off. "I had you and then dropped my dung," said Rabbit.

Ictinike cursed him again. And again. Ictinike left, full of fury. When he reached a certain place, he had to relieve himself, and a young rabbit fell out of his anus and ran away quickly. Then he urinated. Again he said, "He really has made me suffer." Again he reached a certain place and relieved himself. And once more a rabbit burst out and ran off. "That is not going to happen again," said Ictinike. Then he was uneasy about relieving himself again, so as he stooled and let it drop on the ground, he held his robe down over the feces and the rabbit to keep it from getting away. But in spite of his efforts, the little rabbit jumped over the robe. He soiled the robe with the feces at his feet.

"Oh, my embarrassment gets worse and worse." But in spite of his nakedness he walked on.

But it happened that some boys were playing with throwing sticks. He met them and said, "Ho! Younger Brothers."

"Ho!" said the boys.

"Have you heard any news at all?" he asked.

"Yes," they answered.

"Tell me what you have heard," said Ictinike.

"Yes," they said. "It has been reported that Rabbit managed to mount Ictinike. That is what we have heard."

"Oh no! They have already heard that story," thought Ictinike, and he walked on. And again he met some boys playing with throwing sticks as they walked along. "O Younger Brothers, tell me something," he said.

"We have nothing to tell you. Only that Rabbit has mounted you," said the boys.

He walked on. "Oh no! That story certainly has gone around," he thought.

And along came some other boys. And again he asked them, "O Younger Brothers, tell me something."

"We don't have a thing to tell you, except that Rabbit mounted you," they said.

"Oh no! That tale has even come this far," thought Ictinike and he walked on.

Finally he took his ragged breechcloth and began to give an alarm. He then came in sight of a village. "This man," they said, "has been attacked by some enemy." He ran into the village and they surrounded him.

"Find some place to hide your children," said Ictinike.

"They have even robbed him of his robe as they chased him," the villagers said.

"Yes, that is so," and he stood panting heavily, for he was a deceiver.

"We want to see them. Come tell us about them," they said.

"Oh no!" said Ictinike. "Bring me a robe. I want to go see."

"The old man speaks well," they said, and they gave him a robe—a thick summer robe. He left, following the stream.

"Ha ha! day after day I have done that to them. One person did not treat me well at all," he said. And he meant Rabbit.

COMMENTARY
Ictinike can draw little pleasure from having played upon the villagers' sympathies and thereby cheated them out of a buffalo robe—a summer robe at that, never the quality of a thick winter robe—because his own humiliation is all the greater; he should have known better of Rabbit. It is certainly bad enough to have been sodomized by Rabbit, but to have further cursed the world with even more of Rabbit's offspring as a result of this sexual abuse is truly humiliating!

Ictinike and the Buzzard
Told by Mantsunanba

It once happened that Ictinike was going somewhere. And a buzzard kept flying around. And Ictinike wanted to go to the other side of the broad water. He begged Buzzard, "Grandfather, carry me on your back. Carry me to the other side of the water."

"Yes," said Buzzard. "I will carry you on my back," and he carried him on his back. As he was carrying him, he searched for a hollow tree. Finally he found one. Buzzard carried him there and kept passing close to the hollow tree, tipping his wing.

As he wheeled over, Ictinike said, "Oh, Grandfather, you might make me fall."

"This is the way I always fly," said Buzzard. Finally Buzzard twisted himself around and set Ictinike down in the hole in the tree. Ictinike was put in head first in the hollow tree, so he eventually got very thin and ill.

A hunting party of many lodges came there. And whenever these women found a hollow tree, they would hit it, making it give out the sound "dackee." Now Ictinike was inside that hollow tree and he thought someone had come for wood. By chance Ictinike had some raccoon skins with him and he made the tails show by sticking them through some cracks of the hollow tree.

Three women approached; they struck the tree to make it give out the sound "dackee." And they saw the tails.

One said, "Stop, O Husband's Sister! There are a lot of raccoons here! I have found some raccoons!"

"O Brother's Wife! Will you please give me one?" said another. She said, "Let's cut a hole in the tree!"

Finally they cut a hole in the tree. Ictinike said, with a hollow voice, "I am a very big raccoon. Make it a big hole."

"O Brother's Wife, the raccoon says he is big," she said, and they made the hole in the hollow tree large. And Ictinike came out again into the air.

"As a big raccoon I come out to you again, to my real home, the out-of-doors," he said.

"O Brother's Wife, it is Ictinike coming out," said one. And Ictinike got out again into the world.

"I, the big raccoon, will go home with you! Get back!" he said, and the women ran off.

After he had come out, he sat a while, forming a plan. He sat thinking, "How can I get even with Buzzard?" He sat planning. He thought, "Only if I pretend to be dead can I do it easily."

Later he saw a crow. And after seeing the crow, he saw a magpie. And he begged them, "O Friends, pity me! Help me!" he said. "I will pretend to be dead. Help me! Eat me!"

All the birds came, having heard the call. And the eagle came too.

Crow said to him, "Friend, you have a sharp knife. Cut him up for us."

And Eagle bit a hole in the skin of Ictinike's rump. The fat could be seen inside the ham.

They said, "It is an elk, and he is very fat."

Only Buzzard had not come yet. But finally he arrived too. "Shame on you! This is Ictinike," he said.

"No, Friend, hurry. Cut it with your knife. You have a sharp knife," said Crow.

"No, it is Ictinike," said Buzzard.

But before Buzzard could eat any, the magpie entered Ictinike's body and went very far inside to eat the fat. Buzzard went to the head and tried it. Having tried it, he bit the nostrils. Ictinike did not stir at all. And when he bit the eyelids, Ictinike lay without stirring.

Buzzard went to Ictinike's rump and ate a piece of fat that was there. And then Buzzard bit off a piece of fat that was near the edge of the hole. He said, "It is true. This is an elk lying here, but I certainly doubted it at first. Finally he entered [his anus] and went far inside and bit off a piece of fat. When he entered a second time, Ictinike squeezed him and stood up.

"Just as you injured me, I will also get you," said Ictinike.

"O Friend, let me go," said Buzzard.

"No, I will not let you go for a long time," said Ictinike. And when he did let him go, it was suddenly, so that Buzzard had no feathers left on his head because they had been stripped off. This is why Buzzard has no feathers on his head; it is very red. That is how it was.

COMMENTARY

This explanation of how the buzzard lost his head feathers may lack delicacy, but the humor of the final scene is undeniable.

Ictinike and Chipmunk
Told by Francis La Flesche

After punishing Buzzard, Ictinike resumed his travels. He stopped somewhere for the night, wrapping himself up in his robe of raccoon skins and lying on the ground. Just before he woke up that morning, he had an erection which carried his robe way up into the air. That robe was waving around to and fro high above Ictinike's head. When he woke up, he saw the robe, and it worried him.

He said, "Oh no, that must be Buzzard! You won't be able to have revenge on me now, for I am awake!" The robe was coming down again, very slowly. Then he recognized it.

"Oh no, how could I be fooled by my own robe?!" So he wrapped his erect penis and set out on his way until he suddenly came upon a striped chipmunk, who said "Tsi-tsi-tsi!"

"Don't say that again," warned Ictinike, but the chipmunk just repeated his cry. "Well, he really underrates me," said Ictinike, and in his anger at Chipmunk he chased him into his retreat in the side of a bank.

Then Ictinicke took out his penis and pushed it hard into the hole until Chipmunk was offended. He bit off the very end of the organ. "Go ahead, bite me. Try to get away. This is good for you," said Ictinike, and he pushed his penis even further into the hole. So Chipmunk bit off another piece, and things continued on that way for some time. And having bitten off yet another piece, Chipmunk called, "Tsi-tsi-tsi!"

"Sure. Just say your 'Tsi-tsi-tsi.' This is good for you," chided Ictinike, pulling his organ back out of the chipmunk's den. "What can be wrong?" he thought, for he found that it had been bitten off and was now quite short. Now his penis was out of the hole in the bank, but he said, "Oh no! He has really injured me."

He took one piece that had been bitten off and threw it to the side, saying, "You shall be called 'Yellow Skin,' " and grapevines grew from the place where it had fallen.

He pushed his hand into the hole and took out another piece and threw it to the side, saying, "You shall be called 'Kande,' " and plum brushes sprang up from the ground where that piece fell.

In this way he created all the different kinds of fruits and vegetables.

COMMENTARY

In another context, Dorsey quotes the Omaha saying, "He is like the membrum virile. . . . This refers to a bad man, who fears not to commit a wrong, but pushes ahead, in spite of opposition, . . . regardless of the consequences to others or to himself."[10]

In direct connection with this myth, Dorsey asks, "Could this have been intended as the explanation of the origin of the verb, tci?" *Tci*—to copulate.

He also adds parts of this same myth as told by another informant, Tepauthikaga:

It is said there was a striped chipmunk, and they sang, "Oh, Ictinike, you going along there, you walking along carrying your thing on your back without bothering it in the least! Heckathatha! Ts! ts! ts! ts! ts!"

Then Ictinike took four sticks (sic), one being part of an artichoke (?), one part of a potato plant, the third a turnip or a part of that plant, and the fourth part of a plum tree. He threw them among the *ja* (vegetation resembling and including sunflowers), saying to the first, "Ho! You who are out of sight! You shall be called *danke*. The Indians will move their mouths because of you! They will eat you!"

Dorsey then gives yet another version as collected from Pathinanpaji:

The striped chipmunk ridiculed Ictinike and ran into his den. Ictinike took sticks, which he thrust into the den in order to reach the striped chipmunk. But the latter bit off the ends again and again till each stick was not more than four inches long. Ictinike threw the *danke* stick among the *ja*. Hollow places like those where there is a spring in the hillside is the place where he threw the potato vine. He threw the piece of turnip on the hill and the plum stick among the very dense plum trees.

Dorsey adds to this last text that "it is evident that the last informant modified his language, not caring to tell the myth exactly as he had heard it."

Ictinike and the Elk
Told by Hupetha

"My Friend, there are some people in a certain place and I want to go there," said Ictinike, and he went there. When he arrived, it happened that a bull elk was sitting there. He talked with him.

"My Friend, I have come to ask you a question," said Ictinike.

And the bull elk said, "What do you want to ask me? My Friend, I sit here with my tired legs and I don't go anywhere at all."

"My Friend, people like to be happy. Why don't you walk?"

"Yes, My Friend, but I am not happy because this woman who used to be my wife was taken away from me, so here I sit," said the bull elk.

"My Friend, let's go over there," said Ictinike.

"My Friend, you will have to go there yourself," said the bull elk.

"My Friend, where are they?" asked Ictinike.

"My Friend, they are nearby. Go over there," said the bull elk.

So Ictinike went there. And a lot of elk were milling around when he arrived.

"Old Man, what might your business be?" asked the elk.

"Yes, my Grandchildren, I would like for one day to eat the food you eat. I have come here for this reason," he said.

"Why, Old Man, our food is difficult. We eat bitter things as we move along. Besides, when it is cold, we sit facing the wind," they said.

"No, Grandchildren, you have said enough; stop talking. No, Grandchildren, you have said enough. Stop talking. In spite of what you have said, I want to live like you," said Ictinike.

"Ho! He may be telling the truth," said the elk. So they made horns for him out of a small oak; they made him a tail out of a root.

"Well, Grandchildren, when it is cold I may freeze if I remain like this. Make some hair for me like yours," he said. So they made him hair out of cattails.

"Ho! Come here and eat these rosinweeds," they said. Ictinike ate them, but they were bitter in his mouth, and he spit them out.

"Pfui! I have joined eaters of very bad things," he said.

"Ho! Old Man, what were you saying?" they asked.

"What could I say? I said, 'I joined the eaters of very good food,' Grandchildren," said Ictinike.

"Ho! Old Man, we want to tell you about one custom. You are supposed to teach the children to use their ears correctly; therefore, we tell you one custom," they said. "Ho! Old Man, when they detect men, they are to cry out in this way."

"Oho!" he said. "That is the way it will be."

It got very cold. The wind blew, and it got even colder. All the elk walked facing the wind. Ictinike walked apart from them, facing the wind. He turned his back to the wind. "Pfui! This is very bad," he said.

Well, after going on for a while, Ictinike detected some men.

"I-u! Look out for him! Look out for him!" he said.

All the elk quickly raised their heads. "What is the matter?" they asked.

"There is a man," Ictinike said. But when they looked for him, he had suddenly turned into grass.

"You mean that?" they asked.

"Yes," he said.

"Ho! Old Man, don't do this again," said the elk. "Don't give a warning cry unless there is truly danger."

Again they moved along, grazing. And again Ictinike sensed danger, the presence of man. "Look out for them!" And when the elk looked, it was indeed true; there were men and they were scouting the elk.

"Well, it was true," the elk said. "Find a way for the children to escape."

"Let me do it," said Ictinike.

"He speaks well," said the elk. "Ho! Come and do it. You shall be the leader. Find a path for the children."

"Oho! I will try," said Ictinike. He went ahead. All of the elk followed him. And as Ictinike moved along, he found men. He moved in that direction. He passed right alongside the men. When he discovered them, he talked with them.

"Do not shoot at me. It is me."

They shot the elk. They killed the elk. They shot down all of the elk. They exterminated them.

One small bull elk and one small cow—not counting Ictinike—were left alive. Fleeing with them, he reached a place far away from the slaughter site. When they got there, Ictinike took off the horns and threw them away. He commanded the young elk to go, and said, "Why do you follow me? I want to cut a piece of fresh meat for myself. Go away! You shall be called A^npa^n." That was that.

Ictinike, the Turkeys, the Turtle, and the Elk
Told by Pathinanpaji

There were once a great many turkeys. They were feeding on a high ridge among the arrow-weeds. Ictinike went there. He discovered the turkeys and ducked down and crawled back a ways.

"How can I catch them and eat them?" he thought. And he made a decision. He quickly rolled up a raccoon-skin robe, making it into a pack for carrying things. He put it on his back and hurried along.

As he ran, he came very close to the feeding turkeys. "Wuhu! Something is wrong with that old man. Look at him," the turkeys said.

"Old Man, what is the matter?"

"Yes, you are right," said Ictinike. "Some villagers said that I was supposed to sing dance songs for them. They are coming after me, so I am carrying my songs in my backpack," he said.

"O Old Man, we would like to dance a little, too," the turkeys said.

"No, I'm in a big hurry," said Ictinike.

"We would like to dance a little, too, Old Man, and then you can continue on your way," the turkeys said.

"Wuhu! What trouble! I am really in quite a hurry, but if you want to dance, you will," said Ictinike. "Well, let's see. Come together into a group." And they gathered together.

Ictinike opened the robe. "Turn as you dance and circle around me. You big ones, as you dance along, come very close to me as you dance by. Close your eyes. Be careful not to open your eyes, or your eyes will turn red," said Ictinike. "Lift up your tails; open and close them. Come on! Dance!" he called.

Then he sang:

Hé! wa-daⁿ'-be ȼiñ-ké,   i - ctá-ji-dé, i - ctá-ji-dé Hiⁿ'-be-hnaⁿ ȼi-'á-ni,

hiⁿ'-be-hnaⁿ ȼi-'á-ni.

Alas for him who opens his eyes!
His eyes will be red!
Spread your tails!
Spread your tails!

He caught the very big ones and twisted off their heads, one after the other. Ictinike sat filling his bag. He filled it very full. He filled it four feet high. A small, half-grown turkey was suspecting what was happening as he danced along. He opened his eyes a little now and then.

He cried out, "He is killing the largest of us! This is terrible! This is Ictinike standing among us! We didn't recognize him. Ku!" And they all ran away.

"Ha ha! How easy it is to get food for myself," laughed Ictinike. He laughed so hard he could hardly catch his breath. He tied up the robe into a bag. He cut roasting sticks. He put the birds around the fire to roast.

When they were done, a tree branch rustled in the wind, "Innnn."

"I am roasting them to eat. Why do you cluck at me?" asked Inctinike. "Do it again and I'll hit you."

He stuck his fist into the tree several times and it closed on his hands. "Friend, I was only joking when I said and did those things. Friend, let me go," he said. But the tree would not let him go.

"Hey, you there," he said to some big wolves. "I put those there for myself."

"Ictinike says that he put those pieces away for himself," the wolves said. They decided that whoever got there first would get to eat the stomach fat. They ran toward it. They ran fast, racing toward the turkeys. When they reached them, they chewed the meat. They swallowed it. When they had eaten it all, they left in different directions.

And what had closed on Ictinike opened up again. Ictinike crawled down to his camp again, sat down, and after licking the sticks, dropped them. He left and walked along the shores of a row of round lakes.

It happened that a big turtle was sitting there by the shore of the lake. He caught it by the tail. He dragged it off to one side. "I'll be full again in a moment," he said.

Again he broke some branches. He piled the wood up very high and set it on fire. He made the fire blaze up, and he pushed the turtle into the fire. It baked and he was about ready to start eating it. When it was nearly done, Ictinike grew sleepy.

"I am sleepy. When it is done, wake me up, Anus," he said, and he went to sleep. As he slept, someone came along, took the big turtle, and ate it. When he had finished it, he took the feet and put them back in their places in the turtle shell. He made Ictinike's hands all greasy; he also smeared his mouth with grease, and then he left.

Ictinike woke up. He jumped to his feet.

"I'm afraid I've burned my supper," he said. He pulled out the feet and they fell right out. "It has already been eaten," he said. "Why, I wonder if I ate it already. I must have eaten it and then gone to sleep."

He looked at his hands and said, "I must have eaten it." He ran his hands over his stomach. "Yes, I'm very full after eating so much," he said.

When he left, he ran across a great herd of elk. Ictinike spied them. "Stop! I will trick them," he thought.

The elk saw him and said, "There is Ictinike."

"Friend, Younger Brother, it is me. Friend, Younger Brother," said Ictinike, "I want to live like you do."

"Well, Old Man, there is no reason for that," said one. "When the only vegetation is bitter weeds, I eat them all as I walk along. How could your stomach possibly feel good if you ate them?"

"Not at all, Younger Brother. I want to live just as you do," said Ictinike.

"You can have your way if you find a path for our children, for you understand the ways of the Indians," they said.

"Yes, I'll do as you say," answered Ictinike.

"Come, Pronghorns, you are the one to do it," they said.

"Well," he said to Ictinike, "come stand with your back to me." He tried to ram him, but he couldn't because Ictinike jumped away.

"Wuhu! I can't get it done, Old Man," the elk said.

"Oh no, Friend, Younger Brother. I jumped away because I was afraid he would run over me," said Ictinike.

It happened the same way four different times. The fourth time the elk said, "This is the last time I will try it."

"Yes, Friend, Younger Brother, I won't jump aside this time," said Ictinike. When the elk hit him, Ictinike ran along with him, just like him. Ictinike had become an elk. Because he was proud, he walked about lightly, pretending to discover men. He kept crying, "Eeeen."

"Behave, Old Man. Don't do that all the time," said the elk.

"Oh, no, Friend Brother, I'm just doing that because I'm proud," said Ictinike. "Friend, Younger Brother, now I'm living the way I want to." As he went along eating, however, he spit out the bitter weeds in large amounts. He kept spitting them out. "Wa! I think I have joined those who eat very bad food," he said.

"Wa! Old Man, what were you saying?" they asked.

"I didn't say anything. I was saying only, 'I think I have joined those who eat very good food,'" he said.

Finally, as they went over a hill with a very flat top, the elk scented some men.

"Eeeen!" they cried. "Come here, Ictinike. Check this danger for your grandchildren."

He went there, and there were men. He came to them. "Go home and say he is coming with them," Ictinike whispered to the men.

"Wa! Old man, what are you saying?" asked the elk.

"What is the problem? What am I supposed to say? As I walked along I said only, 'A clump of weeds that was there a long time gave them unnecessary trouble,'" he said.

Finally when they went over a flat-topped hill, an elk came running back. "Well, Ictinike, find out where the danger is for your grandchild," he said. When Ictinike got there, there were some men.

Again men were detected in another place. "Well, again go see for your grandchild where the danger is," they said.

He went there and again men were there who were crawling up on the herd. Again he said, "He told the exact truth."

"Come, Ictinike, find for your grandchild a path of escape," they said.

"Well," he said, "even if I go ahead, be careful that you stay together. You must follow me, walking just where I walk."

He followed the headlands of the ridge. He passed close to the many men who were standing close together. "It's me! It's me!" Ictinike said as he walked along.

The men killed the elk. Three elk were left alive after the shooting, and they hid with Ictinike. And soon he pulled off his horns, threw them at the elk, and hit them. "You shall be called 'A^{n}pa^n'—'elk,' Go," he said.

COMMENTARY

It is clear from this tale, or better, an amalgamation of tales, that Rabbit and Ictinike could be confused; both must be viewed as true tricksters.

Dorsey adds comments and variations from several other informants.

"According to L. Sanssouci, it was not the young turkey that opened its eyes and gave the alarm, but . . . a species of snipe. These birds danced with the Turkeys and they, not the turkeys, had their eyes changed to red ones."

Dorsey's informant, White Eagle (Ponca), in his version of the myth told how Ictinike caught Big Turtle.

"When Ictinike saw Big Turtle, he drew back very quietly and went a little distance. Then he raised his voice and called to Big Turtle, 'Hey, you over there!'

'What is the matter, Old Man?' asked Big Turtle.

'You are in great danger,' said Ictinike. 'The Wakonda have decided to make a great flood, and the ground will be covered, and you will be drowned.'

'But I can live in the water,' said Turtle.

'But I tell you that there will be great danger this time for even you,' said Ictinike. 'This time you will not be able to live in the water.'

Finally, after much talking, Ictinike persuaded Turtle to leave the place where he was near the water and to go to the hills. Ictinike went ahead and hid himself in a ravine, and when Turtle came crawling along after awhile, Ictinike hit him on the head with a stick as he came up the hill and so killed him."

And finally, the person who stole the turtle meat was Coyote, according to Omaha and Ponca versions. But the Dakota version makes him Mink. White Eagle says that when Ictinke found the thief, he punished him by sodomizing him.

It is worth noting that in Radin's Winnebago version of this tale, the Trickster's anus is not onerous. It farts vigorously to warn Trickster that someone is stealing his meat, but then Trickster punishes it by burning it with a hot coal.

Ictinike and Turtle
Told by George Miller

Ictinike went traveling once and when he came in sight of a bend of a stream, he found Big Turtle sitting there in a sheltered place warmed by the sun. Ictinike drew back out of sight, crouching along, retracing his steps, and came running back down the hill to where Big Turtle was.

"Why aren't you paying attention to what is going on? They say that this stream is going to dry up and that all the animals that frequent this water will have to move more toward the channel," said Ictinike.

Big Turtle said, "Why, I have been coming down here every day, but I haven't heard anything about this. I usually come down here and sit in this place when the sun gets as high as it is right now."

"Hurry!" said Ictinike, "for some of the young men have already died for lack of water. The young otters died, and so have the young muskrats, the young beaver, and the young raccoons."

"Come, let's go," said Big Turtle. So Ictinike left with him. As they ran along together, Ictinike was looking for a dry bone. When he saw one that would make a good club, Ictinike said, "Friend, go ahead. I have to urinate."

When he was alone, Ictinike took the bone up and then overtook Big Turtle and walked along beside him. "Friend," he said, "when someone has to walk a long way, he should stretch his neck out often." So Big Turtle began to stretch his neck out very far, his legs bent. And as he was going along like this, Ictinike gave him a hard blow on the neck, knocking him senseless, then beat him until he was dead.

As he carried the body away Ictinike said, "Haha! There are days when I do such things for myself."

He lit a fire and began to roast Big Turtle. Although he was looking forward to eating Big Turtle, he became very sleepy, and said, "Ho! I want to go to sleep, so you, O Anus, must stay awake. And when you are nicely cooked, Big Turtle, you must say 'Puff!'" And he went to sleep.

Then Coyote came creeping up. He grabbed the turtle, pulled one of the legs out of the coals and sat there biting off the meat. When he had eaten the meat on all the limbs, he pushed the bones back into their former places, arranging the fire over them and leaving only after putting everything just as he had found it.

When Ictinike woke up, he pushed around in the ashes looking for Turtle. He took a limb and pulled it and the limb pulled right out.

"Pfui," he said, and tried another limb, with the same result, and still another, but still only the bones came out of the fire. He was really confused when he pulled out the fourth limb.

"I am amazed, Anus! I said to you, 'Do not go to sleep,' but you disobeyed me." Then he tried to attack his anus, but it kept running away from him. "Don't run away!" said Ictinike.

Then he exclaimed, "I don't understand it. I must have eaten Big Turtle, but I don't remember it at all."

COMMENTARY

Although this is clearly a fragment of the preceding tale, it does include some elements lost from it.

Ictinike And The Woman And Child
Told by George Miller

Once upon a time Ictinike was going somewhere. It was near a place where two women lived in a lodge. Ictinike traveled along until he reached the bank of a stream, and then he went along the bank. Beneath the water there appeared to be a great many plums, and they were red. "Oh," he said as he undressed; putting aside his miserable clothing of raccoon skins, he dived down after the plums. But he got only a handful of dirt.

When he returned to land, he saw that he had only dirt. Again he looked down into the water, and there were the plums. So he dived again, but the same thing happened. Returning the fourth time with nothing but dirt, happening to look up at the cliff above the stream, Ictinike saw many plum trees filled with fruit hanging down over the stream. It was the reflection of these in the water that had deceived him.

Then he put on his clothes, climbed the cliff, and gathered the plums, with which he filled one corner of his robe. Then he went down to the lodge. He rubbed semen all over the plums and threw them down one by one through the smoke hole of the lodge. A woman saw the first plum and said, "Oh, Sister-in-Law, I have found a plum!" and she scrambled for the plum.

When Ictinike entered the lodge, he observed, "Whew! My relatives, my grandchild, and her sister-in-law have finally returned. Why, there are plums everywhere, but you two haven't picked any of them."

"O Grandfather, we haven't gone anywhere. If they are close around here, we will pick some for ourselves," exclaimed one of the women.

"Ho! Go pick them," he said.

The child of one of the women was still in the cradle, and the mother had set the cradle up against the side of the lodge. So Ictinike said, "When you go, just leave the child in the cradle with me, for it might get hurt if you take it out into the plum trees."

"O Grandfather, I will do so," said the mother. Ictinike promised to watch over the child as his own relative, so the women left.

Presently Ictinike jumped up to his feet, took the kettle that was sitting there full of water and put it over the fire. Then he killed the child, cut the flesh into narrow strips, and boiled them. But he put the head back in the cradle, wrapping it with the head covering, and arranging it as if it were still alive. He put wood on the fire again and then went out of the lodge now and then to see if the women were coming back.

Finally the meat was cooked, and he sat down and ate it. He then departed, having finished the meat before the women returned. When the women got home, Ictinike had gone.

"O Sister-in-Law," said one, "the old man is not here. But my child is sleeping, just as he was when we left." She took up the cradle and was returning with it to the other woman when the baby's head fell to the ground. "Oh, my dear Child!" she cried, and both women mourned.

And as they sat crying, Ictinike, who had painted his face with clay, disguising himself, entered the lodge. "Strange! What is the reason that you are crying?"

"Oh, Grandfather, Ictinike came and told us about plums, and when we went to pick them we left the child here in the cradle. He ate it and then left after putting the head back on the cradle and wrapping the head-covering around it."

"Really!" he exclaimed. "Let me see. Hand me that ax, so that I can chase after him." They gave him the ax and he left, running very fast.

He ran to a place deep in a dense forest, where he looked for some wood mice. He pushed the butt-end of the ax along a rotted log in which there were some wood mice. Thus he killed them and covered the ax with blood.

He took this ax, streaming with blood, back to the lodge, and when he entered he said, "I killed him and have now returned."

"O Grandfather," said the women, "was the place you found him near here?"

"Not at all, but I overtook him by running very fast."

This is why there is a gray haze on ripe plums. Ictinike was the cause of it.

Ictinike and the Brothers and the Sister
Told by Francis La Flesche

There were four brothers. Their sister was the fifth child. The four brothers were very good marksmen, and their sister used to make animals come by calling. The woman loved her brothers.

"Come, Elder Brother, and comb my hair for me," and he combed it for her. He combed it very smooth for her. He made a scaffold for her, and he put her on it. And all of them stood ready, each with a bow.

The woman called and called again. When she called a third time, one could see dust, as if from the trampling of many feet. "Elder Brothers, get ready. They are coming," she said.

The fourth time they were in sight, and Ictinike was there. Animals came, all of them: buffalo, elk, deer—all were there. They stood there and killed them. Finally they were through, and they had plenty to eat, but eventually the provisions began to run out. The brothers talked about going out hunting.

The eldest brother said to his sister, "If anyone comes here—no matter what he says—do not do anything for him."

"Elder Brother, I cannot be that way," she said.

They prepared some provisions for their sister and then left her. After they had gone, Ictinike came with a bow of hard willow and a quiver full of reeds. "Second Daughter, please do for me whatever I ask. Pity me, your relation, your grandchild."

"No, Grandfather, I don't want to," said the woman.

"Please, my Grandchild, pity me. I made these new arrows and wish to try them out. They say that you can call animals. Please do it."

The woman did not want to, but he would not stop talking. Finally, the woman let him have his way. "Let's see! Comb my hair for me," said the woman, and Ictinike combed it for her. He even finished painting her face and head for her. He made her sit on the scaffold which had been made for her.

And the woman said, "They generally come when I call the fourth time."

"Let's see! Call!" said Ictinike, and the woman called. When she had called the third time, the dust from the trampling of the ground could be seen. "Oh, they are coming, Grandfather. Get ready!"

At the fourth call they came into sight, and finally they arrived. Ictinike shot at them. He shot at them with reed arrows that went wobbling.

"What!" said Ictinike, and so he shot at them—always missing. At length he had emptied his quiver. The very last to come was a huge bull elk. He pushed over the scaffold. He carried the woman home on the space between his horns.

Then her brothers came home. When they arrived at their home, their sister was not there. Although they looked all over for her, they did not find her.

The youngest brother went looking for her, making a shortcut across the country. He reached a very large hill and sat down there. When he had been there for some time, he lay down.

Then he heard a woman crying. When he looked around, he could see neither men nor women. But he looked around, thinking, "What can it be?"

He lay down again, and once more he heard the crying. This time he recognized his sister's voice. At once he ran home as fast as he could. When he got there, he told his elder brothers.

"Elder Brothers, I heard our sister crying. I found her and came home."

"Ho! Let us go there where she is," and they did go there. They reached the place.

"It is here," said the younger brother. "Come listen," and they all did.

"Yes, he has taken our sister to his home in the ground, but how do we get her back?" they asked.

"Well, Elder Brother, tell us whatever is on your mind," said the youngest.

The eldest said, "My grandfather said that I should do this whenever I get into trouble of this sort," and he hit the ground with a club that he was carrying. He barely made a crack.

"Ho!" he said to the next brother. "You try it."

He said, "My grandfather said I should do this whenever I get into trouble of this sort," and he hit the ground with a club that he was carrying, but he barely made a crack. So the third tried it. Then the youngest said, "My grandfather said I should do this whenever I get into trouble of this sort," and he hit the ground with a club that he was carrying, and the hill suddenly split wide open from top to bottom.

It so happened that their blows also made all the animals appear. And their sister had been made into a door; her arms had been tied and in this way she was hung up.

"You and your elder brothers spare a male and female of each kind," said the elder brother to the rest, and they stood shooting them. And they gave names to those that remained after the killing. Finally they exterminated the rest. They took their sister back, and that is the way it was.

COMMENTARY

Alan Dundes uses this tale as an example of what he calls a "four motifeme sequence": first the girl is warned by her brothers not to use her power for strangers (Interdiction). Ictinike comes to her when she is alone and persuades her to call the animals (Violation). Then an elk carries her off (Consequence). Then she is rescued by the brothers (Attempted Escape of Consequence).[11]

Ictinike and the Deserted Children
Told by Nudanacha

Grizzly Bear was chief of a very large tribe. He pitched his tent in the very center of the tribal circle. Grizzly Bear took an old man home and said to him, "Tell them to send the children out to play."

So the village crier said, "He says that you are to send the children out to play." And all of them went to play.

When they had gone, Grizzly Bear called the old man and said, "The children are troublesome to us. We sent them away so that we could abandon them. Let's break camp." He commanded them to strike camp.

"He says you are to strike camp!" said the old man.

They quickly took down their tents and put them on the horses. All rode horses, and they left not a single trail. They scattered in many directions away from the children. They were afraid that the children would follow them if the trail were at all clear, so they scattered widely as they moved away. When they came upon the clear trail of one of the others they pitched their tents.

Near dusk the playing children stopped their games and returned to the old camp site but found no one there. The children cried and screamed. They went to the places where the tents had been. The older girls went about finding deer sinew and awls that had been dropped. The boys who were related joined together in family groups.

They put bark in a circle, covered it with grass, and then made a lodge. They built other large lodges. They were quite crowded.

Soon winter came. One of the two grown boys said, "Friend, let us two go together and make us some arrows." First they made bows, one for each of them. They made one hundred arrow heads, enough for both. They made arrow shafts and when they were dry, they glued on feathers and mounted the heads. They finished all one hundred. One glued on the feathers while the other put on the heads. Then that was finished.

Then they slit a skin lengthwise for quivers. When each had finished his quiver he filled it with arrows. One said, "My Friend, let's go traveling," and they did.

They arrived one night at a place where there were a great many lodges. They stole horses. Since these Indians were a warring tribe they had made shields, and the boys stole these and quivers and quiver straps too.

Then they returned to their home with the many horses they had stolen and gave a good number of them to the boys who had grown to about four feet tall. They gave the mares to the girls and colts to the boys who were only about three feet tall.

"Friend, that is enough," said one boy.

They did not move their camp but stayed where they had been abandoned. Finally winter came, and the buffalo came too. The two boys who had reached manhood took their bows and arrows and attacked the buffalo, each killing four.

When they reached home, ponies were brought out to meet them and loaded with meat. The people sat in equal numbers in the seven grass lodges they had made. The hunters moved around the camp circle distributing the fresh meat until they came back to that point in the circle where they had started. Because they had killed a great many buffalo, they gave a great amount of fresh meat to each lodge and divided the skins for beds. They gave each lodge an equal share of deer sinew.

Again they went out to surround the buffalo. Each chief killed six. They were very happy for they had plenty of good meat. Again they shared with those who had not had any green hides.

Summer came. By then two, three, or ten of the boys had grown and the same number of women. The boys counciled.

"Friend, we are still unhappy. Let us get married."

The two boy-chiefs had sisters and each gave his sister to the other for marriage. And they had all the rest marry, too. That summer all who had grown, twenty some, were married. They built skin lodges out of buffalo hides. Those who were still too young dwelt in the crowded lodges.

Eventually they went on the warpath again, and the two boys who had gone before went again. They took two hundred horses from the enemy and brought them home. They gave equal shares of the horses to the grown boys and ponies to the smaller boys.

When winter came again they once more shot many buffalo. All of the men who had taken wives shot at the buffalo. Everyone had plenty of beds and sinew; in fact, there was plenty of everything for everybody. All were then married and nothing of note happened until the next summer.

Again they shot buffalo and dwelt in tall lodges—one-hundred-seventy of them. And this was the way they lived.

Finally, however, there was the warning cry, "We are attacked!" and the two chiefs prepared for battle. Lodges had been made for them in the very center of the tribal circle. (The boys had said to their people, "When you make the circle, make lodges for us in the center.") Then, as has been said, they were attacked. The horses' mouths were tied with lariats. Both went forth and attacked the enemy. Each seized an enemy and held him alive. They frightened them and drove them away. Each killed a foe. They chased them until it was night.

"Come, let us stop," both said, and they returned home. They had cut off the scalps of the enemy they had killed and they were very happy. The women danced around in a circle. They danced for ten days.

One evening someone said, "A visitor has arrived." It was Ictinike.

"Where is the main lodge of the chief of this tribe?" he asked.

"Here it is," they said, and he stepped over to it.

"I have come, Friends, because you have become very famous. I came to talk to you. And you are men. Be strong, Friends," he said.

And one said, "Elder Brother, I give you a horse."

"No, Younger Brother," said Ictinike. He did not want this. "I only want bows and arrows, for it is difficult to get food with only a horse."

"Yes," they agreed.

He said, "I will make arrows," and he made two hundred, which he finished and gave to the young chiefs.

"Elder Brother, that is enough," they said, and they made Ictinike a police servant, one who goes on errands or acts as a crier.

And they were attacked. Ictinike killed one of the attackers and seized him. Ictinike cut off his scalp and took it. He sang for the women dancers. Ictinike made himself very black; he put out the fire-brands, rubbed them to powder, and blackened himself with it.

It is now said that Ictinike originated this custom. Whenever Indians who are enemies kill each other, they lay the blame on Ictinike, for Ictinike blackened himself with charcoal, painted himself with it when he killed a person. They say, therefore, that he was the one who taught this to the Indians.

Soon many of the children grew up, a great many lodges were erected, and the abandoned children grew to two thousand.

Ictinike said, "My Younger Brothers, I want to go visiting."

They asked, "Where do you intend to go?"

"I just want to go," he said, and the people assembled. He entreated the two grown boys who were chiefs, "Tell me who the fathers of these grown boys are."

"Both grown boys answered, "My father is such a one," and described his features and dress, and so forth, giving also his name. The rest answered that they did not know their fathers, and Ictinike left. Each night he slept in some deserted place. During the day he walked every hour, sometimes even at night, for four days. On the fifth day he reached a circle of tents.

"Where is the chief's lodge?" he asked.

"Over there," they answered, and Ictinike stepped over to it.

"A visitor has come," someone said. Everyone said, "Tell us the news." The tents were very close in a circle.

"Yes," he said. "There are some people. They may be people you have abandoned."

"Yes," they said. "We abandoned some people, some of our children. Grizzly Bear made us do it. We were afraid of him, so we did it to them."

Ictinike said, "One of the two chiefs is left-handed," and the chief said that was his son. The mother cried when they told her about it. And the other boy was the other chief's son. He too said, "That one is mine." Ictinike said, "One woman was such a one," and so he described the others. And when they heard their children described, they cried loudly.

"In four days I will go home again," Ictinike told them and in that many days he did return home. Before leaving he said, "They have invited you to move your camp and join them. They hope that you will come in seven days."

And so they broke camp. In seven days they were close to the other camp.

Ictinike arrived home and he said, "My Younger Brother, I am sad."

"Yes, Elder Brother, you should tell me that problem, whatever it is," said one of the two chiefs.

"When your father was chief, he listened to the words of a total stranger and abandoned you, which was wrong. I am sorry for both of you."

It made the hearts of both pain with his words and they sat with bowed heads. Both sat thinking, "He is telling the truth."

Night fell. The left-handed one went to talk with Ictinike. "Elder Brother, come here," he said, and Ictinike did. "Go for your Younger Brother," said the chief. When he arrived at the other's lodge, he said, "Please go to your wife's brother."

"Yes," he said and he went there.

When he arrived, the left-handed one said, "Oh Sister's Husband, I am sad because of what my elder brother said. Think about it."

"Yes, it is so," said the other. "When they come, let us do it."

Day came and Ictinike went to the bluff. Finally he arrived back home. "My Younger Brother, they have moved their camp and are coming." he said.

They came and pitched their tents on both sides of the creek, the tribal circle extending over a large area of land. And the people who had recognized their own children came and pitched their tents.

As each one tried to find his own child they moved back and forth. And they arrived to invite the two boys to a feast. "Grizzly Bear invites you," they said, but the children would not go.

Finally a woman came to the left-handed one and she said, "You are invited."

"Come to the lodge," he said and he made the woman sit in the lodge.

Eventually another woman came, and she said to him, "My Sister's Husband, you are invited."

"Come to the lodge," said the left-handed one, and he made her sit in the lodge. And again he did not send her home.

Then when a good part of the morning had passed, again a woman came to him saying, "My Sister's Husband, you are invited."

"Come to the lodge," he said, and he made her sit in the lodge. The left-handed one was determined not to go.

Then a fourth came. "My Sister's Husband, you are invited," she said.

"Come to the lodge," he said, and he made the woman sit in the lodge.

At length Grizzly Bear came. "Your Wife's Sisters came for you earlier," he said. Ictinike sat looking at him and he did not like him. Grizzly Bear went home, but soon came again.

"Why Younger Brother, have your Wives' Sisters come?" asked Ictinike. He had a sharp hoe and he came into sight. He said to Grizzly Bear, "Get away from here!"

Then his younger brothers came in sight. The left-handed one had a bow, and then the other came running, and he had one too. Grizzly Bear ran away and Ictinike ran after him. He crushed his head with a blow of his hoe. "Yu yu!" cried Ictinike, and this is why one does this when striking a fallen enemy. Then they tried their horses and killed those who had come, had pitched their tents, and had searched for their children.

COMMENTARY

Dorsey explains that the obscure conclusion of the second paragraph means that after the people had scattered they began to reassemble in a prearranged site. "Whenever any party came across the trail of others, leading in the right direction, they kept in it for the rest of the way, pitching their tents in it."

This tale provides a point of departure for explanations of several other features of Omaha culture. The institution of the village crier, for example, still remains, albeit in an abbreviated form. Whenever gifts are given at powwows or hand games—and that is virtually constantly, for the Omahas are a very generous people—the donor quietly tells an elected spokesman what it is he is giving, to whom, why, or any other information the giver would like to have known, and then the crier makes the announcement with appropriate commentary on the generosity of the giver.

It is significant that the chief has his lodge in the center of the tribal circle, for that is a very honored spot, usually reserved for holy tipis housing sacred objects like medicine bundles. Every clan and sub-clan had a specific place in the tribal circle where its tents were erected, and everyone within the tribe had to observe the customs quite precisely. Today camping sites on the Omaha powwow grounds are still considered to be exclusive, but now they are arranged according to family or geographic distribution, and the individual family still retains the exclusive right to the use of that camp site.

The making of arrows was a very precise craft, and different types of arrows could be made. Some were made with stone heads (later iron) for killing large game, some were only sharpened at the end and then tempered in a fire, and others had a knob ending, used for stunning birds and small game. The arrow shafts were straightened through a grooved stone or hollow bone, and wavy lines were etched along the shaft. Fletcher says that the purpose of the grooves was neither to allow blood to run nor to give the appearance of lightning but rather to "prevent the wood from springing back to its natural bent." Feathers were split and the sprays then tied onto the shaft with sinew strings.

I am not normally one to impose psychological analysis on folktales, but I feel that here the social tensions of the Plains Indian child are too obvious to ignore. When the people were tenting and moving daily from hunting site to hunting site, the children must certainly have felt a fear of abandonment. What if the villagers were attacked, as they most certainly might be while on this strange ground? What if they fled from the attack while the children were playing or gathering berries away from the camp? What if in the bustle of a move a child should simply be forgotten?

Of course these stories were more the property of the adult tribal population than that of the children, but it is still hard to ignore the terror of abandonment in this story and the fantasized heroic recovery and brutal revenge.

Ictinike and the Four Creators
Told by Francis La Flesche

Ictinike got married and lived in a lodge. One day he said to his wife, "Hand me that tobacco pouch. I must go visit your grandfather, Beaver," and so he departed.

As he was entering Beaver's lodge, Beaver said, "Ho! Go around to the side," and they seated Ictinike on a pillow. Then Beaver's wife said, "We have been without food. How can we give your grandfather anything to eat?"

Now Beaver had four young beaver, and the youngest said, "Father, let me be the one who shall serve as food," and so the father killed it.

After boiling her son, Beaver's wife gave the meat to Ictinike, who ate it. But before Ictinike ate, Beaver warned him, "Be careful not to break any of the bones by biting them. Don't crack a single bone." But Ictinike broke one of the toes.

When Ictinike was full of the food, Beaver gathered the bones and put them in a skin, which he plunged under the water. In a moment the youngest beaver came up alive from the water. When his father asked him, "Are you all right?" the son answered, "Father, he broke one of my toes by biting." So from that time on every beaver has had one toe, the one next to the littlest, that appears to have been split by biting.

When Ictinike was about to go home, he pretended that he had forgotten about his tobacco pouch, which he left behind. So Beaver said to one of the children, "Take that to him. But don't go close to him. Throw it to him when you are still some distance away, for he is always very talkative."

The child took the tobacco pouch and started after Ictinike. When he came in sight of him but was still some distance away, the young beaver got ready to throw the pouch to Ictinike, but Ictinike called to him, "Come closer! Come closer!" When young Beaver took the pouch closer, Ictinike said, "Tell your father that he should come visit me."

So when young Beaver got home again, he said, "Father, he says that you should go visit him."

Beaver replied, "I was afraid of that very thing. That is why I told you to throw him the pouch from some distance away."

So Beaver went to visit Ictinike. When he got there, Ictinike wanted to kill one of his own children as he had seen Beaver do. So he hit him many times, making him cry. But Beaver did not want him to do such a thing, so he said, "Let him alone! You are hurting him." Then Beaver sent down to the stream where he found a young beaver and he brought him back to the lodge, and they ate it.

On another day Ictinike said to his wife, "Hand me that tobacco pouch. I must go call on your grandfather, Muskrat," and so he left.

As he was entering the lodge, Muskrat said, "Ho! Go around to the one side," and Ictinike was seated on a pillow.

Muskrat's wife said, "We have been without food. How can we give your grandfather anything to eat?"

Then Muskrat said, "Bring some water," and the woman brought water. He told her to put it in the kettle and hang the kettle over the fire. When the water was boiling very fast, the husband upset the kettle and instead of water, out came wild rice! So Ictinike ate the wild rice.

When Ictinike left, he dropped his tobacco pouch as before. Then Muskrat called one of his children and said, "Take this to him. Don't go near him though. Just throw it to him when you are still some distance from him, for he is always very talkative."

So the child took the tobacco pouch to give it back to Ictinike, but when he was about to throw it to him, Ictinike said, "Come closer! Come closer!" and as he took the pouch, he said, "Tell your father that he should come visit me."

When young Muskrat reached home he said, "O Father, he said that you should come visit him," and Muskrat replied, "That is precisely what I was afraid of. That's why I said, 'Throw it to him when you are still some distance from him.'"

When Muskrat went to see Ictinike, Ictinike said to his wife, "Bring some water," and she brought some, which she put into the kettle and hung over the fire until it was boiling. But when Ictinike upset the kettle, only water came out. Ictinike had wanted to do the same thing as Muskrat, but he was not able to.

So Muskrat had the kettle refilled, and when the water was boiling he upset it, and there was a great abundance of wild rice, which he gave to Ictinike. And then Muskrat left, leaving plenty of wild rice.

On another day Ictinike said to his wife, "I am going to see your grandfather, Kingfisher." When he got there Kingfisher stepped on a bough of the large white willow bending it down so far that it was horizontal. He then dived down into the water and came up with a fish which he gave to Ictinike to eat.

And as Ictinike was about to go home he left one of his gloves, pretending that he had forgotten it. So Kingfisher directed one of his boys to take the glove and return it to the owner, but he told him not to go close to him, for Ictinike was very talkative and might keep him too long.

Just as the boy was about to throw the glove to him, however, Ictinike said, "Come closer! Come closer!" So the boy carried the glove closer, and Ictinike told him, "Tell your father that he should come visit me."

So the son told his father, "O Father, he said that you are supposed to visit him," and Kingfisher said, "That is exactly what I was afraid of. That's why I told you, 'Throw it to him when you are still some distance away.'"

So Kingfisher went to see Ictinike. When he got there, Ictinike climbed up on a bough of a large white willow, bending it until it was horizontal. He jumped from it and plunged beneath the water. He had such a hard time that Kingfisher had to seize him and bring him back to land. Ictinike had swallowed more water than he liked.

Then Kingfisher plunged into the stream, bringing up fish, which he gave to Ictinike. But Kingfisher left without eating any of the fish himself.

On another day Ictinike said to his wife, "I am going to see your grandfather, Flying Squirrel," and so he went. When Ictinike arrived, Flying Squirrel said to his wife, "Hand me that awl." He took the awl and climbed up on his lodge. When he reached the very top, he stabbed himself in the scrotum, causing a great many black walnuts to fall to the ground. Thus he provided the black walnuts that Ictinike ate.

When Ictinike left, he left behind one of his gloves, as before, pretending that he had forgotten it. And, as before, Flying Squirrel sent the glove to Ictinike with one of his sons and Ictinike sent an invitation to Flying Squirrel with the son that Flying Squirrel should visit.

When Flying Squirrel reached Ictinike's lodge, Ictinike took an awl and climbed to the roof of his lodge. He had barely reached the top of the lodge when he stabbed himself in the scrotum. He was bleeding very badly. Flying Squirrel said, "Why, he has really hurt himself badly." And so Flying Squirrel took the awl, climbed up on the lodge, and made a large quantity of black walnuts for Ictinike.

COMMENTARY

In regard to this tale Dorsey comments, "Ictinike married after his adventure with the chipmunk, as told in the preceeding part of the myth. The order of his adventures is as follows: 1. With the Buzzard. 2. With [Chipmunk]. 3. With the Beaver. 4. With the Muskrat. 5. With the Kingfisher. 6. With the flying Squirrel.

"The four Creators were the Beaver, whose deeds are told in the myth; the Muskrat, who made rice out of water, roots of trees, and men; the Flying-squirrel, who made nuts of his 'cande' [testes]; and the Kingfisher, who made all the fishes."

Ictinike's assumption of hospitality is a part of Omaha culture. Open hospitality was a reality long before the white missionaries brought the theory in the form of the Golden Rule: "Before considering the new economic attitudes which have been introduced with the concept of ownership of land and of property inheritance, it is necessary to discuss one other trait which the Antlers [Omaha] share with most primitive [sic] peoples and which Morgan called the Law of Hospitality. This is the compulsion to provide freely for anyone who enters one's house, those who feel free to enter being for the most part relatives only."[12]

Margaret Mead was of course right, but the restriction of the home must be noted. In all *social* situations the Omaha still to this day practice open hospitality. When I go to a meeting of any kind, I carry along as a matter of course my dishes and salt, for I can assume that there will be food and that the food will be divided equally among everyone who is there. Even when someone like Ictinike takes advantage of this policy, there is no restriction of the hospitality.

The motif of eating one of the family and then restoring him to life—cautioning a guest not to crack the bones, the violation of this injunction, and the resulting maiming—is one of those motif cycles that amaze newcomers to the study of folklore. This same tale can be found all around the world, even in medieval Icelandic folk tales. There has been some thought that because of the universality of the human spirit, various minds have, at various times and places, arrived at the same narrative formulation; but most scholars today believe that in the passage of many, many hundreds of years man has simply passed such tales from one group to another, even across wide geographic, cultural, and linguistic distances.

Ictinike, Coyote, and the Colt
Told by Francis La Flesche

Coyote was standing, looking at a two-year-old colt that lay sleeping. "Well, Friend," he said to Ictinike, "since this horse is dead, we wanted to drag him away and eat him, but we have not been able to move him. Help us, my Friend. I will tie your hands to his tail, and when you pull, we will grab his legs, and together we can drag him away."

"Yes," said Ictinike. "Come tie my hands for me."

Coyote tied Ictinike's hands very tightly to the colt's tail. Then he said, "Come, My Friend, pull on it," and Ictinike pulled.

The colt woke up and jumped to its feet. He dragged Ictinike along, kicking him. Ictinike cried out as the colt kicked him. Coyote laughed until he could hardly breathe. And the colt kicked Ictinike, sending him flying through the air. He gouged out great pieces of flesh.

"How will I ever be able to get even with him?" said Ictinike, thinking of Coyote.

The next day Ictinike was eating a fish. Coyote came along. "Oho! My Friend, it is truly a pleasure to see you," said Coyote.

"Indeed it is," said Ictinike.

"My Friend, how did you catch that fish?"

"My Friend, I knocked a hole in the ice and sat with my tail through the hole in the water. A fish suddenly bit me on the tail and so I caught it."

"My friend, where was that?" asked Coyote.

"My Friend, over there. But they bite in the evening after it is cold."

Evening came and it grew cold. "Come, My Friend, let's go," said Coyote. Ictinike agreed and they went. When they reached the ice, Ictinike knocked a hole in it.

"Come. Sit and put your tail in the water," said Ictinike. And Coyote sat with his tail in the water through the hole.

After a while he said, "My Friend, there is a bite!"

"My Friend, they are small. Wait until they are large to catch them. Sit still," said Ictinike.

Soon the ice started to freeze over. "My Friend, there is another bite," said Coyote.

"My Friend, sit still. They are all small," said Ictinike. "After a while the big ones will come."

Soon the ice froze over. "Now, My Friend, one of the big ones is biting," said Coyote.

"Now! Now! Pull! Pull!" said Ictinike. Coyote pulled. Though he pulled ever so hard, he only slipped on the ice.

"Try harder! It *is* a big one," said Ictinike.

"Help me!" called Coyote.

"Take my hands," said Ictinike. They joined hands and pulled hard. "My Friend, pull hard. It is a big fish and I'm afraid we're going to lose him."

They said, "Now!" and pulled hard. Suddenly Coyote's tail was pulled off. Coyote looked at his tail. "My Friend, you have done me wrong," said Coyote.

"My Friend, just as you did to me," said Ictinike.

They parted in different directions, and Coyote made himself a new tail out of twisted grass.

COMMENTARY

As I mentioned with the previous tale, some stories appear spread all over the world, among all sorts of cultures, even where contact with other peoples seems virtually impossible. The motif of fishing with one's tail through the ice, only to have it frozen and pulled out, is almost universal.

Coyote

The Trickster commonly appears in the form of the coyote in many American Indian cultures, but we have only the few tales here from the Omaha. The coyote was plentiful enough on the Plains, and his slinking characteristics gave him a bad reputation here too. But apparently the personality of the Trickster simply was not so often applied to Coyote.

Why did the coyote, of all creatures on earth, carry a part of the load of the Trickster's ambiguity and duplicity on his narrow and mangy shoulders? Why was this miserable creature the star of tales told around the Omaha campfires?

Anyone who has seen a coyote scurrying up a Plains draw with his tail between his legs knows why he is here the hapless victim of so many disasters, mostly of his own making. We have a survival of this view of the coyote in our own modern cartoon series, "The Roadrunner." And yet it must be remembered that the coyote enjoys a certain amount of respect in these tales too, if nothing more than as a result of his being the principal protagonist of the tales.

Many Indians and their white compatriots today share a real admiration for the coyote (and his alter ego, Rabbit). I do. When I hear the song of the coyote—never a bark or a howl but a *song*—I still admire the songster as a Trickster, a culture hero, simultaneously a hero and a villain, a coward and the very essence of courage. The coyote (and, again, the rabbit) has been the target of a warfare reminiscent of that waged by America in Indochina. On the Plains, man in his fanciful madness reckons the coyote The Enemy and uses airplanes, speeding all-terrain vehicles, semiautomatic weapons, indiscriminate chemical warfare, electronic detection, trained dogs, and a scorched-earth policy to eradicate the coyote. Every possible advantage of technology, mobility, and manpower—I purposely omit "intelligence"—is brought to bear in the drive to kill a single coyote. Nothing is spared.

Yet today the range of the coyote is expanding.

The message is plain to me and some of my Indian friends, who feel painfully akin to the coyote in this regard. The coyote/Trickster lives on. The hunted is cleverer than the hunter. There is hope for the dogged, be he coyote or Indian.

Coyote and Puma
Told by Mawadanthi (meaning Mandan), an Omaha

There was Coyote and Puma—just these two. They met.

"My Friend," said Coyote, "I want to talk with you about something I have on my mind." They talked about a very large tribe. Coyote said, "My Friend, do what I am asking you."

"Yes," said Puma.

"They have been wanting to get the chief's daughter, but they have failed again and again. I want her. My Friend, you act like a horse and I will ride on you," said Coyote.

And he put a bridle on Puma and mounted him. "My Friend, please do a good job. Show your skill. Practice acting like a horse—prancing, jumping, arching your neck, champing at the bit, walking, and bucking. I will put on my large leggings, blackened mocassins, and a winter robe with the hair on the outside. I will carry an osage orange bow and I will fasten very white feathers on one end of it. And I will ride you around the village when we come near it," said Coyote.

He rode up and stopped at a place where they were playing the game called *bathingjahah*. He sat on his horse as it pranced, jumped, arched its neck, and ran in short spurts.

"Look, Friends. Someone has just come up. Whew! Someone has come whom we haven't seen before, a man quite different from those we know around here. He is very well dressed. He is on an excellent horse. Stop! Who is he?" they said.

Coyote had disguised himself well. They did not think it could be Coyote. They said to him, "Well, why are you traveling?"

"Well," he said. "It is because I want the chief's daughter."

The people went to tell the chief. "He says he has come because he wants your daughter."

"Come," the chief said to his sons. "Go to your Sister's Husband." They went for Coyote and saying, "Come, Sister's Husband, I have to invite you to go with us. We have come for you."

"Yes, Wife's Brothers," said Coyote. He got on his horse, pulled on the bridle hard to make the horse jump, and the horse jumped as he went along. All the people stood back and looked at him.

"The man moving along is certainly well dressed. Whoever he is, he is indeed well dressed," they said.

Finally they reached the chief's lodge. "Ho! Come! Bring your Sister's Husband to me. Tie his horse over there. Give him hay," said the chief.

"My Wife's Brothers, and also my Wife's Father, that horse doesn't eat hay," said Coyote. "He eats only fresh meat," and they entered the lodge.

Coyote approached the woman whom he was to marry and sat down by her.

Night came, and the chief said, "O First-Born Daughter of the House, make a couch for your husband."

When they had copulated, Coyote said to her, "I must urinate," and he went outside. He went to Puma and said, "Friend, I have done it. If you want, you can have a turn with her," and one after the other they did it to her, it is said. Powerfully and frequently they copulated from evening until morning.

At daybreak the chief assembled all his relatives. They gathered all sorts of gifts and took them to the lodge, firing guns.

When Coyote heard that, he was afraid. "Ku! ku!" He jumped outside and ran away.

"Why, it's Coyote! Hit him! Hit him! Kill him!"

Coyote ran, fouling his path heavily and frequently with his droppings. Puma stole off and went home.

The people killed Coyote. They burned him. He had done a great wrong.

COMMENTARY

Marriage was a very sanctified institution among the Omaha, all the more so because so much of Plains survival depended upon a division of labor between the husband and his wife or wives. Therefore, Puma and Coyote's casual violation of the institution is all the more foul, and all the more typical of Trickster.

It is not surprising that the chief's daughter marries an animal—actually two of them in this tale. "In tales of American Indians, . . . and, indeed, of primitive peoples everywhere, the marriage of human beings to actual animals is of very frequent occurrence."[13]

Of the game *bathingjaha*, Fletcher says only: "*Pathinzhahe* was a game adopted from the Pawnee some generations back. It was played with a hoop and a peculiar stick which was thrown so as to intercept the rolling hoop."[14]

But Dorsey offers a somewhat more complete account of the contest:

Pathinjahe is a game played by two men. At each end of the playground there are two *buda*, or rounded heaps of earth. A ring of rope or hide, the *wathigije*, is rolled along the ground, and each player tries to dart a stick through it as it goes. He runs very swiftly after the hoop and thrusts the stick with considerable force. If the hoop turns aside as it rolls it is not so difficult to thrust a stick through it. "The stakes are eagle feathers, robes, blankets, arrows, earrings, necklaces, &c."[15]

Coyote and Snake
Told by George Miller

Once upon a time a snake was lying across the road, at right angles to it. Coyote came along and said to him, "Snake, move off. If I step on you, you will die."

To this Snake replied, "This path isn't big enough for both of us. You can just move over to one side."

"Well," said Coyote, "you'd better do what I say. Move away."

"It's you, not me, who's going to have to move from the path," said Snake.

"Well then," said Coyote, "I will step on you and you will die."

"No," said Snake, "when someone steps on *me*, *he* is the one who usually dies."

"Oh sure, I will die. Let's just see which of us is telling the truth," said Coyote. And when he jumped over Snake, he bit him on the leg or foot. "Ho!" said Coyote to Snake. "You are certain to die because I jumped over you."

"*You* will die," said Snake.

Then Coyote went off and as he went he said, "Well, my body has never been in this condition before. I am so fat!" He stretched his neck as far as he could, looked over his back, and examined himself all over. Despite his condition, he gave the scalp-yell often.

When he found himself gasping, his mouth wide open, he said, "Well, Snake was telling the truth!" Finally his whole body was so swollen that his skin was tight on him and the tip of his nose was puffed up. "Snake told the truth," he said again.

He sat down at a sheltered place warmed by the sun, coiled himself as far as possible as a snake does, fell into a sound sleep from which he never woke, and so died. Because of this event, whenever a snake bites an animal, its body swells up and the animal dies.

COMMENTARY

Dorsey provides a second variation of this tale as it was told by Francis La Flesche, but it is abbreviated and fragmented.

Coyote and Gray Fox (a Ponca tale)
Told by One Horn, an Omaha

Gray Fox was very fat. Coyote said, "Younger Brother, what has made you so fat?"

"Elder Brother," said Gray Fox, "I lie down in the path of those who are carrying crackers along and I pretend to be dead. When they pick me up and throw me into their wagon, I just lie there and kick crackers out. Then I jump out and start on my way home, eating all the way. It's the crackers that have made me so fat. Elder Brother, you should try it. You have such big feet that I think you should be able to throw out a lot of crackers."

So Coyote went to the place and lay down in the road. And when the white man came along, he threw Coyote into the wagon. The white man thought, "I'm up to this guy's tricks." And so he tied Coyote's feet; then he threw him into the wagon and took him to his home. When he got there he threw Coyote out by a miserable out-building.

Then the white man brought a knife and cut the cords that bound Coyote. Now he didn't cut Coyote's feet—just the ropes that he had tied him with. He pretended that he thought Coyote was dead; he threw him over his back and started for the house. But Coyote managed to get loose and run home.

He went back to get Gray Fox. "Younger Brother," said Coyote, "You have made me suffer."

"You yourself are to blame. Be quiet and come with me," said Gray Fox. "You brought the trouble on yourself by lying down where the white man comes along with his load of goods."

"O Younger Brother, you tell the truth," said Coyote.

Gray Fox had tricked him.

Coyote and the Buffalo
Told by Francis La Flesche

Once Coyote was walking along. Buffalo were also grazing around. Coyote went to them and begged them, "O Grandfather—and you, my other grandfathers—pity me. I want to live just like you."

"Don't say that again," said Bull Buffalo.

"No, Grandfather. Pity me. You live by eating the food that grows most abundantly, without working for it, and I would like to live like that too."

"How can you mean that?" asked old Bull Buffalo that was standing a ways off. But Coyote would not stop talking.

"Oho! Blunt Horns, you start it," said Bull Buffalo.

"Come, stand with your back to me," Blunt Horns said to Coyote. "Be careful that you don't make the slightest effort to evade me."

"O Grandfather! O Grandfather! O Grandfather! Oh! Why would I do that?"

Blunt Horns kept pawing the ground and bellowing. He jammed his horns into the ground, sending pieces flying in all directions. Coyote stood looking at him out of one corner of his eye. "Whew! It would be impossible for him not to kill me if he should touch me," thought Coyote as he stood there. So when Blunt Horns came running, Coyote jumped out of his way, and he went on by without touching Coyote.

"Really!" said Blunt Horns, "I thought you were telling the truth, but I don't think so now."

"No, Grandfather, I did that because I was afraid of you. But pity me. I want to live just like you."

Every time a buffalo tried what Blunt Horns had tried, Coyote jumped aside. Finally Bull Buffalo said, "Ho! Young Bull Buffalo, you try it."

"Ho!" said Young Bull Buffalo. "Stand with your back to me. If you jump aside this time, I will kill you."

"Ho! Grandfather. I will not flee," said Coyote.

And Young Bull Buffalo went backward, step by step, pawing the ground, bellowing, thrusting his horns into the soil, throwing up dust. Then he came charging at him. When he got to him this time, Coyote did not jump aside. Young Bull Buffalo hit Coyote right in the side, and Coyote flew along with him, a young bull buffalo, just like him, and they ran off together.

As they grazed along, they reached a certain place. Coyote ate grass of every sort, and as they grazed along, Coyote fell back of the herd.

"Ho! Come on! Speed up!" Bull Buffalo kept saying to him.

"No, Grandfather. I cannot get enough of this grass, and I just want to eat, so I fall behind," Coyote answered. As they moved on, Coyote kept falling further behind.

They reached the crest of a hill, and four buffalo bulls went down to the foot of the hill. The four buffalo bulls reached a certain place and waited there for Coyote. "He isn't here yet. It would be good to wait for him," they said. But after they had waited for him for a long time, he still had not arrived.

"Ho! Young Bull Buffalo, go after him," they said.

"Oho!" answered Young Bull Buffalo and ran back. He even reached the place where Coyote had been changed into a buffalo, and Coyote was not there. Young Bull Buffalo turned back. As he left, he saw a coyote running along as if looking for something.

"You, running along there! Wait!" said the young bull buffalo who had been a coyote. "Would you like to live like me?"

"Yes, Elder Brother," answered Coyote. "I would like to live like you."

"Well, stand facing the other way."

"Yes, Elder Brother."

The young bull buffalo went backward, pawing the ground, thrusting his horns into the soil, throwing up dust. "Be careful that you don't try to evade me." Then he came running as if to attack him. He passed right by, for Coyote had jumped aside. He charged in this way three times, but Coyote jumped aside each and every time.

On the fourth charge Young Bull Buffalo said, "I will kill you." Then he came running. He hit him on the side and they both ran on, but Coyote was again a coyote just like his companion. "You have done a terrible thing to me," he said. "Go!"

Again he went looking for the buffalo bulls. He followed them and finally reached them. Again he asked the favor of them, "My Grandfathers, pity me. Someone did me wrong."

"Ho! Young Bull Buffalo, you begin."

"Ho! Come, stand with your back to me," said Young Bull Buffalo. "Be careful that you don't jump aside."

"No, Grandfather. Why should I jump aside?" asked Coyote.

The young bull buffalo backed off and came running at him. When he reached him he gored Coyote and threw him up high in the air. He killed him with the shock of the fall. And that is the way it was.

Coyote and The Turkeys
Told by Francis La Flesche to Franz Boaz

Once Coyote awoke from his sleep to find that he was hungry, for he hadn't had anything to eat for several days. He arose and wandered about in the woods. Eventually he came on a flock of turkeys. He knew that he could not catch one of them by attacking the whole flock, so he followed them until they came to some open ground where he would have a better chance in running one of them down.

As the turkeys moved on to the prairie where they found their best feeding grounds, Coyote followed them at a distance without their knowing it. They went further along into the open area, still followed closely by Coyote.

When they eventually saw Coyote, the turkeys moved along faster, but he kept his same pace, only wanting to keep them running and in sight. But he did stay fairly close to them.

When the turkeys had gone a long way from the forest, Coyote made an attack. For a while the race was on foot, but then, as Coyote came closer, the turkeys spread their wings and flew away.

But again the turkeys came down to the ground and Coyote moved along even faster to keep the birds in sight. This was repeated three times, but on the fourth time the turkeys were not able to take to the air, so they tried to escape by running along the ground. When they began opening their mouths as they ran along, Coyote was sure of his game.

He ran faster and faster until he came very close to the turkeys, and then they scattered in every direction. This was Coyote's chance. He made for the biggest one. It was nip and tuck, Coyote doing most of the nipping.

Finally he caught the big bird by the tail and brought it to the group and killed it. Just then, from the corner of his eye, he saw his worst enemy, a man.

Now the race was between Coyote and the man. Frequently Coyote would turn his head to see if the man was gaining on him. At last he fell to the ground exhausted. He lay flat on his back on the ground, prepared to die, but no man stood over him.

Coyote got up and was surprised to find that what he thought was a man was a turkey feather that had become wedged between his teeth and was sticking from the corner of his mouth.

COMMENTARY

The text of this tale, sent to Franz Boaz by Francis La Flesche on June 6, 1928, shows La Flesche's extraordinary skill. Unlike Dorsey's translations, La Flesche's version needed very little reworking. La Flesche's style is smooth. Indeed, if there can be a complaint, it is that he uses too much skill in his "free translation." In the original Omaha, the audience is told about the feather being mistaken for a man even before Coyote flees. La Flesche has moved this element in the story to present greater suspense. Also, the pun based on the expression "nip and tuck" does not appear at all in the original Omaha text.

The Raccoons and the Crabs
Told by Francis La Flesche

Raccoon was walking along, and as he walked he sang:

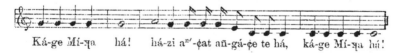

Ká-ge Mí-ʞa há! há-zi aⁿ'-ȼat añ-gá-ȼe te há, ká-ge Mí-ʞa há!

Younger Brother Coon,
Let's go eat grapes,
Younger Brother Coon.

The younger brother responded, "But, Elder Brother, I don't want to because my teeth chatter so whenever I eat them."
Then the elder brother sang:

Ká-ge Mí-ʞa há! ʞan'-de aⁿ'-ȼat añ-gá-ȼe te há, ká-ge Mí-ʞa há!

Younger Brother Coon,
Let's go eat some plums,
Younger Brother Coon.

The younger brother answered, "Elder Brother, when I eat them I get sick to my stomach, so I don't want to."

The elder brother then sang:

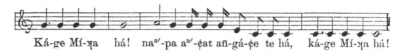

Ká-ge Mí-ꭹa   há! nan'-pa an'-ȼat an-gá-ȼe te há,   ká-ge Mí-ꭹa há!

Younger Brother Coon,
Let's go eat some chokecherries,
Younger Brother Coon.

"Elder Brother, whenever I eat them I get cold, so I don't want to." Finally, the elder brother sang:

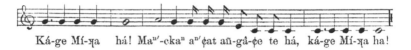

Ká-ge Mí-ꭹa   há! Man'-ckan an'ȼat an-gá-ȼe te há, ká-ge Mí-ꭹa ha!

Younger Brother Coon,
Let's go eat some crabs,
Younger Brother Coon.

"O Elder Brother! O Elder Brother! O Elder Brother! I always like *them*."

So they went off. They reached the place where the crabs would get water for their village. They pretended to be dead.

"Be careful not to move a muscle. When I say, 'Oho!' jump up. Be careful. Even if they tickle you, don't move at all. Even if they push their claws up your nostrils, even if they reach into your eyes, don't stir. Move only when I say 'Oho!' " said the elder raccoon.

Soon some crabs came there for water. After they had been there for a while, they found the raccoons. They ran home to report this. "Two *Wathakukuche* are lying dead over there. Hurray!" said some of the men.

They went to the lodge of the crab chief to tell him about it. And the crab chief went over to look at the raccoons. He sent some over to them to attack them. And an old man went with them to act as a crier and to sing for the dancers. They went up to the raccoons, and one said to himself, "Let me see. I will tickle him in the side," but when he tickled him the raccoon didn't move a bit. Just as the raccoon was about to laugh, the crab stopped.

Then the crab went over to the other raccoon and pushed his claws up his nostrils. He lay without stirring one bit. Then the crab went back to the other raccoon and took hold of his eyelids by the very edge. The raccoon didn't move but just lay there.

The old crab proclaimed loudly, "Ho! He says that you are to dance!" and so they all danced. They danced around the raccoons. The old man sang:

Wa-¢á-qu-qu'-xe na'ⁿ-ba t'é a-ké, Á-ma si-¢é-de sne-dé, Á-ma ïn'-dje q¢é-xe, u+.

Soon the whole crab village was dancing around them. Then the elder raccoon shouted "Oho!" Both raccoons jumped up and attacked the crabs. The crabs ran for their lodges with all their might. The raccoons walked along killing and eating them.

Soon only two crabs were left. "Go on," said the raccoons. "From now on you shall be called *manka*, 'the ground-scramblers.' "

COMMENTARY

Another version of this same tale as told by Pathinanpaji is also given by Dorsey. It is very close to this version except for the reasons given by the second raccoon for not liking the first suggested foods:

"O Younger Brother Coon! O Younger Brother Coon! O Younger Brother Coon! Let's go eat grapes, O Younger Brother Coon."

"O Elder Brother, whenever I eat those, I get a stomachache, and then I drink too much water, and then I have diarrhea so bad that I have to go at nearly every step I take," said the younger.

"O Younger Brother Coon! O Younger Brother Coon! O Younger Brother Coon! Let's go eat hackberries, O Younger Brother Coon," said the elder.

"O Elder Brother, whenever I eat them, I am constipated for such a long time. I get tired of that," said the younger.

"O Younger Brother Coon! O Younger Brother Coon! O Younger Brother Coon! Let's go eat buffalo berries, O Younger Brother Coon," sang the elder.

"O Elder Brother, whenever I eat them, I get a sore bottom and have to scratch all the time. I get tired of that," said the younger.

Adventurers And Culture Heroes

It is not surprising that in many cases Indian tales refuse to fit neatly into folktale categories formulated primarily by Europeans in the nineteenth century. These adventure tales show some of the characteristics of the trickster tales. The heroes' powers frequently transcend those of ordinary man, and they might be minor gods, which means that the tales should be treated as myths. Some are etiological and quasi-historical, which suggests the legend. The tasks, trials, and fantastic creatures remind one of the fairytale or *Märchen*. Therefore, while I have put them together and apart here as a separate unit, I do not mean to separate them from the larger narrative tradition of the Omaha.

Orphan's Adventures as Rabbit
Told by Mary La Flesche

Orphan lived with his grandmother. "Oh, Grandmother, let me go to the village."

"Why, Grandchild! They will mistreat you. Do not go."

"No, Grandmother. I want to go anyway," and he did go there.

He reached the village. "Ho! Ho! Rabbit has come." Take him to the chiefs!"

"Rabbit has come to see you," they told the chiefs.

"Come, bring him here. Put him in the center. Gather around him." The chiefs said to Rabbit, "Come, you will dance."

Rabbit said, "Sing for me."

"Come, Rabbit. You are nice and fat only on your shoulders. You won't satisfy anyone's hunger." They sang for him and he danced.

When he stopped dancing, he said, "I will break in the heads of four chiefs on one side."

"He said, 'I will strike them and break in their skulls,' " bystanders said. "Surround him and cut off his retreat!"

He struck four chiefs and broke in their skulls, and ran home. They could not catch him. He ran home and ran into a hole the size of a hen's egg. He was home with his grandmother.

"Grandmother, give me a piece of iron," he said.

And she said, "I have no iron at all. There is only this piece of hide scraper."

"Let me have it," he said, and he threw it quickly through the door and it closed the entrance of the lodge. When his pursuers came up, he said to them, "How can you possibly kill me? Go away. You are standing around for nothing."

That is how it happened.

COMMENTARY

Orphan is a mysterious creature who appears throughout Sioux and Plains folklore (Omahas are a distant member of the Sioux linguistic unit). In his formlessness, his uncertain character, he is like Ictinike, but he is not usually a true trickster. This story offers a rare and interesting anomaly in that regard. Orphan is usually a true culture hero, a benevolent demigod. But in this tale, Orphan is described explicitly as Rabbit. The title suggests that he is only passing for Rabbit, but it is hard to know if the title was provided by the informant or the collector. Omaha songs, for example, have no names, and it would not be surprising to find that their nineteenth-century stories also went without title.

Orphan and the Water Monster
Told by Joseph La Flesche

A boy went traveling. He was very poor. He wandered continually without a lodge, with no relatives. At length he found a small writing. When he found the writing, it said, "I will give you a gun." And as he walked on, he found the gun and picked it up.

Having the gun, he looked at the small writing and it told him what the gun did. The boy took the gun and put powder and shot in it. He found a prairie chicken and shot at it. He knocked it down and killed it.

The Indians knew nothing about guns at all. When he departed he saw a deer. Having seen it, he shot at it and killed it. The boy thought, "This gun is certainly a fine thing."

Again he saw a deer, and he shot it. Again he was glad. He thought, "This gun is good," and he was very glad.

Then he heard someone talking. He was in some dense woods. The intruder quickly urged his dogs on. He called "Hu! hu! hu! hu!" He had his dogs seek game.

The boy, who was Orphan, stood leaning behind a tree, hiding himself. Since he was afraid of being seen by the dogs, he stood there with his gun. But at length the dogs found him, and then the man came up to speak with him. "Why do you have that?" he asked him about the gun for he did not know what a gun was.

The boy said, "When I see an animal, I can kill it with this, and then I can eat, so I keep it."

And the man said, "Let me see! Shoot at that prairie chicken standing over there."

When the boy shot at the prairie chicken he killed it, and the man said, "Let me see, O Friend. Let me see that thing you have there." When the boy gave it to him he looked it over and said, "Friend, this is certainly a good thing to have." And then he said, "Teach me how to use it."

He taught him, and when the man shot at a prairie chicken he killed it. "O Friend, I wish to buy this gun from you," he said.

But the boy was not at all willing to sell it. "No, I cannot spare it," he said.

The man said, "I will give you something better."

"And what could you give me better than this?" asked the boy.

The man had two dogs, and he said, "I will give you both of these dogs."

The boy said, "What could I do with these dogs?"

He answered, "You can have them hunt game."

"Come now. I want to see that. Command them to hunt."

The man called the dogs by name. "Here, Walks-Following-the-Stream, go for deer. Here, Breaks-Iron-with-his-Teeth, go after a black bear!" And soon Walks-Following-the-Stream came back with a deer, and Breaks-Iron-with-his-Teeth returned with a black bear.

The boy liked the dogs, and he gave the gun to the man and the man gave the dogs to the boy. The man said, "I have given you something very good. I will give you a sword too."

The boy said, "I have also given you something good too. Whatever animal I shot at with it, I killed, so I kept it."

The man said, "Teach me how to use the gun," and Orphan taught him. He wanted to know all about the gun.

And Orphan said, "My Friend, teach me about the dogs."

He said, "If you want the dogs to do something, call them by name, and when you say, 'Do this thing or that,' they will always do it."

"And teach me about the sword too."

The other said, "If you get into any trouble, think of me, grab this sword, and threaten to strike with it. No matter how difficult your problem, it will do the job."

When they parted, the boy took the dogs and the other the gun.

The boy approached a nearby tribe. When he got quite near, he commanded the dogs to go after rabbits. "Walks-Following-the-Stream and Breaks-Iron-with-his-Teeth, hunt for rabbits," he said. The dogs hunted for rabbits and killed a great many. The boy carried the great number of rabbits on his back.

There was an old woman who pitched her tent far from the village. The boy went there. When he arrived there, he said, "Take these rabbits."

"Oh, my grandson has brought rabbits to me," she said.

"Grandmother, first give one of the rabbits to each dog. You can eat after that." And the old woman did that.

Soon the people who dwelled in the large village nearby began to cry loudly. The boy asked, "Grandmother, why are they crying?"

"Yes, the Water Monster with seven heads has said that he will swallow the chief's daughter, and if he doesn't get her, he will devour the whole village. So they are taking her to him. That is why they are crying," she said.

The boy said, "Grandmother, why don't they kill the Water Monster with seven heads?"

"Oh, Grandchild, don't say such a thing! He is holy, so he hears whatever is said," she answered.

"Even if he does know it, Grandmother, it would be a good thing if he were dead," he said.

Finally the soldiers went to the Water Monster with seven heads, taking the chief's daughter. And the boy went there too, but he went a different way. As the soldiers got close with her, they stopped and sent the woman ahead. The boy, Orphan, got to the shore first. He got to the place of the

Water Monster with seven heads before the woman did. Then the woman arrived where Orphan stood.

The boy had made some very good clothing for himself. He had his sword too. He said to the woman who was standing there, "Why have you come here?"

"Oh, it is possible that you haven't heard about it?" the woman cried.

"Yes, it is true. I have not heard," said the boy.

"I have come because the Water Monster with seven heads wants to eat me. If he does not get to eat me, then—I dread to think about it—he has threatened to eat the whole village. So I came," she said.

And the boy said, "Go home!"

The woman said, "Oh, you should go home yourself, you who are so handsome. Be careful that the Water Monster does not kill you."

"No, go home," said the boy, and the woman did go home.

And when she had left for home, the boy went to the edge of the water and stood there. "Breaks-Iron-with-his-Teeth, you go to the base of his neck, and Walks-Following-the-Stream, you go to the root of his tail," he said, and both of the dogs went under the water.

Finally they forced one of the heads of the Water Monster with seven heads to appear. The boy seized his sword and cut off the head of the Water Monster with seven Heads. He said, "Stop," and he cut the tongue from the head of the seven-headed Water Monster. He threw the head down at the edge of the water, but he took the tongue.

When he again approached the village, he said, "Hunt rabbits," and Orphan took the rabbits and put them in a sack. He carried them home to the old woman. "Grandmother, I have come with some rabbits."

"Oh, my grandchild has carried home some rabbits for me," said the old woman, and she took the rabbits.

"Grandmother, put that on something for me," he said, and she took the tongue and put it at the side of the lodge. "Grandmother," he said, "first give the dogs one rabbit a piece and then the rest are yours."

In the morning there was a great crying among the villagers, and the boy asked, "Grandmother, what is the matter?"

"Oh, how can my grandchild sit there and say such a thing? They are crying because the chief's daughter came home and they must take her away again."

"Grandmother, they should kill the Water Monster with seven heads. Why don't they do that?"

"My Grandchild, he is very holy. They are afraid of him. Everyone is afraid of him," she answered.

Again the boy went there. He went to the water and stood there before the soldiers got there. The soldiers brought the woman there. When they got close, they sent the woman ahead, and the soldiers went home.

The woman went on to the water, and there was the boy standing by the edge of the water. And the boy said, "Why have you come here?"

"Oh," she said, "you should have stayed home, you who are so handsome. Be careful that the Water Monster with seven heads doesn't kill you."

"No, go home," said the boy, and the woman went home. Again the boy went to the water. He said to his dogs, "Walks-Following-the-Stream, go to the base of his neck! Breaks-Iron-with-his-Teeth, go to the very root of his tail," and the dogs went headlong into the water.

After they had gone into the water, they made two of the seven-headed Water Monster's heads appear, and the boy cut off both heads. He took the tongues, threw the heads down on the bank, and went home.

When he got near the lodge, he hunted rabbits again. "Grandmother," he said, "take these rabbits," and the old woman did. "Grandmother, put these tongues on something for me." Then he went to sleep, for it was night.

In the morning the villagers cried again, making a great noise. "Grandmother, why are they crying?" he asked.

"My Grandchild, the chief's daughter came home and they are mourning for her."

Again the soldiers took the chief's daughter away. And again the boy reached the edge of the water first. He had made very excellent clothing for himself. The woman went there again.

The woman said, "You shouldn't have come. Be careful that the Water Monster with seven heads doesn't kill you."

The boy said, "No, you go home."

Well, the woman went home. When she was gone, the boy said, "Breaks-Iron-with-his-Teeth, go to where the base of his neck is, and Walks-Following-the-Stream, go to where the root of his tail is," and both dogs went under the water. The dogs bit the seven-headed Water Monster, causing three of his heads to appear. The boy cut off the three heads and went home.

Although the girl had always wanted to tell her story when she got home, she never had. When the boy was coming home, he hunted rabbits. He caught a great number of them and took them home in his pack. When he got back to the old woman, he gave her the three tongues.

"Grandmother, put these away for me. Ho! take these and give each of the dogs one."

Well, they slept. In the morning the people again made a great noise crying. "Grandmother," he asked, "Why are they crying?"

She said, "My Grandchild, the chief's daughter came home again, but they have to take her back again. That is why they are crying."

"Grandmother, they should kill the Water Monster with seven heads. Why don't they kill him?" asked the boy.

"Don't say that again to anyone. If you say it, he will kill you," said the old woman.

And again the soldiers took the girl away. The boy went there and arrived at the edge of the water first. Then the girl came, and the boy said, "Go home. Why did you come?" The woman did go home, and he said, "Walks-Following-the-Stream, go stand at the very base of his neck! Breaks-Iron-with-his-Teeth, go stand at the very root of his tail," and both dogs went down into the water. They bit off the one remaining head, causing it to come up from the depths. The boy cut off the head and took the tongue. He placed all the heads in a row on the bank of the stream, and when he had gone homeward, it happened that a black man came along the bank of the stream. Black Man found the heads and carried the heads away.

Black Man said, "I killed the Water Monster with seven heads," and the people said, "Really! This black man came here carrying the heads of the seven-headed Water Monster in his pack. Take them to the chief's tent," and he carried them there.

The chief said, "Where did you get those heads?"

Black Man said, "There was a Water Monster with seven heads, and I killed him."

And the chief said, "Well, if you killed him, you shall marry my daughter," and they cooked. They prepared a great feast.

All the people were invited to the marriage feast. And the chief said to the people, "If you say that the black man should marry my child, then he shall marry her."

The people said, "Yes, he has saved us, the whole tribe; therefore, if you say he may marry her, let him marry her."

The boy sat in his lodge knowing this. He was sad because Black Man was to marry the woman. The boy said, "Breaks-Iron-with-his-Teeth, go there. Bring back a slice of the meat that has been cooked for the marriage feast." And the dog went there.

When the dog came in sight, the people said, "Here comes a very fine dog!" The dog went to the table and then ran home carrying a slice of meat in his mouth.

"That dog has done a very bad thing. Chase him!" the people shouted. He reached his home at the old woman's lodge, carrying the meat in his mouth.

The chief said, "Come back with the dog and his owner too." This is what he told the soldiers, and when they reached the old woman's lodge, they found that the dog's owner was a very good-looking man and he was wearing very fine clothes. And the soldiers were ashamed before this man; he was so respectable that they could not express their business.

The boy said, "Why are you here?"

"We were sent here to find the dog that ran from the marriage feast with a piece of meat he had stolen," they said. "The chief told us that we should bring back with us the dog's owner too."

"Come! I will go with you," said the boy. He made himself the very best clothing, and he went there, taking along the tongues.

Black Man had not yet reached the chief's lodge. He was in a lodge somewhere else.

Finally the boy reached the chief's lodge with the tongues. He said, "What did I do wrong that you sent soldiers after me? A Water Monster was about to devour your whole tribe in spite of all that you could do, but I killed him for you. Why did you have soldiers take me?" He added, "These are the tongues of the Water Monster with seven heads," and he gave them to the chief.

The chief said, "This is the one who killed the Water Monster with seven heads. This is my daughter's husband." He had him sit with the girl, the wife of the black man.

"Yes, Father, this is the one," she said, pointing to Orphan.

They returned with Black Man. They gathered around him and the chief asked him, "How did you kill the Water Monster with seven heads?"

He answered, "I went there and killed him."

The chief asked, "What did you kill him with?"

He answered, "I killed him with a knife."

Then the woman came to the lodge with the man and came up to the gathering. "Father, this is the one, the man who killed the Water Monster with seven heads. This is the one, my rescuer," she said, indicating Orphan.

And the chief said, "Seize Black Man," and they carried him outside and burned him.

COMMENTARY

The writing and the gun are clearly recent influences on this tale. In another version of the same story, as told by Frank La Flesche, Joseph's son, the marvelous weapon traded for the dogs and sword is an infallible bow-and-arrow. It is curious that the younger man's version should display what must be assumed to be the older form. The great power of the sword is altogether lost in Joseph La Flesche's version, but in general the tale seems to be more complete.

In Frank La Flesche's version, which is not given here, the dogs' names are "Breaks-Iron-with-his-Teeth" and "Shatters-Stones-with-his-Teeth." The conclusion of that tale is more dramatic: Orphan sends one of his dogs to the wedding site, and the dog snatches a piece of meat from the feast. The wedding party chases him to Orphan's lodge, where the black man's deceit is revealed.

Of the introduction of firearms to the Omaha, Alice Fletcher says: "Guns were introduced toward the close of the first quarter of the nineteenth century, receiving the name *wahutonthe*, 'to make noise with.' The bullet was called *moncemon*, 'metal arrow'; gunpowder was called *monchude*, 'ashes.' The first guns received by the Omaha were flintlocks; rifles did not reach them until the third or fourth decade of the last century."[1]

Orphan and Buffalo Woman
Told by Mary La Flesche

When Orphan's mother and father died, he lived with his sister. And his sister married a man who was an excellent marksman. He went hunting, and he returned every day carrying a deer on his back.

Orphan said, "Surprise! O Sister, my Sister's Husband is coming home with something on his back. I want to eat some very fat meat."

And when he reached the lodge, she took some of the fat from around the kidneys after she had taken them out of the animal. She gave them to Orphan, along with the liver. "Eat that. It is clear that you *do* want fat! When you are through eating," she said, "go and guard the field."

He ate and then left for the field. He departed feeling very sad. And when he reached the field, he climbed into a tree and said, "Birds, come and eat the corn in these fields!" And when it was night, he went home again.

When it was morning again, the sister's husband again brought home a deer. Orphan said, "Ho ho! O Sister, my Sister's Husband is bringing home a deer on his back. This time I want to eat a piece of *very* fat meat," and so again she gave him the same pieces.

Having taken the fat wrapped around the kidneys, she gave them to him along with the liver. "Eat that. You really *do* want the fat piece." And then she added, "Go and guard the field." And so it happened for four days. On the fourth day she said, "Sit here and keep an eye on things. We want to take a look at the field."

As soon as he was alone in the lodge, Orphan lay down to sleep, but suddenly a very beautiful woman appeared and woke him by tugging at him. "Get up. Why are you sleeping?" she asked.

He got up, and she said, "You should eat a piece of those very fat pieces of meat. Why don't you eat one?"

"That is easy for you to say, but it is my sister's. I am afraid to eat it because she would scold me," he said.

She said, "Cut off a piece with a knife. Eat it."

But the boy said, "That is easy for you to say, but I don't want to."

So the woman got up and cut off part of the best piece, just about the size for one person to eat. She roasted it. She gave it to the boy and said, "Eat it." Then the woman replaced the slice she had cut off just as it had been, restoring that which she had taken from the meat. And so it happened for four days in a row. When the woman finally went home, she left a plain trail.

Orphan followed the trail. He walked all day and finally arrived very late in the evening at a fine lodge, a white lodge. When he entered it, there sat the woman. She was sitting on a fine couch. She gave him a small wooden bowl filled quite full with dried and pounded buffalo meat.

As she gave it to him he thought, "I have been very hungry. How will I ever get my fill?"

The woman said, "No, eat as fast as you like. You are certain to have enough."

He ate and was filled up, but there was still some left in the small bowl. He gave the small bowl back to the woman.

At night he lay down, she having made for him an excellent couch, and even a pillow. He slept very soundly, and when he woke up, it turned out that he was no longer in a lodge; he was lying on the grass. This same thing happened four days in a row.

She was Buffalo Woman. She was pregnant and delivered a child. When she gave birth to the baby, it was very short and white all over.

Ictinike was walking along, and suddenly he came upon the place at that very moment. "O First-Born Daughter of the Household, what is the matter with you?" he asked.

"Grandfather, my stomach hurts," she replied.

"Oh no, dear little Grandchild! Your stomach hurts you," he said.

Then a little buffalo calf was born, and he stood there, very white. Ictinike quickly pulled him under his robe.

Buffalo Woman said, "O Grandfather, where is your grandchild?"

He answered, "It hasn't come out yet."

"Grandfather, your grandchild did come out just before you came," she insisted. She told him this again and again.

But Ictinike said only, "It isn't here." Then Ictinike said, "O First-Born Daughter of the Household, I must go. It hasn't come out yet."

But Buffalo Woman said, "Grandfather, you are lying," and Ictinike left.

When Ictinike had gone, he went some distance, well out of sight. When he got there, he took the buffalo calf and wiped him with grass. He was very white and handsome. "Ha ha!" How easy it was for me to do what I wanted to do! They are saying, 'We have been robbed of a very fine buffalo calf,'" said Ictinike, and the buffalo calf ran around him. "Ho! O Third-Born of the Household, come here! Come here!" Ictinike kept calling and the buffalo calf came back to Ictinike.

The next time Buffalo Calf ran about, he went a little way off. "Why, O Third-Born of the Household, be careful not to run too far away. You are mine," he said. It happened this way four times, and on the fourth time he just kept on running toward his mother. When Ictinike called, "Come back.

O Third-Born of the Household! Don't run so far!" Buffalo Calf just kept right on running. And Ictinike went away feeling very sad.

Finally, as Buffalo Calf ran on, he came upon an old buffalo bull sitting on the ground. And the old buffalo bull said, "O Third-Born of the Household, they took your mother in this direction. They have already taken her down that long bluff extending beyond the horizon. And, Grandchild, you will go through occasional drops of rain." He said these words to him because he wanted to make him strong. And when Buffalo Calf left, there were occasional drops of rain.

When he reached the foot of the bluff, again there was a buffalo bull sitting there. He said, "O Third-Born of the Household, they have just passed this way with your mother. They have gone to the foot of that long bluff extending beyond the horizon. You will go through dense, misty rain." He said this to him because he liked him. When Buffalo Calf departed, he walked through dense, misty rain. And when he reached the foot of the bluff, a young bull buffalo—very young and small, of the sort that have very sharp horns—was sitting there. And the young buffalo bull said, "O Third-Born of the Household, they have just taken your mother this way. They have gone to the foot of that bluff nearby, the one after the next. You will pass through a very dense fog." And when Buffalo Calf departed, he went through a very dense fog.

When he reached the bottom of the bluff, there were a great many buffalo. They sat in a circle and his mother had been placed in the center. And they said, "Ho ho! Here comes the child! It missed you and so it has come here to you."

And then a very old buffalo cow, very scabby and decrepit, was sitting with her own calf directly in line with the approaching calf. And when white Buffalo Calf reached the old buffalo cow, he sucked at her teats, for he was very hungry.

One said, "Let four buffalo go after that one a little ways away. He is nursing there."

"We have come for you. The one right over there is your mother," they told him. But Buffalo Calf did not want to go. They wanted to take him home, but they failed, and the four returned to the herd.

When they got there, they said, "Leader, we have failed."

"Unsplintered Horns, go at once and kill the old woman," he said. And he went there and killed her, but when he tried again to take Buffalo Calf home, he too was unsuccessful.

"The one right over there is your mother. Let's go home," he said, but Buffalo Calf did not want to. And he went home, having also failed. "Leader, we failed once more," he said.

And the leader said, "Let four go at once and erase all traces of the buffalo cow," and they went there and tore the buffalo cow into small pieces, leaving not one trace of her. And they took white Buffalo Calf home to his mother. When they got home with him, they made him sit with his mother. They sat around her, a great many buffalo.

Then Orphan came in sight on the bluff, having been hunting for his wife for some time. And the leader said, "Although that is your husband who has just come in sight, you shall sit beside a buffalo cow just like you. If he recognizes you, you shall go home with him; if he does not recognize you, we will kill him."

His wife secretly told him, "They will make a buffalo cow just like me sit beside me. And when they say, 'Where is your wife?' say, 'That is she.' I will move my right ear. They will do the same thing with the child, but he too will move his right ear, and you take him."

They did make her sit with a buffalo cow just like her. "Come," said the leader, "take whichever one is your wife." He looked at them, and one did move her ear. He said, "That one," and took her. And the same was done with the child. "This is my child," he said, and took him.

The leader said, "Come. That will do. Go with him."

COMMENTARY

The implication of the parts of meat given to Orphan by his mean sister may not be clear; she is giving him cuts that are considered very poor indeed.

The reference to the field is not an anachronism. Omaha women kept corn fields in the Missouri River bottomlands for many centuries before the coming of the white man.

Dried and pounded buffalo meat was a common trail food because it was light and kept for long periods of time. Finely grated beef is still a part of the ritual breakfast of the Native American Church, sometimes referred to as the Peyote Cult.

Two variant texts follow. The first, as told by Mikasinazi, is very fragmentary. Dorsey explains: "The translation of this version is fuller than the [Omaha] text, because it was easier to keep pace with the narrator by writing in English; and he would not repeat any of the original that the collector failed to get. The words of the song are in Iowa, not Omaha."

It is precisely because of the song and other small but significant details in this splintered text that I have chosen to reproduce it; it contributes, I believe, to a fuller understanding of the myth.

The second variant, as told by Pathinanpaji, offers a substitute conclusion. As Dorsey says this "variation from the first version begins after the meeting of the Orphan and the Buffalo-woman in the white tent on the prairie. In the morning he found himself lying on the grass, the woman and tent having disappeared. He followed her all day and overtook her at night. This was repeated three times."

He adds in connection with this same version of the myth, "The Omahas imagine that the upper world is like stone, and that ground is there. The ground rests on the stone. The Orphan pushed his way through both stone and ground, when he pursued his wife."

Orphan and Buffalo Woman
Told by Mikasinazi

When Orphan went to the field at the request of his sister, he sang the following song.

Hiⁿ'-yu-no+! hiⁿ'-yu-no+! wí-taⁿ-haⁿ' ta qaⁿ-yé cé-wa-há-nyi ki+

hiⁿ'-yu-no+!

Sister mine, Sister mine,
My Sister's Husband is bringing home a big deer,
Sister mine.

Then he said, "Hu-hu-hu! Come, birds, eat. Eat this field. I am very poor. All birds! Come here! All you animals, too, of every sort, come gather around. I want to go wandering."
[omission]
Buffalo Woman gave birth to two babies.
[omission]
They stuck their father's side as they ran to meet him. Their mother was put in a row with three other white cows and Orphan was directed to identify her.
[omission]
"They say they will dance with you," she said.
[omission]
The buffalo sat for awhile, and then they went up high. They went flying. "They will go to the upper world," said Buffalo Woman.
[omission]
Buffalo Woman blew a horn, saying "T-t-t-t."
[omission]
The buffalo reached the shore of the Great Water and sat there. Orphan arrived there. And it happened that there was a lodge there.

A very old man was sitting there. "Yes," he said, "you are very poor. I heard you. The buffalo have gone across the Great Water. Shut your eyes and take a big step and you will be across the Great Water." He took the step and found himself on the other side. His two sons came running to meet him.

The woman told him, "They are going across the Great Water again. They will pass to the other side. They will land down there on the earth." [omission]

She came to the place where the boy was standing. "If you are completely unable to recognize me, I will move my right ear." [omission]

She moved her right ear briskly. [omission]

The next day the buffalo had a dance. Orphan went to it. He changed himself into a martin and darted back and forth among the buffalo. He kept making sudden thrusts at the buffalo. "You will get hurt thrusting like that. Stop it," he said.

The buffalo kept suddenly falling down on their knees. He went about, causing them to kill themselves by tearing themselves open.

Orphan and Buffalo Woman
Told by Pathinanpaji

On the fourth night the woman said, "Though I go home, please keep following me. When I reach my home on the other side of the Water, come there. When you reach the shore, say, 'Well, my Wife, here, just as you said, I am coming to you.' As you say that, close your eyes and take a step over the water. The next thing, they will make sharp thorns for you all over the ground. When you get there, say, 'Well, my Wife, here, just as you said, I am coming to you.' As you say it, close your eyes and take a step across the thorns. Next they will put down a road to the Upper World. Go there. When you get there, say, 'Well, my Wife, here, just as you said, I am coming to you.' As you say it, close your eyes and take a step into the air."

The woman then left him. She reached her home and walked among the buffalo. The buffalo had reached their home on the other side of the Water. Orphan came into sight.

"Really! Here is Orphan," they said. He went on following his wife and child. "Find something to stop him," said the buffalo.

They made four buffalo cows lie in a row. "Come," they said to Orphan, "which one lying there is your wife?"

She moved her ear briskly.

"That one is my wife," said Orphan.

"Well, find something else hard for him to do," the buffalo said.

The next morning when Orphan awoke, he lay alone on the grass. The woman had gone with the buffalo. The buffalo went across a very deep canyon hollowed out by a stream.

Orphan reached the canyon. Closing his eyes, he said, "Well, my Wife, here, just as you said, I am coming to you." He took a step and he was across the canyon.

"Really! Orphan has come here too. Find something more difficult for him," they said. And the next morning, when Orphan awoke, he lay alone on the grass. The woman had gone with the buffalo, and they had spread a bed of sharp thorns all over the surface of the land.

Orphan arrived at that place. He said, "Well, my Wife, here, just as you said, I am coming to you." He closed his eyes, took a step, and was across.

"Orphan has come here too. Find something even harder for him," they said.

The next morning Orphan woke up, and he lay alone on the grass. The woman had gone with the buffalo. They had gone, making a road to the Upper World. Orphan followed the road uphill. "Well, my Wife, here, just as you said, I am coming to you." He closed his eyes, took a step, and moved off. He went far beyond the clouds and he reached the other side.

"Really! Orphan has come here too. Stop trying!" they said to him. "Go home! You will fail!" they called. They went downhill from the Upper World to this earth. They reached their home at the bottom.

"Well, scatter in all directions," they said.

Orphan said to his wife, "Come, let's go home. Let me see your Husband's Sister."

When they were home, he put the child and woman by the outside of the tent. But his sister was very poor. She and her husband had been, and still were, apt to die of starvation.

"O Elder Sister, and my Sister's Husband, I have come home," he said.

"With no cause for complaint, a boy, our relation, went to some unknown place. We have not found him and we are very unhappy. There is no need to ridicule us," she said.

"But, Sister, it is I!" he cried.

Then his sister rubbed her eyes repeatedly with her hands and looked at him. She recognized him. "Hiho! my dear Younger Brother has returned," she said, pulling her husband to attract his attention.

"O Sister, your Brother's Wife is sitting outside, out of sight, holding your Brother's Son. Go for her," said Orphan.

She brought her in, and having done that, all of the animals came back again. And again his Sister's Husband killed them at will. Finally his sister was kind to him.

That is how it was.

The Orphan (a Pawnee tale)
Told by Big Elk, an Omaha

Long ago the Pawnee knew the Great Spirit. There were always many of them. Once they went on the hunt. A real orphan lived in a lodge with his grandmother, who was a very old woman. The grandmother used to carry her tent skin, one that was very worn. Orphan had his bow. His skin robe was unsightly, and his hair was always uncombed. He lived only by going to other lodges and begging. He would go throughout the camp from one end to the other, stopping in at lodges and begging for food. They called him "Beggar" and made him use that name. Even though they called him such names, they feared Beggar, so he was able to continue going around through the camp.

One morning they broke camp when it was still very early in the morning. He was still sleeping. He was left among the litter and rubble of the old camp. He slept until they were all gone, leaving the place abandoned. He was still sleeping.

Then he heard some white men say, "There is the one we are looking for." When he got up, he found four white men there. The white men went off again, and Orphan departed too.

Now he was wide awake, and he followed the trail left by the moving village. The young men said, "You said that Orphan would not follow, but here he is again." Once more they broke camp. But again he went begging at the lodge of the head chief, whose daughter had not yet taken a husband, and so she gave food to Orphan.

But the chief said, "The people have no food. Only we have plenty of food. Whenever you wish, just come here."

Not long after that he came begging again. "What?" said the chief. "There is so little food that the people can only eat once each day and here you are again, when you only left with some food a few moments ago." But his daughter gave Orphan some food again, because she knew about him.

Again they broke camp, and the daughter of the head chief said, "Mother, when we break camp and go this time, please pitch our tent at the very front of the path."

All the young men used to court the chief's daughter, but she acted as if she did not want to get married. When the mother pitched the tent, the daughter, in anticipation of Orphan, went to find fuel. They went out, you see, for wood. They came back carrying wood on their backs, and the chief came up.

"You should have pitched the tent among the others," he said.

His wife said, "That is true, but the girl, your daughter, told me to pitch it here."

When the chief's daughter came back carrying wood, she put it at the side, not right at the lodge. Then Orphan's grandmother came along carrying her worn tent skin. "Old Woman, come over here," said the chief's daughter, who was sitting by the wood, waiting for her to come along. The old woman was so ashamed that she could not speak. She put the tent skin by the wood. The chief's daughter pitched the tent for her, and the old woman sat there, being able to say nothing but "Oh!"

All the young men were talking, "Why, the chief's daughter has put up the tent for Orphan's grandmother. My Friends, I think that she is intending to marry him."

When she had finished with the tent, she carried her robes and bed to the Orphan's tent.

"It is just as I thought," said one.

When Orphan arrived at his tent, he did not enter it. In spite of all that had happened, he was reluctant to go into the tent because the woman was in it. "Oh, come on in," she said, and so he did go in. She had made a very good bed for him. She sat down with him. She ate with him. She married him.

And the young men all said, "Why, Friends, the chief's daughter has married Orphan."

Orphan said to his wife, "Please tell your father to have them stop and rest tomorrow," and the chief sent the criers around.

The people thought, "Why should we stop to rest?"

But the criers said, "He says that you are to stop and rest tomorrow, hey!"

The people asked, "Why should we stop to rest when we are without food?"

Then four white men came along. The boys shouted, "Four white men have arrived."

The criers announced, "He says that you are all to assemble, hey!" the Orphan having commanded this.

The chief commanded everyone to dress up. "He promises to give you all sorts of things, hey! He says, "'Yes, you will paint yourselves, hey!'" The white men, it seems, had promised to give a silver medal to the head chief.

On the next day the white men came into the village. The wagons came and stood right outside the camp. The head white man was in the front. All the Pawnee went outside the camp, and the four white men came up.

The head white man said, "Go get the one we promised to make a great man."

The white men looked for him in the line of the middle-aged and old men. They went to their leader. "Why, Leader, we did not find him," they said.

"Come now. You saw him before, so you should recognize him. Ho! Come on. Go again and look for him," said the white man who was the leader.

So Orphan put on his robe. He also took his bow. He stood among the young men. When the white men finished looking at the line of the elder men, they went over toward the younger men to look at them. Soon they found him. They said, "This is the one," and went back to report that they had found him.

"That is the one," said one. "Ho! Leader, he is there," they said when they returned.

So the white men went there, sitting in the wagons. They had a medal and a robe too. They came up and stood there. The head white man said, "It is our job to come here." He promised to say something to his superior, the President. "He has promised to make one man head chief, so we have brought all these things to him. Since he alone will be your head man, do not be jealous of him. Even though we have brought these things to him, it is just as if they were for you, too. Go get him. Put him in a robe and bring him back."

Four went to get Orphan. They went to the end of the line for him. They put him in a robe and took him along. All the chiefs were unhappy. The white men made Orphan sit in the middle. The principal white man said, "This is the one. Let's make him the head chief. We have brought this for him to wear around his neck." And they went to Orphan and put the medal around his neck.

"Bring the goods for him," said the white man, and they brought the wagons to him, with different kinds of goods: kettles, guns—in fact, all things—and they were placed in a pile in front of Orphan.

Orphan pulled tobacco out of one box. He put his arms around everything and stood up. He stood up with his arms around two large pieces of tobacco and said, "Although people sometimes make fun of someone, they usually stop their ridicule. You have been ridiculing me, but now it is time for you to stop." And he took the tobacco and scattered it about, making them scramble for it.

He gave most of the goods to his wife's father. But his wife's father was unhappy because they did not give a medal to him. Orphan sent a great many goods, piled very high, to his lodge.

The white man said, "We have been sent here to make this man the head chief. When you are out of goods, ask favors of him. We will come back from time to time to do whatever he wants."

The woman's father called her relatives together and they gathered what good clothes they could. The chief gave one good horse, the one he had had before, to the woman for Orphan.

When everything was finished, they broke camp. Orphan ruled the whole village when they ventured out to hunt buffalo. Orphan rode horseback with his woman. Although the people knew him well, they talked against him.

They surrounded a herd. When they came back and reported seeing the buffalo, Orphan promised to help in surrounding the herd. The woman's relatives surrounded their own part of the herd.

And when they returned from surrounding the buffalo, the women talked about going out for chokecherries. Orphan's wife mentioned going out, and Orphan said, "Do so." So the woman went out on a very fast horse. Orphan did not go with her.

Soon there was a great uproar. "It is said that they are killing the ones who went out looking for chokecherries and are chasing them about."

So they went out after the enemy. Orphan said, "Tie up my fastest horse, the one with white hair. I must ride him." Orphan had only one arrow, but he went out after the enemy.

People returned and said, "They nearly got Orphan's wife." And by the time he got there, the Dakotas had nearly captured her. He arrived just in time.

"I have come," he called to his wife.

"You talk big," she said. "This one has nearly captured me."

"Oho!" he said and attacked the Dakota. He pushed one off his horse. He stabbed him with the arrow. Still many of the enemy were pushing them back.

The woman said, "This one behind me has nearly grabbed me. You have talked big before."

"Oho!" he said and attacked them. He pushed a Dakota, making him fall off, and stabbed him with the arrow.

The fourth time the woman said, "This one behind me has nearly got me. You talked big before."

"Oho!" he said and attacked them. Then his horse got winded. He pushed around among them and stabbed a Dakota with his arrow. They could tell that he was hurting them fairly regularly. They closed in on him, gathering very closely around him, and he disappeared.

When everything was over, they said that they had killed Orphan. People came from the Pawnee camp to look for Orphan, but they couldn't find the slightest trace of the struggle. They didn't find the horse, and the man himself was nowhere to be found. They stopped searching.

When the woman got home, she made good clothes for herself, and when night came, the daughter of the head chief disappeared. Although they were curious about where she had sneaked off to, they could not find out. The first white men who had come to the Indians had known something about this, so the Indians thought that Orphan might have gone on high. They thought that, perhaps, the woman, too, had gone on high. They have never heard anything more about them on this earth.

COMMENTARY

Dorsey reports that Sanssouci explained that "Orphan had so great an appetite that the Pawnees grew tired of him. They put him on the ground, flat on his back, and fastened down his hands and feet with tent-pins. A wolf approached him. The Orphan told his trouble; whereupon the wolf pulled out the tent pins and took him to camp."

The Omaha were frequently in alliance with the Pawnee who hunted to the west and south of them because they were common enemies to the powerful Dakota Sioux to the north. Even today memories of Sioux raids for women and horses remain; only a few years ago at an Omaha powwow I heard an Omaha remark jokingly to some young Sioux who had come to join the dancing, "Are you in Omaha country for women or horses?"

This tale of Orphan provides a remarkable documentation of the clash between white and Indian cultures. Orphan becomes a chief by means of the arbitrary choice of the white outsiders, in spite of the contempt the tribe feels toward Orphan. The favors of the whites were as mysterious as those in our western folklore of the fairy godmother, and often as powerful. Silver peace medals were precisely the badge of office given by the whites to "paper chiefs."

It is also interesting that Orphan, a symbol of Omaha ways, beliefs, theology, and folklore, should disappear before the wave of white immigration, in part as a result of having been touched by white culture.

The Adventures Of Orphan
Told by George Miller

Once upon a time there was a village of Indians, and an old woman and her grandson, called Orphan, lived in a lodge a short distance away from the village. The two were very poor, living in a low tent made of grass. The grandson used to play games.

One day he said, "Grandmother, make a little bow for me," and she made him a bow and some arrows. The boy went out to hunt birds. And from that time on he used to bring back many birds, putting them all around his belt. The boy became an excellent marksman, usually killing whatever game came in sight of him.

About ten o'clock each morning all the people in the village used to make a great noise. Finally Orphan asked, "Grandmother, why do they make such a noise?" and his grandmother answered, "There is a very red bird that goes there regularly, and when he lands on a very tall cottonwood tree, he makes a bright red glare over the whole village. So the chief has ordered the people to shoot at the bird, and whoever kills the bird can marry the chief's daughter."

"Grandmother," said Orphan, "I want to go there."

"Of all the places in the world, that would be the worst place for you to go. They like to abuse strangers. They will pick on you. There is no reason for you to go there."

But the boy paid no attention to her. He took his bow and went out of the lodge. "You had better not go there," warned his grandmother.

"I am going out to play games," said Orphan, but he went straight to the village. When he drew near the village, he noticed a red light all around. He also saw a great crowd of people who were moving around, shooting at the bird. Orphan approached them.

One man said, "Come on, Orphan, try shooting at it," but Orphan was hesitant, for he was afraid of the people.

But the people kept approaching him, telling the others, "Stand back! Stand back! Let Orphan shoot." So Orphan shot at the bird, and he barely missed it.

At that very moment, Ictinike shot and sent a reed arrow alongside that of Orphan. The people said, "Oh, Orphan came very near to killing it!"

But Ictinike said, "I am the one who came near to killing it."

When the bird flew away, the people scattered, returning to their lodges. Orphan went home too. He said to his grandmother, "I came very near to killing the bird."

"Don't go there again. They will abuse you. Didn't I tell you not to go there?" scolded the old woman.

The next morning he went back there again, and the people were making a great noise. And the same thing happened as the previous day. He was told to shoot at the bird, and he barely missed it. On the third day he met with the same kind of bad luck. But on the fourth day he hit the bird.

"Oho! Orphan has killed it," said the people.

"Nonsense," said Ictinike. "I was the one who killed it. I killed it. Don't make such noise. Stop complaining." And Ictinike would not let the people do what they wanted. He snatched the honor of the occasion from Orphan.

People came in droves to see the spectacle, the body of the famous bird. And when Orphan approached the place, he pulled out a feather, so the people thought, but he really took the whole bird and carried it home.

The chief said, "Bring my new son-in-law here," so the people took a bird they thought had been killed by Ictinike and took it and Ictinike to the chief. Ictinike married the elder daughter of the chief and made his home in the chief's lodge.

In the meantime Orphan reached his home. "Grandmother," he said, "I killed the bird."

"Oh, Grandchild! Oh, Grandchild!" she cried.

"Grandmother, make me a shield support between the fireplace and the seat at the back of the lodge," said Orphan, and after she had made it, Orphan hung the red bird on it. So Orphan and his grandmother had their lodge filled with the red light.

By and by the young man said, "Grandmother, make me a hide hoop," and she made the hoop, placing it aside to dry. But Orphan could hardly wait for it to dry. Finally it was dry, and he said, "Grandmother, sit in the middle, between the fireplace and the seat at the back of the lodge. Then Orphan went out of the lodge and stood at the right side of the entrance.

Then he said, "Grandmother, you must now say, 'Grandchild, one of the buffalo people is coming to you,' " and the old woman did this. Then she rolled the hoop out of the lodge to Orphan, and as it rolled from the lodge it suddenly changed into a buffalo, and Orphan shot and killed it right at the entrance of the lodge.

He and his grandmother cut up the body, and his grandmother then cut up the rest of the meat for drying. At this time the people in the village had nothing to eat. The grandmother prepared some of the dried buffalo meat by mixing it with fat, and Orphan told her to take it to the lodge of the chief and to say to the chief's daughter, "O Daughter-in-Law, this is for your father to eat."

The old woman tossed the bundle into the lodge, turned quickly around, and went home. When the bundle was thrown in, the chief said, "Look! Look! Look!" And when one of the daughters went to look, she could not see anyone; Orphan had used his magic power to make his grandmother invisible. On the fourth day he had said, "Grandmother, you will be invisible until you return."

But Ictinike said, "There is only one old woman who lives apart from us and she must be the one." And so it happened four times in a row.

On the fourth time, the old woman carried a sack of buffalo meat on her back, and on top of the sack she was carrying the red bird. Orphan said, "Grandmother, now you shall be visible when you return." So the old woman left.

When she was very near the chief's tent, the tent began to shine with a red light. As she passed along by the lodges, the people said, "Oho! We thought that Orphan had killed the bird, but Ictinike said that he had killed it. Now Orphan's grandmother has brought it here. Where is she taking it?" The people were watching. "Oho! She is taking it to the chief's lodge!"

When she got there, she threw down the sack, letting it fall with a sudden thud. "O Daughter-in-Law, that is for your brothers and father to eat," she said.

"Look! Look! Look!" said the chief, "She keeps doing this."

And Ictinike said, "There is only one old woman around here, and she must be the one. Who else could it be?" and they went to see, and they found that it was indeed Orphan's grandmother.

One of the daughters said, "It is Orphan's grandmother."

"Ho! Bring my new son-in-law to me," ordered the chief, and they took the pack that the old woman had brought and they hung it up with the bird. They put it beside the one that Ictinike claimed he had killed and which had also been hung up. And as they sat in the lodge it was filled with a very red glare.

They returned with Orphan, and he married the chief's daughter and also made his home in the chief's lodge.

Orphan's hair had not been combed for a long time and so it was tangled and matted. So Ictinike's wife said to her sister, "Sister, if he sits on the rug, he will drop lice on it. Make him go sit somewhere else. How can it be that it doesn't make you sick just to look at him?"

Orphan and his wife were unhappy about this, but when Orphan's wife wanted to comb his hair, Orphan would not let her.

Finally one day when the sun was approaching noon, he and his wife left the village and went to the shore of a lake. As they sat there, Orphan said, "I am going beneath this water, but do not return to your father's lodge. Be sure to stay here even though I am gone for some time. I will return. Examine my forehead."

Now, in the middle of his forehead was a depression. He had been a poor orphan and was brought up accordingly, so he had been hurt somehow, causing this scar on his forehead. Then he waded out into the lake. He waded until only his head was above the surface, then he turned and called to his wife, "Remember what I told you. That is all," and having said this, he plunged under the surface.

His wife sat weeping, and after a while she walked along the shore, weeping because he had not returned. At last her eyelids became weary and she went to sleep at the very place where they had first reached the lake. Her husband returned while she was still sleeping soundly. He took hold of her and woke her up. "I have returned; wake up!"

She jumped up and looked at him only to find that he was now a handsome man and his hair was nicely combed. The woman hesitated, thinking him a stranger, and she turned away from him. "Oh, you just like to fool people. I married a very poor man, who dived under this lake, and I have been sitting here crying while waiting for him to return," she said.

"I am he," said her husband. But still the woman would pay no attention to his words. "Why, look here at the place I told you to examine before." When the woman turned around she saw it, she no longer hesitated but threw her arms around him and kissed him. Then the husband went down to the shore and pulled up some green scum that gathers on the top of the water and from it made a robe and skirt for his wife.

Orphan had birds resembling short-eared owls over his mocassins and robe, and he had some tied to his club too. Whenever he put the club down, the birds would cry out.

Late in the afternoon he and his wife left for the village. When they arrived, the people exclaimed, "Why, Orphan's wife has returned with a completely different man. I think Orphan has been killed. He went off this morning. Why, this one is a very handsome man."

When Orphan reached the chief's lodge, all the birds made a great noise. Then Ictinike's wife said, "Sister, let my sister's husband sit on the rug."

"Why, Elder Sister, your Sister's Husband might drop lice on your rug," said the younger sister as she turned up one end of the rug and threw it toward her elder sister. Then Ictinike's wife began to cry, and she cried and cried.

At last her father said to Ictinike, "This world is very large, but you are known everywhere as one who possesses various kinds of knowledge. Use some of it and make my daughter stop crying."

By and by Ictinike said to Orphan, "Younger Brother, let's go cut arrow shafts. Let's make some arrows for your wife's brother."

But Orphan did not answer, so Ictinike said to him again, "Younger Brother, let's make arrows for your wife's brother. Let's go cut arrow shafts." Then Orphan said, "All right, Elder Brother, let's do it." And Ictinike was delighted because Orphan had agreed to go with him.

But when Orphan said that he was going to take off his magic clothing, Ictinike objected. "Wear them anyway. Why take them off?" Therefore, they went off together.

When they reached the edge of a very dense forest, some turkeys flew off and alighted in a tree. "Oh, Younger Brother, shoot at them! I want to eat roasted turkey as we lie around," said Ictinike.

"No, Elder Brother," said Orphan. "We are in too much of a hurry for that."

"Oh, Younger Brother, kill one of them for me," said Ictinike.

"When my elder brother talks about something, he apparently has so much to say that he hardly ever stops talking," said Orphan, who then went toward the tree, taking his bow to shoot the turkeys.

Just as he pulled back the bowstring, Ictinike whispered, "Let it lodge in the limb!" and when Orphan shot, he sent the arrow through the bird, but Ictinike was saying, "Let it lodge in a limb! Let it lodge in a limb!" and it fell and lodged in a limb.

"Oho! Younger Brother, climb up there for me. Get it and throw it down," said Ictinike.

"No, Elder Brother. Let's just go on ahead," said Orphan.

"Why, you shouldn't leave you arrow and the bird up there too. Go up there and throw it down."

"When my elder brother talks about something, he has so much to say that he never seems to stop talking!" said Orphan. He had decided to go climb the tree, so he went to its base.

"Ho! Lay your clothes down there. If you get caught in the branches, your clothing will be torn," said Ictinike, referring to the magic garments. So Orphan stripped off his clothes, putting them at the foot of the tree. And as he climbed Ictinike said in a whisper, "Let this tree shoot suddenly up into the sky!"

Orphan heard him whisper, so he turned and asked him, "Why, Elder Brother, what did you say?"

Ictinike answered, "I didn't say anything important, Younger Brother. Just, 'When he brings that bird back I want to eat it.' " So Orphan kept climbing.

When Ictinike whispered the same thing again, Orphan repeated his question. "I didn't say anything important," answered Ictinike. "Just, 'He has nearly gotten it for me now.' " And then Orphan climbed even higher.

Ictinike whispered again and gave the same answers to the question of Orphan, who was beginning to guess that there was some mischief going on.

When Ictinike whispered the fourth time, Orphan said, "Hey, Elder Brother, I think that you have been saying something."

But Ictinike just answered, "I didn't say anything important at all. I was just saying, 'Let this tree shoot up into the Upper World!' " Then Ictinike ran around the tree, hitting it at short intervals and saying "I say, 'Let this tree shoot up high very suddenly,' " and the tree extended up into the Upper World.

Now Orphan was standing on a very narrow place between the limb of the tree and the Upper World. "Oh no!" he cried, and he was weeping for some time. His hair became terribly tangled. At length a young eagle came up to the weeping man.

"O Man, what arc you saying?" he asked.

"O Grandfather! O Grandfather! O Grandfather!" said Orphan to the young Eagle.

"Come! Speak up! Tell me your story," said Eagle.

"Yes, Grandfather, I am one of those who at the timber at the foot of the bluff left some part of a young bull elk for you to fly over and eat."

"That is true. One of your grandfathers will come over and rescue you," said Eagle, and Orphan stood there weeping, being very sad indeed.

Finally Buzzard came over to him, and when Orphan told him of another animal that he had left out for the buzzards, he was told, "That is true. One of your grandfathers shall come to rescue you." And then Buzzard left, leaving Orphan weeping once more.

By and by Crow approached, and when Orphan told him about an animal that he had left for the crows to eat, he was told that another grandfather, a crow, would come to rescue him. After the departure of the crow, Magpie came. He made a similar promise and flew off.

Then came the promised eagle. "Oh, Grandfather! Oh, Grandfather! Oh, Grandfather!" said Orphan, praying to him.

"Ho! Catch hold of my wings at the shoulders and lie on my back with your legs stretched out. Be careful not to open your eyes. Keep your eyes closed," said Eagle. And so he flew off with Orphan on his back, flying round and round the tree until he grew very tired. He would alight from time to time to rest, and when he was rested, he would resume his flight. Finally he left Orphan standing on a lower limb.

Then came Buzzard who took Orphan on his back, after giving him instructions similar to those issued by Eagle. Then Buzzard flew round and round the tree, going lower and lower, alighting from time to time to rest and then resume his downward flight when he was refreshed. Finally he, too, left Orphan on a lower branch.

Then Crow, who took Orphan even lower. But when he was on Crow's back, he opened his eyes slightly, and he saw the ground emitting a yellow light. So he lay there on Crow's back and begged him to continue to help him, but about then Magpie came along and carried Orphan lower and lower until they finally reached the ground. When they got there, Magpie lay insensible, for he was utterly exhausted. When Orphan went to get his garments, he found that Ictinike had taken them, leaving his own garments at the foot of the tree.

Now, when Ictinike returned home wearing the magic garments, the birds on them would not cry out at all, so Ictinike pretended that they wanted to cry out, saying, "Keep quiet! You make too much noise for these people's ears!" But when Orphan returned on Magpie's back to the foot of the tree, the birds on the garments knew about it, and they cried out with a great noise for some time, for Ictinike had the garments on. Then Ictinike cried, "Do be quiet! You are making far too much noise for these people's ears."

When Orphan looked for his quiver, he found that Ictinike had taken it, leaving instead his quiver with reed arrows. When he looked at the arrows, he found among them some wooden arrows with points carved with a knife. He also found that Ictinike had left his robe of raccoon skins there. Orphan was very mad, but he took the arrows, straightened the wooden ones, and with them killed all the animals he had told his rescuers about. Then he started back to the village wearing the robe of raccoon skins and taking Ictinike's quiver.

When he approached the village, the birds knew it, and they cried out and flew about now and then. This made Ictinike feel very proud, and he commanded the birds to keep quiet.

Finally Orphan returned and entered the lodge. He sat there a while. Ictinike was still wearing his magic garments. Finally Orphan said to him, "Hey! You used to wear this thing, so wear it again," and he threw him the raccoon-skin robe, and so Orphan took back his own clothes.

But his hair was still a mess. And nothing happened for some time after his return. Then Orphan had a drum made. Then he said to his wife, "I have returned after being in a very lonely situation. Tell your father that I want all the people to dance."

His wife did tell this to her father, and her father commanded an old man to go around among the people and proclaim all the words that Orphan had told. So the old man went through the village as a crier, saying, "He says that you should dance! He says that all of you in the village, even the small children, are to dance!"

Orphan, his wife, and his grandmother took the drum and went into the circle of lodges. Orphan fastened his belt very tightly around his waist and then said to his wife, "Grasp my belt very tightly. Be careful not to let go!" Then he told his grandmother to take hold of the other side of the belt, saying, "Don't let go!"

The people assembled inside the circle of the lodges and Orphan sat in the very middle, surrounded by the people. When he started to beat the drum, he had the people rise about a foot from the ground and come down again. The people were enjoying themselves as he beat the drum. When he beat it again, he made them jump even higher.

Then his grandmother said, "O Grandchild, I usually dance quite well." He made her jump and come down suddenly as he beat the drum, just as he had done with each of the others.

When he gave a third beat, he made the people jump still higher, and as they came down he beat the drum before they could touch the ground, making them leap up again. He beat the drum rapidly, sending all the people so high into the air that one could not even get a glimpse of them, and when they came down again after a long time, he killed them all as they hit the ground. He killed all of the people with the concussion from his drum beating.

Although Orphan's wife and grandmother were also taken up into the air at each beat of the drum too, it turned out that only their feet went up into the air and their heads and bodies were held down because the women were holding him by the waist as he had ordered them.

Of all the people only three others survived: Ictinike, the chief, and the chief's wife. When the chief was falling down, he begged Orphan to spare his life. But Orphan's mind could not be changed. He sent him up into the sky again and again, until he grew tired of hearing the chief's entreaties, and then he let him fall to the ground and die. He caused the chief's wife to die in the same way.

Only Ictinike was left. "Oh, Younger Brother, I beg you and my wife's sister! Pity me!" said Ictinike, but Orphan beat the drum once more and when Ictinike fell to the earth, the concussion killed him, too.

COMMENTARY

Again one must detect something of Rabbit in Orphan. This story is very similar to some Rabbit tales. His living situation is identical to Rabbit's, his powers and personality are much the same, and, like Rabbit, he is in conflict with Ictinike.

This is one of the longest and most coherent of the Omaha tales published by Dorsey.

Haxige's Adventures
Told by Pathinanpaji

Haxige lived alone in a lodge with his younger brother. The elder brother used to go out hunting, shooting deer. It happened that he feared some unknown danger, and he said to his younger brother, "If any animal passes along on the ice by the place where we get water, let it alone."

The elder brother went out hunting. The younger brother took a kettle and went for water. At length two otter came along. The younger brother ran along the ice and attacked them. He was carrying a stick, and when he reached the place where they were, he hit them again and again. And he chased after them.

Finally he reached their home, the den of the Water Monsters, and they went headlong into it with him. They closed the entrance.

The elder brother reached home, carrying a deer which he had not skinned. When he got home, he threw the deer by the door. But his brother did not stir.

"Here! Take it, Brother," he said, but he received no answer. "I guess you are asleep," he said. But when he pulled back the door, he could see that his brother was not there. "Oh, my poor little younger brother! I knew this would happen and it has," he said.

He ran to the place where they got water to look for him. When he got there, he could see that the footprints of his brother went on further. As he followed the trail, he came to the place where he had attacked the otters. He could tell that he had struck them, and he said, "Alas!" The kettle had been dropped between the two places, and the elder brother continued to follow him. When he could not find him, he cried. "My younger brother! My younger brother! My younger brother! My younger brother! When I think of your spirit I cry. Woe, my younger brother! Alas, my younger brother. If it had been me, friend Younger Brother, I would have made it home."

He wandered over the whole earth looking for his brother. As he cried, the water flowed very rapidly in many long streams, making very large creeks. His tears were the rivers.

On the bank of one stream the grass was very good and he lay down there. As he lay there, two ducks came along. They were diving. And they came up again.

One said, "My friend, when Haxige's younger brother was killed, I had plenty of food. How was it with you?"

The other duck replied, "My friend, I did not have a good time. Only his little finger was left for me, and I swore that no matter when I saw him I would tell him about what happened to his relative."

When Haxige heard that, he turned into a leaf. He fell on the water and floated between the two ducks. When he reached them he grabbed the two ducks by the neck. "You two! What have you been saying?"

"Yes, Elder Brother, it is true," said the one. "Elder Brother, I have been saying that I would tell you the news. Elder Brother, do loosen your hold on me. I have been saying that I would tell you about your brother. Elder Brother, they took your younger brother home by a row of very high cliffs, to the land in that direction."

He tore the first duck into many pieces, and threw them away. He asked the other duck, "When do they come out of their den?"

"At noon, when the fog is blowing very dense and when it is very warm, they lie to make the fat on their bellies firm by exposure to the heat of the sun. During the day it is so," he said.

Haxige turned into an eagle and flew away. He found the monsters lying flat on their backs. He came back to earth to attack them. There was a warning, "Haxige is coming at you," and he failed. They went back to their lodge, and Haxige went home again too.

When he reached his home, he thought, "What can I do to get even with them?"

Well, he went again on a similar day. When he got to a very great height, he turned into a leaf again. Then, as a leaf, he fell back toward earth to attack them. There was a warning, "Haxige is coming at you," and once more he failed to attack them, for they returned to their lodge. Having failed again, Haxige went home.

Again such a day came. And he turned into a blue-backed bird hawk. Then, having become a blue-backed bird hawk, he returned to attack them again. There was a warning, "Haxige is coming at you," and again he failed to attack them, for they had gone into their lodge. Again Haxige went home, having failed with them.

Finally, on the fourth day, he became a grass snake. He left, slithering alone under the grass. When he reached the cliffs, he could see that they were lying on their backs, making their stomach tissue stiff by the heat. He took his bow, fit the arrow to the bowstring, and sent it with great force, making it land in the middle, wounding two of them.

They grunted very hard, "Ang," and went back into their lodge.

Haxige went home, and when he got there he was very happy. He said, "I got them."

In the morning Haxige went hunting, and as he was returning he saw a person going across the road. He went hunting again the next morning, and he saw another person crossing the road. On the fourth occasion Haxige crouched down and lay in the path of whoever was approaching.

When he was nearly upon him, Haxige jumped up. "Well, the old man walks along as if something were wrong," he said, trying to draw him out.

"Yes, very much so," he said. "How can it be at this late date that you have not heard about it in your travels?"

"Why, old man, whatever can be wrong. I have been traveling about without hearing anything at all," said Haxige.

"Yes, Haxige's younger brother was killed and Haxige killed two of the Water Monster's most dearly loved children. I have been going over there to powwow with them," he said.

"Why, Old Man, it might be so, but I haven't heard a thing about it. Well, Old Man, it might be a good idea to have a witness at your powwowing," said Haxige.

"Yes, that is so," said Buzzard, "but I make it a rule not to have witnesses."

"Well, Old Man, I will watch on. I'm going along your way hunting," said Haxige. "Ho! Old Man, see for yourself. When I finish watching, you can go on."

"Well, all right, you can watch," said Buzzard.

"But, Old Man, I want to hear from you how you do your deeds," said Haxige, trying to egg him on.

"Just watch," said Buzzard, and he sang and danced.

Hé-ke tá-ko, hé-ke hé-ke tá-ko. Hé-ke tá-ko, hé-ke hé-ke tá-ko,

"Well, Old Man, if that's what it is, it looks very nice. Old Man, how do you usually do it? I want to learn all of it from you," said Haxige.

"I said that I would do the cure when I get up there. There are four peaks that are flat on top. When I reach the fourth, they usually come there for me. They put me in a robe and carry me in it. When I get there this time, I will say, 'Let the water stand hot.' When I heat two irons red-hot and press them against the wounds again and again, they will be alive again," said Buzzard.

Haxige made him do the dance about three times because he wanted to be able to perform all of the ceremony well. After the fourth time, Buzzard stopped dancing. "Well, that is enough. I suspect that you have had more than enough looking at me," said Buzzard.

"Yes, Old Man, that is enough. What sort of person are you that you despise Haxige?" Having said this, Haxige broke in his head with a blow, and so killed him.

He took all of Buzzard's clothes and put them on. And he carried the gourd-rattle on his arm. He practiced the ceremony. He thought, "I am doing it quite well," and he traveled until he came to the fourth peak. He danced.

Hé-ke tá-ko, hé-ke hé-ke tá-ko.   Hé-ke tá-ko,   hé-ke hé-ke tá-ko,

"Well, the old man was nice looking, but he never had anyone to admire him," he said.

"Oho! The old man who is the doctor has come in sight," said the people. "Servants, go after him," said the chief, and they went after him.

When they got there, they spread out the robe for him. He sat on it and they carried him off on it. "Make room for him by moving away from the door," they shouted. They pulled open the outside door, and when they did so he could see that the whole of his brother's skin had been stripped off and made to hang inside as a door flap.

Haxige stood at the door, facing it and dancing. He stopped dancing and entered the lodge. He took hold of his brother's skin at the wrist. He was pulling open the door flap with some force. "Alas, my dear younger brother," he said in a whisper. But the servants detected him. "Hey, friend, what did the old man say?" said one to the other in a whisper.

"Friend, he said something like 'Alas for my dear little younger brother!'"

"Pfui, Friend, that is no cause for concern. The old man has been coming here as a doctor for a very long time before now."

"Well," said Haxige, "I said that this one last time would be enough. Ho! Servants, bring two very large kettles filled with water." They went for it and came back carrying them on their backs. The kettles were fastened over the fire and were very hot, boiling hard.

"Sharpen two knives and put them here. Put two irons in the fire and make them very hot. After I press these hot irons repeatedly against the wounds, they shall come alive again. Ho! Get out of my way. Don't look in here at all, even when you are close by. Don't let them get up and get away from you. Walk down to the other side of the four peaks where you come to get me when I come here," he ordered.

Everyone went at once and he was left alone. The water was boiling hard.

"Ho! Lie down side by side. When I stick a very red-hot iron into your wounds you will get better. Be careful not to move. Lie with your sides held very stiff," he said.

When they were lying the way he wanted them, he pushed into the wound on either side with sudden force, "Tchu! Lie still."

Both said, "Ah!" and died from the pain. He took the knives and cut the bodies into very narrow, long strips. When they were all cut up, he put them into the boiling water. Then he put the cooked meat into a pile.

The people who had gone said, "The old doctor has never taken so long before. He has certainly been taking his time. Grass snake, what did you say he said?"

"Yes, I was saying that when he took hold of the door flap and went in at the side of the entrance, he said something like 'Alas, my dear younger brother!' " said Grass snake.

"Grass snake, run home. Look in on him. Make extra eyes with your nose, flatten your head out, curved like a dish," they said. And Grass snake left, crawling along under the grass. When he got there, he peeped in at a crack in the lodge. Haxige spotted him.

"Come! Come! Come!" said Haxige, and Grass snake came in. "Fill yourself up on food," and Haxige put a narrow strip of meat about two feet long into the throat of Grass snake, where it stuck very tight. "When you get back, tell them that it is Haxige and that some time ago he cooked the Water Monsters until the meat was nicely done. Go and tell them that." And the Grass snake went to tell them.

"Haxuka! Haxuka!" he said in a voice barely above a whisper.

"What? What is the unseen moving one saying?"

Finally he had come directly to them, crawling along in the grass. "Haxuka! Haxuka!" he said.

"Aha! He says 'Haxige.' Take out the piece of fat meat which he has put in his mouth. Hurry! It must be as we have suspected. Give it a try." They then set off to attack him.

When they got very close to their home, Haxige went rushing away, carrying his brother on his arm. As he went along, they went to attack him. But even though they changed themselves into all kinds of swift animals, they did not overtake Haxige and his brother.

"There is good reason to be mad. Try harder. You are about to fail," they called. They ran along after him.

It so happened that Haxige, on his way home, drew near a spring which always boiled up. It was in a very dense forest at the foot of a cliff, a very high hill, whose perpendicular face was concave.

"Try harder!" they called. "You have almost caught him."

Finally Haxige turned into a bullet and went headlong into the water, "Tchu!" Instantly he became a stone under the water. Though Haxige and his brother were taken hold of, he had become a solid stone, so they could not loosen him, and they went home. "Let's quit and go home. We've failed," they said. So they went home, having failed to catch him.

As they went along home, Haxige came out again into sight after a while. And he, too, went home, carrying the skin of his brother on his arm. Finally he reached home. "Brother," he said, "let's go into the sweat lodge."

He went for four stones that were about one foot in diameter. He stood on a very high headland and picked up a stone. "Ho! Old Man, I have come to powwow with you," and then he took another. "Ho! Old Man, I have come for you to powwow over me." He put it in his robe, and he took another, and said, "Ho! Old Man, I have come for you to cause a person to bathe." And when the fourth time came, he said, "Ho! Old Man, I have come for you so that you could cause a person to bathe all over. Ho! Old Man, I have come to you to cause me to bathe. I have come for you so that you may throw out from me all bad affections, impurities. I want to come into view on many different days. I want to come into sight, Old Man, with my young ones on the four peaks. Superior Diety on either side, I pray to you. On different days may I, with my young ones, come in sight!" he called.

He carried them home. He built up the fire. "I will go for lodge poles," he said, and he brought them home. "I will make sticks for pushing the stones straight," and he placed them by the edge of the fireplace. Then he went for water too.

"Ho! Water, I have come for you to make a sacred thing of you." He placed the water too at the door. "I will send the stones to you, Brother," he said, meaning the empty skin of his brother, which had been put inside the lodge.

He pushed the stones straight in a moment. He placed them in a heap. They became very red from the heat. He took the water and threw it very quickly into the lodge. "That water goes to you," he said. "Ho! I will go to you," said Haxige. He went into the lodge. The stones were still red-hot. "Ho! Old Man, I have come here in order to bathe by your grace," he said, and he dropped large drops of medicine on the fire. The fire sent out sparks.

He seized his brother and had him bathe by pouring water over him. He made him as he had been before. "That will do, Younger Brother," he said.

"Yes, Elder Brother, that is enough," said the younger brother.

But when Haxige let his brother go, he floated on up into the air: he was a ghost. So he repeated his treatment three more times, all without success.

Finally Haxige said, "Well, Friend Younger Brother, apparently you want to have your own way." So he stood holding him and talking to him. "Ho! Younger Brother, you shall have your way. That being so, Younger Brother, we must separate. No matter what size this island, the world, as you now go into the sky and disappear, so also shall the red man go and never return." And Haxige went away.

Once there was an old Beaver-woman making a boat. "Hu!" she said. "Haxige's odor is very strong."

"Old Woman, there is no reason for complaint. Since his brother was killed by the Water Monsters, Haxige is wandering about aimlessly, killing himself with his grief," he said. "Aren't you making a boat there?"

"Yes. Haven't you heard about it before?" asked the Old Woman. "Because his younger brother was killed, Haxige killed two of the chief Water Monsters. And since they were not able to kill him, they have threatened to cover the whole earth with water. So I am making myself a dugout," she said.

Then Haxige replied, "Old Woman, Haxige always wants to do the clever thing. He has made a canoe, and if he piles up wood at the bow, fills the bottom with earth, then he can have a brightly burning fire. He can seize the animals that come floating along, and he will have plenty to eat."

"Even if they fail in that plan, they say that they will send a plague of snakes over the whole world," said the Old Woman.

"Then he will put shells of red-breasted turtles on his feet, and his hands too. Then when the snakes come to bite, he will be able to crush their heads by stepping on them with his new thick skin. He will walk all over them," said Haxige.

"Even if they fail in this, they threaten to cover the whole earth with darkness. They say that if he stumbles into some canyon accidentally, he will die from the fall," said the Old Woman.

"Old Woman, Haxige wants to be as clever as possible. As he sits in that canyon, he will gather much wood and sit by a nice fire. Any animal that falls down to him will die from the fall, and he will take it and sit there eating it."

"Even if they fail in this, they threaten to cover the whole world with snow. They say that he will die from the snow crushing him," she said.

"That Haxige," he said, "always wants to be as clever as possible. He will make himself a grass lodge, gather a good pile of wood, and then he will make himself snowshoes. Whenever animals get accidentally buried in the snow, he will kill them at his pleasure and eat them. What sort of person are you that you hate Haxige so?" he asked, and he hit her many times with an axe, crushing her head and killing her.

Haxige then left and went home. When he got there, he built a sweat lodge again. They were about to practice some medicine again. "Shall we powwow, Younger Brother? Shall we treat ourselves?" he asked, talking to his younger brother as if everything were normal.

"Yes, Elder Brother, let's do that," said the younger brother.

And when he had finished the sweat lodge, he began to work again on his relative. He worked very well on his brother. Though he made the body as it had been before, whenever he let it go, the younger brother would float up into the air without touching the ground. Finally Haxige again grew impatient with his brother. He wanted to end this trouble.

"Well, Friend Younger Brother, you shall have your way," he said. "Though this island, the world, remains this large, you will always be just as you are. We shall change our forms. You shall go as a young male big wolf with very long blue hair on the space between your shoulders. And as for me, Friend Younger Brother, I will go as a very large male deer with horns full of snags and with hair, which has been made yellow by heat, scattered over my forehead. Red men shall eat me. By means of me mouths shall be caused to move," he said, and so it was.

COMMENTARY

Dorsey comments on several features of this long and intricate tale:

"Note that water and ice existed before the alleged origin of rivers from Haxige's tears."

"Haxige crouched down suddenly, and lay across the path of the person who was approaching. It was Ictinike, disguised as *Hega*, Buzzard."

"The behaviour of Hagixe's brother made the elder brother determine that the souls of Indians should never return to this world. 'Well, Younger Brother, as I have failed to keep you here, when red men die, though the earth be this big around, as you go thus, so shall it be with them. They shall never come back.' "

"Haxige may be the mythical ancestor of the *Tada* or Deerhead gens [clan]; and his brother, of the *Mathinka-gache* or Wolf gens. The Beaverwoman and Grass-snake spoke of the hero as *Haxuka*. This latter is the *Tsiwere* form of Haxige."

The term "powwow" is used in the nineteenth-century white usage, "to cure by means of folk and primitive medicines," rather than the more modern "to gather the tribe."

Haxige's Adventures
Told by Francis La Flesche

[There were two Water Monsters who killed the younger brother of Haxige. They flayed the body and hung up the skin for a door. They invited all of the animals in for a feast, when they cooked the body and divided it among the animals, bribing them to silence. Haxige missed his brother and went out in search of him. He reached a creek where two wood ducks were swimming. The conversation of the ducks and the transformation of Haxige into a leaf are given in the preceding version. When he caught them . . .]

"What did you say?" he asked.

"O yes, Elder Brother. Loosen your grip on me and I will tell you the news. Loosen your hold on me," he said.

And Haxige said, "Come on. Tell me."

"Yes, Elder Brother. When Haxige's younger brother was killed, I received nothing but the little fingers as my share. And so I said that no matter when I might see him, I would tell Haxige about his brother. All of the animals were invited to eat part of his body, but only his little finger was left for me at the distribution."

And Haxige said, "What do they usually do?"

"Well, Buzzard goes there every day to powwow over them," said Duck.

So Haxige made the duck's feathers next to the outer corners of his eyes white. He made the feathers on the top of his head into a crest. "You shall be called 'Conjurer Duck.' Go. Think of me whenever you get into any trouble and I will help you," said Haxige. And he left.

As he cried, water flowed very rapidly in many long streams, making large creeks. His tears became rivers. As he walked along, he saw Buzzard approaching. He went up to him. And Haxige said, "Old Man, what business are you on?"

"Well, Grandchild, haven't you already heard?"

"Whatever you are talking about is new to me," said Haxige.

"Well, Grandchild, Haxige had a younger brother who was killed. So Haxige wounded two of the most dearly beloved children of the Water Monsters. Therefore, I have been there to powwow over them," said Buzzard.

"Old Man, what do you usually do when you go to the village?"

"Well, I always do this," and he took his gourd rattle and shook it. He said, "I always do this, Grandchild," and he danced and sang the following song:

Hé-ki-man'-dan, hé-ki, hé-ki-man'-dan, hé-ki, hé-ki-man'-dan.

And Haxige said, "Grandfather, do once again what you do when you arrive at the village. I would like to see that again." So Buzzard said, "I always do this," and he danced.

Haxige asked, "What do you do when you powwow over them?"

"Well, Grandchild, I usually say, 'Let every one in the village get out of sight behind that hill, everyone, including the dogs.' "

"Yes, Grandfather," said Haxige. "And when you practice, what do you do?"

"Well, Grandchild, I take that iron rod, for I intend to thrust it into the wounds after I have made it red-hot."

"Yes, Grandfather. Do what it is you intend to do when you approach the village. Go. I want to watch you." But when Buzzard started to do this, Haxige grabbed a stick and hit him right on the head, killing Buzzard with one blow.

Haxige took the iron and a small pack too and he carried these on his back. He went along. He went to the Water Monsters. When he finally reached the hill in view of the village, he sang the song that had been Buzzard's.

When they saw Haxige, they said, "Oho! There is Doctor Buzzard not too far away coming down to us." And the chief said, "Let four of the most stout-hearted braves go there. Put him in a robe and carry him back." And when they went after him, they thought that he was Buzzard.

When they reached him, they spread out the robe and said, "Old Man, sit on this. We have come for you." And Haxige did sit in it.

But one of the men whispered in the ear of another, "Buzzard is not the same one. I think it is Haxige." He said that because he recognized Haxige. But the other whispered, "It is Buzzard. How could Haxige ever come here?"

So they carried him home to the wounded ones. And when they reached their home with him, he saw that they had flayed the body of his younger brother and had made a door flap from his skin. When Haxige raised the door flap, he recognized the skin of his younger brother, and as he raised it he said, "Alas, my dear little younger brother!" He said that in a very soft whisper, not crying out loud at all. But one of the people standing around said, "Friend, when he raised the door flap, he said, 'Alas! my dear little younger brother!' I think that he is Haxige." But another said, "Do not say that to anyone. It is Buzzard." And Haxige went on into the lodge.

And as he proceeded, he said, "Go. All of you must leave the lodges. Walk out of sight, beyond that hill. Go get some water and hang two very large kettles over the fire for me. When I finish powwowing over these, I must have them bathe." And having done so, all left.

Haxige made the iron very hot. Then he said, "I will powwow over your elder brother first. Lie still for a moment." Then he said to the Elder Brother, "Show me your wound." And when he had made the iron red-hot, he thrust it into the wound. When he did that, Water Monster said nothing but "Han, han."

"Be still. This is good for you." But the one who had had the hot iron thrust into him died.

Haxige then said, "Now, come. Your elder brother is a little better and has gone into a very sound sleep." Then he did the same thing to the brother. And the younger brother died too, having had the very hot iron thrust into him.

When he was dead, Haxige took a knife and cut up the two Water Monsters, and when he had finished he put them in a pile in the middle of the lodge. He cut them into long narrow strips and filled both kettles very full, and sat watching them boil.

The people who had gone out of sight began to say, "Let two braves go over there and see what he is doing." They said, "That doctor is taking a long time."

One said, "Aha! When I said I thought he was Haxige, you doubted me and you said you thought he was Buzzard." So they sat down to decide who should go back.

And one said, "Grass Snake, if you go back, he will probably not notice you, for you are not easily seen. Go carefully so he does not detect you. Go in some small hole and see what he is doing. But don't let Haxige see you."

The Grass Snake said yes and set off. When he got there, he peeped through a very tiny hole, but Haxige did detect him. "Ho! Ho! Come in! Come in! You must eat," he said when he saw him.

Although he wanted to go in, Grass Snake was afraid of him. But since Haxige said, "Come in," the snake did go in. And Haxige said, "Lie down there by the edge of the fireplace. When you eat, you shall have plenty. After you have eaten and you return, say 'It was Haxige, and he has killed both of the Water Monsters.'" And Haxige took a piece of fat meat and put it in a bowl. He made a strip of fat meat about two feet long. And he said, "Bolt it down. Let it hang out of your mouth only this far (about one inch)."

And Grass Snake arranged the piece of fat meat so that it would stick out of his mouth, and since he had no hands he could not pull the piece of fat meat out again.

Grass Snake went back, but he could only barely make it. And at the same time Grass Snake went back to his people, Haxige left for his home. He took his younger brother and he ran home.

But it was hard for Grass Snake to talk. When he said "Haxige, Haxige," it was only in a very faint voice. Even when he was near his people, they thought that he was far away. They said, "That Grass Snake says 'Haxige,'" and when they looked for him, they found that he was really very close. "Ho! ho! it is Grass Snake, but he has a piece of fat meat stuck tight in his throat," they said, and they pulled it out for him. And so the people went back to their village.

When Haxige went home, he ran into an old Beaver Woman and said to her, "Old Woman, what are you doing?"

"Well, Grandchild," she said, "Haxige killed two of the Water Monsters, and therefore they have taken me on as a servant."

So he said, "Old Woman, what kind of work do you do that they have taken you on?"

"Well, Grandchild, they are threatening to make a flood against Haxige. When Haxige is sitting in his boat because of the flood, they say that I am supposed to gnaw a hole in it, and so they have taken me on."

"Old Woman, even if it is so, Haxige will sit in his boat and will get along very well whatever happens."

"And, moreover, if they fail in this, Grandchild, they threaten that they will cause a darkness over the whole earth," she said.

"Old Woman, even if that happens, Haxige will sit in a canyon, deep in a hollow. As he sits in his hollow, he will eat the animals that die from falling into the hole."

"Well, Grandchild, even if they fail with their darkness, they are talking about a plague of snakes," she said.

"Old Woman, even if that happens, Haxige will make himself paws of turtle shells and he will walk about on the heads of the snakes everywhere," he said. "Old Woman, what sort of person are you that you hate Haxige?" and he crushed her head with several blows, then set out for his home.

When he got there, he made a very small lodge. He carried several stones of a certain size and made a sweat lodge. He placed the skin of his brother in a sitting position on one side and he sat on the other. He made the stones red-hot and poured water on them. He made the small lodge very hot. He did this for four days.

On the fourth day he made his brother return to life; once again his young brother lived. And he said, "Ho! Friend Younger Brother, I very much wanted you to live. I have brought you back to life. But let us separate. And I, Younger Brother, will be a big wolf. And you, Friend Younger Brother, will go as a young male deer."

And so it was.

Haxige
Told by Francis La Flesche to Franz Boaz

The first people to walk upon this earth were two brothers, Haxige and his younger brother, who kept house together. The elder brother was fond of travel, and sometimes he would be gone away from home a long time, which left the younger brother all alone. But he liked to hunt and would bring home rabbits and small birds. When the elder brother returned home at the usual time, the boy would get water and cook for his brother.

These two brothers were very happy together and did not get lonely for their family. Sometimes the older brother, Haxige, would again start out after returning home late, but he would only get as far as the ridge when a feeling of fear came over him and his heart would be anxious about his younger brother. This caused him to turn back, and when he reached home he would say, "Younger Brother, I could not go away. There is a feeling in my heart, and for that reason I have come back. When I am away I am afraid that you might wander away. If you do want to go anywhere, go to places close by."

After saying this, he left on his journey.

Because every kind of creature on the earth knew these brothers, Haxige knew that they hated him and his brother, and that is why fear and anxiety were in his heart.

After one of his travels, he came home in the evening and found his younger brother gone. He called and called but got no reply. He followed the brother's footprints from the house and found signs that he had been chasing an animal.

It was winter and the river was frozen. Two tracks were visible and both led into the water. Following them the elder brother kept up his search for his brother. Across the country Haxige went, calling and crying for his brother. Early the next day, as the sky became red from the sunrise, the elder brother came to a gray wolf.

He said to him, "I believe that a boy who is my brother has been taken into the water and I am looking for him. I thought that you might have heard where he is."

The gray wolf only answered in tones that were not pleasing to Haxige and then ran off with his tail blowing in the wind.

Haxige chased and killed the animal and said, "Whoever you are, you may not laugh at Haxige." He went on in his search, crying all the while. His tears flowed so freely that they became the rivers and streams.

Along the way he met an old, old beaver. He said to her, "Ho, Old Woman. What has happened?"

Shading her eyes, she looked at him and said, "Have you not heard that Haxige's younger brother has been killed and for that reason he is threatening people with a flood? That is the reason I am building a boat."

Upon being asked what would happen if the flood were not brought about, the old woman replied, "If Haxige does not make a flood, he will make snakes."

Haxige had great pity for the old woman and therefore did not hurt her but went peacefully on his way.

The next morning at sunrise he went on his way, still crying. He happened to look up and saw an eagle, to whom he appealed with outstretched hands for news of his younger brother. The eagle paid Haxige no attention and started to go on his way. Quickly Haxige leaped after the bird before it could escape and knocked it to the earth with a single blow. He then said to it, "Be you great or small, you may not laugh at Haxige with your indifference."

He went still further searching for his younger brother.

Another morning when the sky was beginning to grow red he approached a babbling creek where he heard voices, and he paused and listened.

One said, "Friend, when Haxige's brother was killed I had a good time."

The other, rather suspecting that Haxige might be near, said, "I did not have such a good time because I did not get so much as one of his little fingers. So, whenever I run into Haxige, I intend to tell him all about the killing of his brother."

Softly Haxige crept up on the two little ducks who were talking to each other and vanished. In the form of a leaf he dropped down between the two birds and caught them in his hands. "What was that you just said?"

Both little ducks cried out, "Hold me gently and I will tell you." The one who said he had a good time at the killing died at Haxige's hand at once. Haxige held the other gently and said to him, "My little duck, tell me the truth. I will decorate you. When people look at you, you, of all the little ducks, will be the most beautiful."

To this the little duck replied, "Now I will tell you what happened. Your brother was killed at the edge of the lake near the white cliffs. They took him to a cave where four monsters live and they killed him. When the sun is high in the sky you can see them sun themselves, and then they always go to sleep."

"You have spoken well, little duck, and now I shall decorate you." He painted the base of its wings blue and he painted the lower lids of its eyes white. "I shall also give you a name; forever you shall be known as 'the traitor bird.'"

Continuing on his weary search, Haxige finally came into sight of the white cliffs and the cave. He could see the place where the monsters sun themselves. He could see all of this from a distance. As he stood there he thought, "What shall I do to catch them in the easiest way." And as he stood looking at the lake he saw the monsters appear and run for their certain particular places, just as the little duck had said they would.

Haxige quickly disappeared again and then dropped in very close to the monsters from above. They were suspicious of him and ran for their cave. Patiently the elder brother waited for the return of the monsters, and, as usual, on the next day about noon they came racing for their usual places.

Again Haxige vanished, but soon came floating down in the shape of a feather, drifting down from above, and when he landed he again took on the form of a man. Seeing the strange man in their midst, the monsters ran for their cave but Haxige wounded them as they were running away. Even though he wanted to get even closer to them, however, he did not want to go into the cave, and so he had to content himself with watching them from a distance.

On the next morning when the sun was high, Haxige saw an old man, ornately decorated, come dancing and singing to himself.

Hegi, daga
Hegi, Hegi, daga
Hegi, Hegi, daga.

When he stopped dancing and singing, four persons went to meet the old man; they spread a robe for him and had him lie down on it. These four men did not appear to see Haxige, but he could plainly see them from where he sat. Approaching the old man (a vulture), Haxige, who had already made plans to kill the vulture, spoke to him. "Wu hu! What a handsome old man this is! What is the occasion for all of this festivity?"

To this the vulture answered, "Haven't you heard that Haxige has wounded the four monsters and managed to escape with his life and that I am their doctor and have come to relieve them of their suffering?"

Again Haxige said, "You are a handsome old man. Let me see you dance."

So the old man began to dance, using a jumping or hopping motion all the while. Haxige watched him carefully. When he had memorized every step and motion he killed the vulture-doctor. Then Haxige went to work and made himself look like the old man. He painted his face to look like him and put on his clothing. When this had been accomplished he began to dance like the vulture, and once again the four men came rushing to meet him and, much as before, spread a robe for him and carried him home on it.

Entering the door of the cave he saw his younger brother suspended, tied completely with robes and cords. He cried out, "My very dearest brother," and then disguising his voice he said to all of the people who had assembled, "I want you to go to the hill and stand behind it."

When the people had left, he—still resembling the vulture doctor— began to examine the wounded monsters. He took a burning torch and pushed it into their wounds, thus killing them. He cut their bodies up into small pieces and put them in a kettle of boiling water and cooked them. When he had finished he broke the ropes that bound his brother and, after they had eaten, Haxige fled, carrying his brother with him. Then the people were very afraid of him and they ran to their homes.

After they had fled some distance, Haxige prepared a sweat bath for his brother. When it was ready, he said, "Do you think it is better to live or die?"

The boy replied, "Death is better."

"Ho! It is good," said Haxige, and he turned his brother into a red stone and placed him on the side of a high hill. Haxige changed himself into a gray wolf and ran away.

COMMENTARY

La Flesche sent this tale to Franz Boas on June 22, 1928, apologizing for its length and making a point of its being a myth rather than a simple folktale.

Indian tales are the result of a culture quite different from that which produced the fairy tales first collected by Grimm, but I have always taken some pride in having associated with my Omaha friends and relatives sufficiently to have acquired some understanding of Indian ways and thoughts. But I must confess that the conclusion of this tale depressed me severely at first reading. What despair follows the success of a long search and struggle!

But, of course, to the Indian, man is not some sort of ultimate, unique expression of nature; he is simply an expression of life, and death does not end that expression but only alters it, perhaps for the better. So the fate of Haxige's younger brother is not at all a sad one; indeed, he makes it quite explicit that death is preferable, and as that red stone on the side of the hill he will probably outlast us all.

Haxige assumes the form of the animal that he killed as he began his adventure, thus closing the full circle of nature.

Icibaji
Told by Joseph La Flesche

A certain man had a wife and one child. The boy did not hunt at all, neither did he do any traveling. Actually, he did nothing at all. He was very fond of women, and so he spent most of his time talking with them. The people laughed at him and ridiculed him as a boy without any sense at all. His father was the only one who did not ridicule him.

He became a man, but he was without a bow or any other weapons. The boy made a four-sided club which he always carried with him. When the people saw that, they laughed at it.

Now hostile nations were always going on the warpath, but Icibaji never went along, for he knew nothing about it. But finally he made sacred two quill feathers of a sparrow hawk. He did this secretly; no one knew that he had them.

Then Icibaji heard the men talking about going on the warpath. He heard this when they were talking secretly to each other, and he thought, "I will go along with them." But he didn't tell anyone.

When his mother was not in the lodge, he took his quill feathers and left. It was night and Icibaji walked along, watching carefully the ones who were going on the warpath. When they got some distance from the village, they sat down. One by one they assembled together. The war chief did not notice that Icibaji had joined the war party.

Soon all the braves were there, and Icibaji stood in the rear, peeking around. Some of the warriors said "Oh, War Chief, someone else is here." And he said, "O Warriors, go see who it is." And two of them caught him and saw that it was Icibaji, so they went back to the war chief and said, "O War Chief, it is Icibaji."

The war chief was very happy. "O Warriors, bring him up here. It was natural that you would laugh at him when he was always talking with the women, but now things have changed."

They brought him forward and found that he had no bow, not even moccasins. "Braves, give him mocassins and arrows," ordered the war chief. So all the braves gave him arrows, two from each, and also mocassins, one pair from each man. They cut down a dry ash tree and made a bow for him. Then they left.

They slept every night, as usual, and when it was day they would go on the move again. At length they had passed many days in this way.

At length the warriors detected a man. They told the war chief, "O War Chief, a man is coming right along our path."

"Ho! Warriors, he is the very one we are looking for. Let's kill him!" and the warriors prepared themselves. They painted themselves with yellow earth and white clay. Icibaji picked up all the pieces of white clay which fell as they rubbed it on themselves.

The war chief asked, "Is this what you want, O Warrior?"

Icibaji said, "Exactly like that." And so the war chief painted his back yellow for him, for Icibaji had told him to do so.

"Is this the way you want it to be?" asked the war chief.

Icibaji replied, "Yes, exactly like that."

The braves pulled off their leggings and mocassins too, and they made Icibaji carry them. "Icibaji, carry these for us," they said.

Icibaji said, "O War Chief, I want very much to see this man."

"Be careful not to scare him off," said the war chief.

"No, War Chief, but I do want to look at him," said Icibaji.

"All right, then, go look at him," said the war chief, and Icibaji peeked at him. Soon the man came very close.

Icibaji said, "O War Chief, I have never come this far," and Icibaji attacked the man, throwing away the bow, carrying only the club. He overtook the man and killed him with the club. "People may make fun of someone, but the time comes when they usually stop. I wish that I could do this same thing to a few of you," he said to the others.

All the other warriors took parts of the man's scalp, but Icibaji did not. So they all started home again. When the warriors came in sight of the village, they called, "We attacked a man and Icibaji killed him," and an old man proclaimed loudly, "The warriors attacked a man and Icibaji was the one who killed him for them, they say. Hey!"

Icibaji's mother heard this, and when she heard it she said to her husband, "Go see if that is really true!"

"How could that possibly be true? They are just making fun of him," said the husband.

And when the party got to the edge of the encampment, the old man said, "The warriors attacked a man, but Icibaji was the one who killed him. Hey!"

The father got up and went outside. Now he knew that they were telling the truth. So the father caused his people to scramble for his horses and, in fact, everything else in his lodge.

Icibaji continued to be like this. Once again they went on the warpath, and this time they discovered four men approaching. Again when they attacked them, Icibaji left his comrades behind and killed all four of the men.

When they reached home, they said, "We attacked four men, but Icibaji killed them."

An old man proclaimed it loudly, "The warriors attacked four men, but Icibaji killed them for them, they say. Hey!"

And so it usually was whenever such a situation arose on the warpath: he always killed the men and usually brought back horses.

His father commanded him to marry: "My Child, take a wife." And although Icibaji did not want to for some time, he finally did take a wife. But after he had married her, he never lay with the woman. He just went to sleep wherever he was when night fell. So his father told him, "My Child, when a man marries a woman, he usually sleeps with her. Do sleep with your wife. You are wrong not to." And his father kept telling him this all the time, until finally Icibaji got tired of it. So when it was night, he slept with the woman.

But when daybreak came he did not get up. All he would do is lie with his woman. The woman wanted to get up but Icibaji would not let her do so. Even when the lodges were taken down and the camp was moved, Icibaji would not get up. It was very late in the evening when he finally caught up with them, and it was exactly the same way the next night. And early the next morning some men from another tribe attacked them.

"Get up," cried the father. "We are being attacked," but Icibaji just lay there, without a word.

Soon the enemy got very close, and a woman cried, "O Icibaji, where are you? I am being captured by a very bad man. Keep him from seeing my parts that should not be seen!" And when he heard her voice, Icibaji jumped up and took his club. He ran out against the enemy, killing a great many, in fact, all of them. There was another brave man beside Icibaji, Unahe, a member of the Honga Clan. Icibaji helped him. They were both very brave. His people loved Icibaji very much.

When they went on the warpath later, one very brave man went along with Icibaji. His name was Techujan, and he was a member of the Kansas Clan. As they moved along together, each one thought, "Which of us has the best heart?"

Soon they reached a very large village. When they got close, they told the rest of the war party, "Warriors, go on home. Go a ways away." And they did so.

Techujan and Icibaji said, "Let's go," for they wanted to test their courage. When they got there, they found a great plain all around the village. When they got very close, they found men playing the game *banangekide* (or shooting at rolling hoops). There was a great crowd gathered around, and it was just noon.

Techujan said to himself, "How will we go down there?"

Icibaji said, "Friend, let's put our heads in these bones," referring to some very white buffalo pelvis bones that were lying there.

So they put them on and went crawling toward the village. Each one was still thinking, "I wonder which of us will fear danger when he meets it."

One of the men playing *banangekide* looked at one of the bones and saw that the bone had come closer, and he said, "Friend, this bone used to be some distance away."

The other scoffed, "Friend, it has always been right there."

But after it had come even closer, the first said "Friend, you said before that that bone was some distance away, and now it is very close."

Techujan said, "They have spotted us. We are discovered," and Icibaji said, "This is it." Then Techujan shouted "Oho!" and they threw away their bones and attacked the men who were playing *banangekide*. Each of them killed two players and then they ran for home.

The enemy shouted, "There are only two of them. Let's chase them," and they pursued them a long ways. They chased them into a very deep thicket where Techujan and Icibaji had dashed. They could not find them, and so Techujan and Icibaji continued along for some time.

COMMENTARY

Dorsey entitles this story "History of Icibaji" and includes it in the section titled "Historical Texts." However, it has the ring of the traditional legend, which in many cases is hard to separate from historical narrative. A legend is usually told as truth, which separates it from stories like the Rabbit tales. But since it is nonetheless traditional, being transmitted primarily by unsophisticated means and representing folklore rather than precise history, it must be treated as folklore. In addition, there are the many features of this story which call forth comment on other features of Omaha tradition.

For example, Dorsey notes: "The father of Icibaji was so proud of his son's success that he let the people scramble for the possession of all his property, as well as for his ponies. Chips were thrown into the air, each representing a piece of property. Whoever caught the chip as it descended won the article. There were other adventures of the two, but I have not preserved them in Çegiha. Only one of these was gained and written in English, and it occurred after the adventures given here in the text. Mothers used to scare their children, telling them that Icibaji . . . would catch them if they did not behave."

It is no wonder that Icibaji's father was concerned about his behavior, for honors gained in war were, and in fact still are, the primary marks of distinction in a man's life. Furthermore, industry was demanded and laziness sternly condemned. Alice Fletcher cites some of the folk sayings and customs regarding the importance of diligence:

"When a boy used a knife in cutting meat the old men said, 'The knife eats more meat; you should bite it.' This saying means, the use of the knife makes one lazy; a man should rely on his own resources; the one who so trains himself is ready for any emergency.

"The old men used to tell the young men that they must learn to make arrows. They said, 'If one does not make arrows he will borrow moccasins, leggings, and robes and be disliked by the persons from whom he borrows.' This meant that one must be industrious in order to have things of one's own. The old men also said, 'If you don't make arrows yourself and a young man who is industrious shows you his arrows, you will be tempted to steal from him.' Also, 'If you are not industrious you will borrow a horse from a young man who may be insignificant [of no position in the tribe], and you may be proud that you ride a horse even if it is not your own; you will borrow a bridle too, and you will be disliked by the men from whom you borrow.' Also, 'If you are not industrious, when a herd of buffalo is slaughtered you may come across a young man whom you may consider of no significance but who has killed a buffalo by his energy; you will look longingly at the best portions of the meat, but he will give to another who is known to be thrifty and generous and you will go away disappointed.'

"I was told: You must not be envious and maim the horse of another man if it is a fine horse to look at. You must not take another's robe or blanket, or his moccasins, or anything that belongs to another. You will be tempted to do these things if you are not industrious and if you yield to the temptation you will be shunned by all persons. A man must be energetic, industrious . . . . If you are not industrious your blanket will be ragged, your moccasins will be full of holes, you will have no arrows, no good, straight ones; you will be in poverty and finally you will go to neighboring tribes to avoid meeting the members of your tribe, who should be your friends. If you are lazy, by chance you may have a horse that is blind and you will think yourself well off. You may have a horse with a disjointed hip and you will think yourself rich. If you are lazy, your tent skin will be full of holes. You will wear leggings made out of the top of an old tent that is smoked yellow; for a robe you will wear a buffalo skin pallet pieced with the fore part of a buffalo hide—such is the lazy man's clothing.

"An industrious man wears leggings of well-dressed deer skin; his robe is of the finest dressed buffalo skin and he wears earrings—such is the dress of the energetic, industrious man. If a man is not industrious and energetic, he will not be able to entertain other people. A lazy man will be envious when he sees men of meaner birth invited to feasts because of their thrift and their ability to entertain other people. If you are lazy, nobody will have pleasure in speaking to you. A man in passing by will give you a word with only a side glance and never stand face to face in talking with you. You will be sullen, hardly speaking to those who address you—that is the temper of the lazy man. The energetic man is happy and pleasant to speak with; he is remembered and visited on his deathbed. But no one mourns for the lazy man; nobody knows where he is buried; he dies unattended. Even when only two or three are gathered to a feast the industrious and energetic man is invited. People in speaking of him say: He is pleasant to talk with, he is easy of approach. Such a man has many to mourn his death and is long remembered. A thrifty man is well spoken of; his generosity, his help are given to those who are weaker than he and all his actions are such as make others happy. Such are some of the things that used to be said by the old to the young men."[2]

Dorsey says of preparations for going on the warpath that "each warrior makes up a bundle composed of about fifteen pairs of moccasins, with sinew, an awl, and a sack of provisions, consisting of corn which has been parched. The latter is sometimes pounded and mixed with fat and salt."

The quiet preparation and nocturnal departure for this war party suggests a connection with a discussion about such parties in Dorsey's work. He states that, "the departure takes place at night. Each man tries to slip off in the darkness by himself, without being suspected by any one. The leaders do not wish many to follow lest they should prove disobedient and cause the enemy to detect their proximity.

"Another reason for keeping the proposed expedition a secret from all but the guests is the fear lest the chiefs should hear of it. The chiefs frequently oppose such undertakings, and try to keep the young men from the warpath. If they learn of the war feast they send a man to find out whither the party intends going. Then the leaders are invited to meet the chiefs. On their arrival they find presents have been put in the middle of the lodge to induce them to abandon their expedition.

"The warriors and the leaders blacken their faces with charcoal and rub mud over them. They wear buffalo robes with the hair out, if they can get them, and over them they rub white clay."

The game of *banangekide*, as described by Dorsey, "is played by two men. Each one has in his hand two sticks about as thick as one's little finger, which are connected in the middle by a thong not over four inches in length. The sticks measure about three feet and a half in length. Those of one player are red and those of the other are black. The wheel which is rolled is about two feet and a half in diameter, its rim is half an inch thick, and it extends about an inch from the circumference towards the center. On this side of the rim that measures an inch are four figures. The first is called . . . 'Marked with a knife,' or . . . 'Cut in stripes with a knife.' The second is . . . 'The black one.' The third is . . . 'Crossing each other.' The fourth is . . . 'The little one,' or . . . 'The little one marked with a knife.' The players agree which one of the figures shall be *wakube* for the game; that is, what card players call 'trumps.'

"The wheel is pushed and caused to roll along, and when it has almost stopped each man hits gently at it to make it fall on the sticks. Should the sticks fall on the top of the wheel, it does not count. When a player succeeds in lodging his sticks in such a way that he touches the wakube, he wins many sticks, or arrows. When figures are touched by one or both of his sticks, he calls out the number. When any two of the figures have been touched, he says, . . . 'I have wounded it twice.' If three figures have been hit, he says, . . . 'I have wounded three.' Twenty arrows or sticks count as a blanket, twenty-five as a gun, and one hundred as a horse."[3]

Curiously, this game is not mentioned in Fletcher and La Flesche.

The Suitor and His Friends
Told by Joseph La Flesche

There was a village once where a very beautiful woman lived, and young men used to go there to court her, for she was very desirable. But none of them could win her.

One young man thought, "Let me see! They all have wanted this woman but have failed to win her. But I too want her; I will go give it a try for myself." And he went off.

There was a person sitting on a high hill, and the youth, who was thinking only of the beautiful woman, drew near the person on the hill. The person on the hill stood up and sat down, and stood up and sat down again at short intervals. And the young man, who was thinking of the beautiful woman, arrived at the place where the man was sitting.

And the young man asked, "My Friend, why are you sitting there?"

The man answered, "My Friend, I want to attack those buffalo, but I always run right on past them, so I am tying stones to my ankles." The stones that he was tying to his ankles were very large.

And the young man said, "My Friend, I can see that when the occasion calls for it, you can do some running. I am without a companion. Why don't you come along with me?"

The man said yes and he went along with him.

Soon they came within sight of two large lakes where another man was sitting. Whenever he was thirsty, he just leaned over and drank, and then he would raise his head again. The young man came up to him. "My Friend, why are you sitting there?" he asked.

"Yes, My Friend, I want a drink, but I never get enough, so I just sit here drinking, and I may just drink up that other lake too," answered the man.

"My Friend, if ever the need arises, it is clear that you can drink quite a lot. I need another companion. Why don't you come along with me?" asked the young man. And the man joined them, making the group now three in number. As they traveled along, they met another person who was walking around looking at the sky.

The young man went up to him and asked, "Why are you walking around?"

"Yes, My Friend, I pulled back on my bow and shot an arrow up into the air. But the arrow hasn't come down yet, and I am waiting for it," answered the man.

"My Friend, I am traveling along, and I need another companion. You can look for your arrow some other time. Come along with us," said the youth.

The man said, "Yes," and they all left together. Now there were four.

They came upon a person lying stretched out on the ground. Whenever he raised his head, he would lie down again. They could see that he was listening to something on the ground. "My Friend, why are you lying there?" asked the young man.

"Yes, My Friend, the different kinds of plants are growing up, and I am listening to their breathing," said the man.

"My Friend, you can listen to that some other time. Come along with us. We are on a journey, and we could use you," said the youth. The man agreed and joined them.

Soon they arrived at a village, and when they entered the village, the people crowded around them and looked at them. "Five people have come," they said. "Why have you come?"

"Well, we have come because we want the woman," said the five.

The people said, "People are always coming for the woman, but they have all failed, for it is difficult to win her. If you want to marry the woman, you must throw this rock so far that it goes to another country. It overshadows the village and keeps away the sunlight."

And the youth who wanted the woman said, "Well, My Friends, this is going to be a hard task."

"My Friend," said He-Who-Tied-Stones-to-his-Ankles, "what is hard about that? That won't be a problem." He went over to the rock, leaned against it, and pushed it away. When the rock fell over, it cracked into many pieces. In fact, it was the cracking of that rock into many pieces that caused there to be rocks scattered all over the earth.

Then the people said, "Let these men eat. Cook for them." And all the villagers cooked for them. They carried many kettles to them; also water.

The youth said, "My Friends, we cannot eat all this." But He-Who-Drank-Much-Water said, "My Friend, we can eat it."

"Yes, My Friend," said the other.

Everyone ate, and while they were eating, He-Who-Drank-Much-Water took a kettleful and poured it down. He swallowed all the water until the people finally stopped bringing it.

"There is one woman who is very fast at running. If you run a race together and you come back ahead of her, you can marry the woman you want," said the people.

Then He-Who-Tied-Stones-to-his-Ankles said, "I will run against her," and he did race her. They ran to the place where the woman usually raced those who had come courting.

The woman said, "This is the place we must run back from. Let's rest a minute." He sat down with her, and she said, "Lie down right there," and then she hunted lice for him. And the man went to sleep lying there.

When she was sure that he was asleep, she left him and ran on home. The woman came in sight again on a very distant hill. "Here they come," everyone said. But they could see then that the woman was coming alone.

The boy said, "Friend, Listener, our friend is missing. Listen for him."

Listener did listen, and he could hear him snoring. "Our Friend lies fast asleep," he reported.

"Ho, Friend, Pull-the-Bow, give it a try," said the youth, and big Pull-the-Bow took an arrow, bit off the end, pulled the bow, and sent the arrow off with great force. And as the man was lying there, fast asleep, big Pull-the-Bow wounded him right on the end of his nose.

He jumped up and could see that the woman was nowhere in sight. So He-Who-Tied-Stones-to-his-Ankles started running back and when the woman had nearly reached home he overtook her. He ran right on toward the village, left the woman far behind, and reached the goal far ahead of her. So he beat the woman in the race and the young man married the beautiful woman.

COMMENTARY

The motif of the magical helpers is one of the most common in world folklore. Perhaps the version best known to Westerners is that of the Bremen City Musicians, in which a group of misfit animals join together to form a successful team, routing some would-be burglars.

The situation of the suitor was a common one in Omaha village life and so plays a large role in the themes of Omaha folklore. Fletcher suggests that usually marriage was by the choice of the couple, but that "when a marriage was arranged by a girl's parents, with or without her consent, it was apt to be with a man in mature life and established position. The would-be husband made large presents to the girl's parents and relatives. When the time came for the marriage the girl was well dressed, mounted on a pony, and accompanied by four old men she was taken to the lodge of her husband. Young men derided this kind of marriage, saying, 'An old man cannot win a girl; he can win only her parents.' "[4]

Ukiabi, the Suitor (a Ponca legend)
Told by Yellow Buffalo, an Omaha

Old Man Ukiabi had two men as his servants. He was sitting with them one day at sunset, and he said to them, "O Friends, I want to marry the single woman who lives over there," and he described her home. "Both of you go over there and court her for me."

But Ukiabi's wife said, "How absurd! Don't say such things! Why should those people give you one of their pretty daughters?"

"Go there," ordered Ukiabi, so the men left. They reached the lodge where the young woman lived and presented their request.

"You have a very pretty daughter whom someone wants to marry, and so we have come here today to speak to you about it."

The father said nothing, but his wife spoke up immediately, "Who is the man who wants to marry her?"

The two men replied, "Our friend, Ukiabi, is the one."

"Phooey! Go back there to your own lodge! He can hardly be considered a human being! I have a pretty child, and I want her to marry a human being. I don't want her to marry some kind of spirit."

And so the men went back. As they were on their way back, they were talking. One said, "My Friend, the woman's words were harsh. Let's not tell our friend about them."

But his comrade replied, "Why, he knows everything. Why shouldn't we tell him about them?"

Meanwhile Ukiabi had stretched out, but when they returned, Ukiabi was sitting up erect. He said, "Ho! You and your friend have come back. Tell me exactly what they said." After hearing their report, Ukiabi told his wife to hand him a plume. Then he blackened the face of one of his friends, put plumes all over his crown, and attached quill feathers to it here and there. He decorated the other man in the same way and made each one wear a buffalo robe with the hair outside. Then he told them how to act. He told them where to go. "Go to that place and make a hole for a pole." Both servants had hoes. "When you have prepared the ground just right, strew plumes on it and draw the figure of a man. Do not come back. Stay there when you have completed your job. I will join you."

At the appointed time Ukiabi went to the place mentioned. When he came into the forest, he changed himself into a wild cat. When he walked, the ground shook and his steps made fire blaze up. His servants heard him coming.

"Your friend is coming," said one.

When Ukiabi arrived, his servants said, "O Friend, we finished our job a long time ago, but you did not come."

Ukiabi replied, "Well, you can go again. Leave the hoes. Take these five plum stones to the young woman's lodge. Stand at the entrance. Patter with the soles of your feet on the ground at the left side, near the tent pole. Show her the plum stones."

The servants left and eventually reached the lodge where the woman lived. She came out of the lodge. They did as Ukiabi had told them, and then they stepped backward, moving toward their home. The woman followed close after them. After walking backward for some time, the two men turned around and ran homeward, closely followed by the woman. Thus the two men drew the woman home behind them.

As she walked along, she acted like a crazy person, tearing her skirt and pulling her hair down over her forehead. She acted like this until she had torn off every shred of her skirt and was completely naked.

Finally they reached the place where they had left Ukiabi. The two men and the woman approached him. Ukiabi and his friends then raped her. Finally Ukiabi had one of the servants fill a kettle with water for the woman and he washed her face for her. With this she came back to her senses.

Then Ukiabi said to her, "Keep the plum stones for gambling. You will always win. You will live for many years. You will be a very old woman before you die. If I had wanted you to die, you would have been gone long before now, but I didn't want you to die. Your mother spoke bad words about me, and it is for that reason that we have done this to you. Well, now you can start home. You must start for home while it is still dark. When day comes, you will be all right again."

Then the woman left for home, but Ukiabi took the form of a prairie chicken and was the first one to start for home.

COMMENTARY

This suitor may have dishonored his chosen one, but he gave her, and thereby the Omaha women for all time, a game they were to spend many an hour with. "One of these [games] was played exclusively by women; this was called *konsi* (*kon*, part of the word *konde*, the name of the plum; *si*, 'seeds'). The appliances were few and simple—a wooden bowl and five plum stones. Two played at a time. First, the number of counts that should constitute the game was determined—50 or 100 points. Sticks were used for keeping tally. The plum stones were 'burned' so as to show certain forms. Two on one side had moons, two on one side had stars; there were three black sides and three white sides. The bowl containing the plum stones was tossed and the combinations of the stones as they fell had certain values. These counts were as follows:

"Two moons and 3 black counted 5 if the game was 50, and 10 if the game was 100. Two moons and 3 white, 2 stars and 3 black, and 2 stars and 3 white had the same count as the above. These counts were called *chube*, and whoever tossed and got any of these throws might keep on tossing so long as she could make *chube*. One moon, 1 star, and 3 white counted 1. One moon, 1 star, and 3 black counted 1 in a game of 50, and 2 in a game of 100. One moon, 1 star, 1 black, and 2 white counted nothing. Two moons, 1 black, and 2 white counted nothing. Two moons or 2 stars, 1 white, and 2 black counted nothing.

"The stakes put up were necklaces, moccasins, earrings, and paint."[5]

It can be seen from the fact that Ukiabi's wife only ridicules the idea of his taking the young woman for a wife that polygamy was practiced by the Omaha. Dorsey comments on this custom.

"When a man wishes to take a second wife he always consults his first wife, reasoning thus with her: 'I wish you to have less work to do, so I think of taking your sister, your aunt, or your brother's daughter for my wife. You can then have her to aid you with your work.' Should the first wife refuse, the man cannot marry the other woman. Generally no objection is offered, especially if the second woman be one of the kindred of the first wife.

"Sometimes the wife will make the proposition to her husband, 'I wish you to marry my brother's daughter, as she and I are one flesh.'

"The first wife is never deposed. She always retains the right to manage the household affairs, and she controls the distribution of food, etc."[6]

Alice Fletcher offers some varying views on the institution of polygamy.

"Polygamy existed, although it was not the rule; in the majority of families there was but one wife. A man rarely had more than two wives and these were generally sisters or aunt or niece. These complex families were usually harmonious and sometimes there seemed to be little difference in the feeling of the children toward the two women who were wives to their father. No special privileges were accorded to the first wife over the others. Polygamy was practised more among the prominent men than among any other class. On the former devolved the public duty of entertaining guests from within and without the tribe. This duty brought a great deal of labor on the household. There was no serving class to render help to man or woman, so that the wife could not hire anyone to assist her in any extra labor or in her daily work or her varied avocations, as in the dressing and tanning of skins, the making of tent covers and clothing, not to mention the embroidery put on garments and regalia. It will be remembered that embroidered garments, robes, pipestems, and other articles were required for gifts that went toward a man's 'count' which led to his tribal honors. Looking at the duties and customs of the tribe, it seems that the question of domestic labor had a good deal to do with the practice of polygamy. 'I must take another wife. My old wife is not strong enough now to do all her work alone.' This remark was made not as if offering an excuse for taking another wife but as stating a condition which must be met and remedied in the only way which custom permitted."[7]

Old Ukiabi
Told by Yellow Buffalo

Ukiabi was a mysterious person, exceeding all others in performing wonderful deeds. He had four sons, one of whom was grown, while the rest were still small. The grown son closely resembled his father in being mysterious. He thought of his father as a rival and wanted to kill him.

One day the son changed himself into a yellow-tailed hawk and flew round and round far above the clouds, very near the Upper World.

That day his father was resting in his lodge. By and by the father looked around and discovered that his son was in the distance. He recognized him at once and knew that his son wanted to kill him. So he said to his wife, "Old Woman, Lodge-Shivers-for-Another-by-Biting is doing something very bad."

"Don't say such a thing," she scolded. "I'm sure that he doesn't mean anything wrong by it."

"You're wrong, Old Woman. He wants to kill me."

Then the father changed himself into a hawk and darted through the smokehole of the lodge. He dashed toward his son. All day long he crossed the earth in close pursuit of his son, turning to the left or right whenever he did. He chased him back to the lodge and in through the smoke hole. The son took on the shape of a feather plume and was lying there when the father entered.

The father recognized him at once and the chase was resumed. He chased him and chased him until the son became a fish and went beneath the water. But again his father detected him.

He chased him and chased him and chased him, until the son reached a water monster that was lying in a stream. The son flew into the water monster's mouth and lay concealed in his body. The father entered the water monster too, driving the son out the other end.

Again Ukiabi chased his son until he dashed down through the lodge's smoke hole. He took on the form of a louse, but his father recognized him. No matter what form he assumed, his father would take on the same shape. Among others, they assumed the forms of a prairie chicken, a grizzly bear, a wild cat, and a very white swan. Finally the son became a hawk. By this time he had used up all of his mysterious power and he had become very tired.

He tried to force his way up through the foundation of the Upper World. When his body from the hips up was through the hole into the upper world and the part below his waist was still on this side, his father stepped on the son's penis and thus killed him. The chase went on all night until half of the sun was visible above the horizon; it was just at that moment that the boy was killed.

Early that morning the people were crying in their lodges. "It is a strange thing, but Ukiabi's son is dead," they mourned, and everyone went to see him.

There he lay, dead, flat on his back. The father took some red Indian paint and reddened the body in spots. He did not cry for some time but just sat there shaking a gourd rattle and singing.

I am walking back and forth,
But I find nothing which can ease my sorrow.

Finally he ended his song and then he cried. First one household and then another took up the wail, until all of the villagers were mourning with Ukiabi. The Ponca have thought there never was such an exhibition of grief as that shown when Old Ukiabi killed his son.

COMMENTARY
According to Dorsey "Ukiabi was the chief of the Hisada, a Ponka gens [clan]. . . . Ukiabi was buried in the side of a high bluff back of Fort Randall. This bluff is known to the Ponkas as . . . 'Where Ukiabi was buried.'

"Yellow Buffalo said that his maternal uncle saw Ukiabi. The face of Ukiabi was exceedingly hideous. Lumps were on his forehead, his eyes were large, and his nose, which was small and turned up at the tip, had an indentation across the ridge, which made it appear broken. It seems probable that a historical Ukiabi is here confounded with the original one, judging from the statement in the [previous] legend about the origin of the game of plumstone shooting."

The Adventures of Fine Feather
Told by Joseph La Flesche

And he said, "We have come to compete with the first-born child of the woman." One of the bad men said this to her. And the boy went there. Even though his father and mother did not want him to, he went there.

When he arrived, they said, "We will compete with you."

"Yes, I agree to that. What shall we play?" asked the boy.

The bad men had planted a very tall, smooth pole in the ground, and they said, "We shall climb that pole and whoever gets back last will be killed," and they started climbing. The bad men got back first and killed the boy.

The woman bore another son and he too grew up. When he was grown, a person came to ask him to go away with him. The visitor said, "We have come to compete with your child."

Again his father and mother were unwilling, but the boy was grown, and he did go along. The boy arrived there. And again they had a contest.

He said, "What shall we play?"

They answered, "Let's play at swinging."

So they played at the swings. One cord was broken in many places, but the other one was in very good condition. They made the boy use the good cord, and the bad man used the cord broken in many places. But soon the cord that was good became bad, for the cord had been cut. The boy fell and was killed.

And the woman gave birth to yet another child, again a boy. The boy grew up and when he was grown they came for him too.

"We have come to compete with your child," they said. Even though the mother and father did not want him to do, he went there anyway.

"Come, we will compete with you," they said. And when they competed, they raced with the boy. Having outrun him, they killed him.

At length the woman bore still another son. He was Fine Feather. All over the land people heard of his birth, the birth of Fine Feather. He never failed getting any kind of animal he was hunting, for he was a very good marksman. In fact, the whole country knew about the boy. He was a fine boy.

Finally, when the boy was grown up, they once more came to ask him to go with them. "We have come to compete with your boy," they said.

His mother and father did not want him to go. "Please do not go," they said.

But the boy said, "O Mother and Father, I want to go there."

"They came this way for your elder brothers and took them away, and they killed them each and every time," said his mother.

He said, "I still want to go there, O Mother," and he did go there.

He arrived, and they said, "You have done well to come here."

The boy asked, "Come, what shall we play?"

They replied, "We will climb that pole."

The boy took his fine feather and put it in his hair. They went to climb the pole, and the boy got to the top first. As they came back down, the boy was the first to reach the bottom. When they returned, he killed a bad man, one of the four.

The boy went home. He got there and found his mother and father there. "O Mother," he said, "I have killed one of those who killed my elder brothers."

She said, "O dear Youngest Child, do be strong. You are quite right; they did kill your elder brothers. Do your best."

The next day, the remaining three bad men arrived. "Boy," they said, "we have come to compete with you."

But his mother said, "Do your best, O dear Youngest Child. You know that they always killed your elder brothers. Do be strong."

The boy went there. When he arrived, they talked about using the swings again. "Use the swing with the good cord," they said to the boy. "The other one is bad. The old cord, which is broken in several places, is bad," they said.

He said, "No, I would like to use it even if it is bad. It isn't true, but you keep saying, 'It is bad.' "

"Use the good one," they said.

"No. No matter what, I want to use the bad one," said the boy.

So they went to swing. The boy did very well. He used the cord that had been broken in many places. The other one, who used the good cord, was killed by a fall.

The boy went home. When he got there he said, "O Mother, and Father, again I killed one of the men who killed my elder brothers."

"O dear Youngest Child, it is true. They did kill your brothers. Do be strong."

The next day the remaining two arrived. "Boy," they said, "we have come to compete with you."

"Yes, I will go with you," he said, and the next day he went there. When he got there he said, "What shall we play?"

"Let's run a race!" they said.

The boy took his fine feather and stuck it in his hair, and he ran with the first bad man. As they were coming back from the race, Fine Feather reached the goal first. He killed one of the bad men.

When he got home again, he said, "O Mother and Father, again I have killed one of those who killed my elder brothers."

"O dear Youngest Child, do be strong. It is certainly true that they did kill your elder brothers," said his mother.

The next day Fine Feather sat waiting for the last man, but he did not come. When it was clear that he was not coming, the boy went to him. When he reached the lodge, the last man was not there. The boy went to look for him. On the way he met a beautiful woman. Fine Feather said, "Why did you leave? You used to compete with me. But now that I want to compete with you, you flee."

The woman said, "No! I don't know who it was competing with you. I am going to take Fine Feather as my husband."

"No, you competed with me, and I want to compete with you. Why did you flee?"

"No! That is not at all true, but you keep saying it. I am going to make Fine Feather my husband," she said.

"Why, I am Fine Feather."

"No! You are he, but you should have told me. Let's sit down," said the woman. He sat with her, and the woman said, "Lie there. I will comb your hair for lice," and she had him lie with his head in her lap. Thus she searched his hair for lice.

So Fine Feather went sound asleep. She put him to sleep with her hands. When he was fast asleep, she took hold of his ears and stretched them out by pulling at them. In this way she quickly turned him into a dog.

So Fine Feather became a dog. And he had mange all over his body. The man who had assumed the form of the woman took the dog with him. He stuck the fine feather in his own hair. They reached a very large village.

"Wonderful," said the people there. "Fine Feather has come. The man we have heard so much about has come."

The head chief heard it. "Bring my Daughter's Husband to me," he said, and he was taken to the chief's lodge.

Now the chief had two daughters, and the chief gave the eldest to the bad man as his wife. And as they had heard that Fine Feather was a fine marksman, they thought that they would test him, so they told him to go hunting. But every time he went out hunting he was unsuccessful. All he brought back was rabbits.

The man said, "That dog smells bad. Old Man, please kill him. He is very offensive."

But the unmarried sister said, "O Father, let him alone. Don't kill him. I want him," and she took good care of the dog.

Her Elder Sister, however, said, "That dog is bad and stinks. You are the only one here who doesn't loathe him."

At length the man went hunting. The dog went along with him. Then, when the man reached home from the hunt, he brought back a wildcat. And the dog, returning too from the hunt, pushed again and again at the girl to get her attention.

She thought, "I wonder why he is doing that?" and she followed him. Finally they arrived at a place some distance from the village where the dog had killed a very large doe.

The girl ran home to her lodge and told her mother and father about it. "O Father and Mother, my dog has killed a very large doe." So her mother and father went to the place where the doe was lying.

The old man said, "My Child, it will do very well."

The girl usually made her bed near that of her elder sister, but she said, "Make it further away. That dog smells bad." She said this because the dog was sitting on the bed. In fact, the girl had let the dog sit on her bed.

The man went hunting again, and as he went out, the dog went with him again. This time the man came home with a raccoon and the dog came home too. When he got there, he kept pushing up against the girl to get her attention, and so she followed him. She followed him some distance from the village and was surprised to find that he had killed a black bear.

She went back to tell her mother and father. "O Mother and Father, my dog has killed a black bear," and her mother and father brought the black bear home to the lodge.

The next day they went hunting again. The man brought home a rabbit. But when the dog got home he kept pushing against the girl to get her attention. They followed him and found that he had killed an elk.

The next day the man went hunting again. He brought home a muskrat, but the dog had killed a beaver. The girl's mother and father were very glad; they loved the dog now. The girl, too, loved her dog very much.

At length the man said, "Old Man, please have them break camp. There is no more game to hunt around here," so they broke camp the next day. But when they left, they did not take the dog along.

When all of the people had gone, the girl remained behind, alone. She was looking for her dog, for he had hidden. And when everyone was gone, she went to where the lodges had been, crying very hard.

When it was late in the evening, the dog appeared, emerging from a thicket nearby. The girl said, "Where have you been? I have been looking for you. Everyone has gone but me. I was looking for you."

"Yes," he said. "It is hard." He continued, "Kindle a fire. Start up the flames. Go to that headland. Say, 'Grandfather, I have come to get some stones for your grandchild!'"

The girl did this, and the ground said, "Kee!" It caused some stones to come to the surface, and the girl took the stones back to her home. When the girl got home with the stones, she said, "These are the stones."

He said, "And finally, go to that cliff. Say, 'Grandfather, I have come after some tent poles for your grandchild.'" And the woman did that too. She arrived at the cliff and some snakes appeared. The woman took them. She took them home. When she got there with them, the dog said, "Come, make a small lodge." The woman made tent poles out of the snakes. She made a grass lodge.

The dog talked with the woman, "You may think you have pitied me, but I pity you. You shall be rich. I am Fine Feather. But that man over there hated me and was cruel to me." And the dog went into the small lodge.

He took a sweat bath. Then he said, "That will do. Uncover me." Then he was a very handsome man. He was no longer a dog; he had become a very handsome man. He went to sleep then. The next day he said, "Let's go," and the woman went with him. Fine Feather took the girl to be his wife.

Eventually they reached the circle of lodges, and when the people saw them, they said, "The girl who was looking for her dog has come home with a man." And one man said to the others, "Friends, this man is very handsome and I think that he is Fine Feather."

When they got to the lodge, the bad man was sitting there with the fine feather sticking in his hair. When Fine Feather got there, he took back his fine feather and stuck it in his own hair. He kicked the bad man and then turned him into a dog and was a very mangy dog that howled terribly when he was kicked.

Then Fine Feather said, "Old Man, please make them kill that dog. That dog is evil," and they took the dog out and killed it.

Fine Feather hunted all the time. He killed all sorts of animals, like bear, elk, deer—in fact, every sort of animal—and he became very rich. Everyone in the tribe prospered and was happy.

The woman whose husband had been killed said to her younger sister, "Younger Sister, let's share your husband."

"But Elder Sister, you once said that my husband smelled bad, that he was very offensive. How could you marry your sister's husband?" All this time the elder sister was crying because she so wanted to marry the man too.

Then the man said, "Now I came here and left behind my mother and father, but now I want to see them again. I want to go to my home."

The woman told her father this. "O Father, he says he wants to see his father and mother. He wishes to go to his home."

And her father said, "Yes, my Child, when a woman marries a man, she must follow him. Go with him." So the woman's father gave his daughter's husband a great many ponies.

But the other woman followed them. When neither the man nor the woman spoke to her, she kept following them, crying all the way.

Then they reached a lodge. His father and mother had become very poor. The crows had picked out their eyes. After a while the other woman, the elder sister, said, "Younger Sister, I would like to heal the eyes of your husband's mother and father. Let me marry him too." The man did not speak.

The woman said, "Elder Sister, you may. They are very poor. My husband will surely marry you too."

And the woman did restore their sight to them.

COMMENTARY

Dorsey says, "The beginning of this myth, as well as the conclusion, could not be given by the narrator, who had forgotten them." Still, the body of the myth seems to be fairly well preserved and when presented along with the next tale, which is clearly related to it, the sense of the tale can be reconstructed.

It is interesting to note the manner in which the father announces his wish for his daughter to marry the young man; he simply refers to him as "my Daughter's Husband."

Corn Woman and Buffalo Woman
Told by Nudanacha

Once there was a tribe. During the winter, as is also the custom now, they moved their camp. The crier called, "He says you are to break camp!"

Now there was one man who had no wife. However, he had four sisters. When they broke camp, the man said, "Leave me behind," and they did.

All the women in the camp were saying, "The sisters of the young man who lay sick have left him and come with us."

All of the tents were moved again. His youngest sister, the smallest one, hid herself among some large trees. She went back. She followed the trail back to the starting point. Finally she came in sight of the lodge. The sister came back crying, but her brother was still alive.

"My Sister, why have you returned?" he asked.

And she answered, "O Elder Brother, I came back to see if you were dead," and she stayed with him.

Then he said, "O Younger Sister, comb my hair for me," and she did. "Get my robe for me," he said, and she got it for him. "I put my fine feather over there in the pack; get it for me, too, O Younger Sister," he said, and she got everything for him. He put on all his clothes, mocassins and leggings, too. The fine feather he stuck in his scalplock. He wore his robe with the hair-side out, and he drew it tightly around him. He painted his face.

He said, "Oh, Younger Sister, since you have no one to talk with, I will go and find a sister-in-law for you."

Four days passed. He stood at his door, so it could not be said that he traveled a great distance. The evening of the fifth day arrived, and he, the elder brother, lay down just as he was.

Finally his sister, who had gone outside, said, "O Elder Brother, a woman has come."

"Come back here with your brother's wife," he said.

"O Brother's Wife, come to the lodge," she said.

Night came, then day, and again evening. As it began to grow dark, the sister went outside. Again someone came.

"O Elder Brother," the sister said, "this woman has come too."

The brother said, "Come back here with your brother's wife," and so he had two wives. Both became pregnant and they gave birth to children, both boys. And they were all happy together. Both of the boys were quick to learn to speak.

Their father said, "You and your brother must never fight," and so it was. They always played games together.

It eventually came to pass, however, that the boys got into a fight. They cursed each other.

"Your mother is Buffalo Woman," said one.

"And yours is Corn Woman," said the other.

When they got home, Buffalo Calf told his mother about this. And the other did too.

"O Mother, My Younger Brother said that you are Buffalo Woman," said one.

The other said, "O Mother, my Elder Brother says that you are Corn Woman."

That night both women were very angry. They would not talk with their husband. But Buffalo Woman copulated with the man.

Day came. The man was lying alone. The women had gone again. He sat for some time. Then he said, "O Sister, I am going to look for your brother's sons," and when the next day came, he left.

He went in a straight line, crossing the land in a direct route. At length, when it was very late in the evening, he discovered the trail, and he followed it. The man was Buffalo and his son Buffalo Calf. He and his mother had gone home to the buffalo herd, running very swiftly.

The man at length reached a creek along which the trees stood very thick, and when a lodge was in sight the man thought, "This must be the place." He approached the grove and sat down. No one was in sight.

Then his son came along. "It is Buffalo Calf," said the man.

"My Father has come," said Buffalo Calf.

"Father or not, you cried all the while we were walking today. Fool! Go to him," said Buffalo Woman.

The man came up and she gave him a very small wooden bowl with water barely covering the bottom. The man sat thinking, "I haven't had any water and am really thirsty. This is so little." He drank but could not drink all of the water. "A little simply would not have satisfied me, and yet I cannot drink all this water," he thought.

Then she gave him a bowl that contained a piece of dried buffalo meat this size [three inches in diameter].

"I have been hungry for some time. She should have given me a bigger piece," he thought, but he could not eat all of the meat. He gave her back all of the meat that was left when he had finished.

"It is really very little food," said the woman. She divided the dried meat into two parts and bolted it down.

When night came, they all went to sleep as they were. Since they had made a fine couch, they went to sleep. In the morning he rolled over and looked around. But there was no lodge at all; he was lying in a deserted place.

He followed their trail. Late that evening he overtook them again. Once more there was a creek and once more a tent. He came up and sat down outside the tent. His son approached him and said, "Father has come."

"Father or not, you cried all day as we walked," said Buffalo Woman. "Call for him."

"Come here, Father!" called the boy, and he came.

The woman gave him a very small wooden bowl in which the water barely covered the bottom. Now the man understood this matter, and so he was not surprised. He drank but could not drink all of the water. And she gave him the bowl which contained a piece of dried buffalo meat this size. Again the man understood the matter, so he was not surprised. But again he could not eat all of the dried meat, so he gave her back the piece that remained.

"This is very little food," said Buffalo Woman. She pulled off a piece of dried meat and bolted it down.

Night came, and they went to sleep. The man had a piece of cord and he tied the woman's feet together with it. Since he had not been awakened when he slept the preceding night, and since he wanted to be awakened, he thought, "When she moves, she will probably awaken me," and they went to sleep.

Day broke. At length he opened his eyes. He was lying in a deserted place, and again he followed their trail. He came in sight of a very large peak. Then he reached a very large stream which they would have to cross.

He hid behind a tree. Then, as they walked along the stream, the man heard Buffalo Calf and his mother speaking.

"Since he prizes his child, let me see if he will cross the water here," she said, and the son and mother crossed the stream, he bellowing and even his mother from time to time.

When he and his mother, cutting straight across the water, reached the middle, the man took out his fine feather. He quickly blew on it and suddenly he was on the other side. He had changed himself into the feather and then blew himself over the water, just that fast.

He stuck to a tree and stayed there, waiting to see Buffalo Calf and his mother. They finally got across. They rubbed their hair dry. They rolled in the sand.

"Since he is so fond of the child, let's see if he will come," said Buffalo Woman, and they quickly ran homeward up the hill. And the man followed them. When he came in sight of the peak, there was a circle of lodges, a large tribal circle. He approached it and sat on the peak.

"O Mother, Father has come," said Buffalo Calf.

"Go there for him," she said, but when he got there he could not find him, for he had changed himself into a fine feather.

Again Buffalo Woman said, "O Younger Sister, go for him," and although she went for him she could not find him.

"O Elder Sister, no one is there," she said.

"Why, that is terrible. You must have been close to him," said Buffalo Woman.

Another went for him. "O Elder Sister, I was not able to find him," she said.

"You are dreadful! You keep going right past him. Stop. I will go for him," said Buffalo Woman. I will see if I cannot find him," and she arrived there.

"They have been looking for you for some time. Where have you been?" she asked.

"Well, hardly anyone has come for me. I have just been sitting here all this time," said the man, and she took him back.

The woman had four sisters, and the fifth was the one who had gone to marry him. They prepared room for her, a lodge all to herself. Her younger sisters were the only ones with her.

Morning came. Her grandmother said to the grandchild, "I have heated stones for your father so that I can take a sweat bath with him," and her daughter's husband took a sweat bath with her.

Eight buffalo came to hold down the sides of the tent. His wife's mother pushed at the stones, which were the size of a man's head. She pushed at them again, and they became the size of a large watermelon. The third time she pushed at them they suddenly became as large as a buffalo calf. She pushed at them again and they were as large as the lodge.

The buffalo bulls leaned against the lodge, causing it to fall in, but the man changed himself into a feather and was quickly blown away. Before the old woman had made the stones grow big, he had disappeared into a fold in the tent.

Old Buffalo Woman said, "O Daughter's Husband, have you become accustomed to the heat?" "Yes, O Wife's Mother," he replied.

After a long time had passed, Old Buffalo Woman asked, "O Daughter's Husband, how are you?" She asked because she hoped that he had been killed by the heat.

He answered, "O Wife's Mother, I am just sitting here as before."

After another time had passed, he was still sitting there, and she asked, "O Daughter's Husband, how are you?"

"O Wife's Mother, I am still sitting here, as always. I am not even sweating much yet."

Finally Old Buffalo Woman got weary of the heat. She was nearly dead, she was so hot. "I am tired of this heat. Open that tent flap for me." They opened it and she came out into the air. As she stepped out, Old Buffalo Woman fainted.

When her daughter's husband came out, however, he was hardly sweating.

"Why, even though I have been taking a sweat bath, the cold bothers me," he said.

His wife said, "You aren't even sweating. But the old woman has fainted from the heat."

"Well, the cold is bothering me," he said.

At length his wife's mother was revived. Having recovered, she went out the next day to call together all of the women.

Buffalo Calf said, "Why, Father, look for my mother among these women and recognize your own."

She and her younger sisters looked exactly alike. They were all beautiful, and looked exactly alike in their beauty. They were all painted and standing in a row. They pushed each other about in an effort to confuse the man. They all got in a line and Old Buffalo Woman spoke.

"O Daughter's Husband, look around for your wife," and the man looked for her.

"That one there is her," he said, and he took hold of her. That was the end of that test.

Buffalo Calf said, "O Father, they say that they are having the boys run a race tomorrow and I will be in it. Look for me. If you don't recognize me, my grandmother says she will kill me. O Father, I will run slowly in sixth place, right after the first five buffalo calves."

When they ran the race, five buffalo calves came running in ahead, and one came in slowly behind them. The man said, "That is my child."

"Which one?" asked Old Buffalo Woman.

"The sixth one, after the first five in the lead," he answered. So the race was over.

"I wonder if they could have been telling him beforehand," said Old Buffalo Woman.

And the next day Buffalo Calf said, "O Father, my grandmother says she is going to run a race with you. If you don't overtake her, she says she will kill you. Be strong."

"Yes, My Child. What your grandmother says must be true," he said.

On the next day she ran a race against her daughter's husband. She ran with him. They ran to a distant hill. "O Daughter's Husband, let's run back from here too," she said, and she ran back with him. She left the man far behind. She appeared on a hill on her way home. Without stopping she went on home.

"The old woman is coming back way ahead of him," everyone said.

When the old woman came near the lodge, she said, "Get my spear ready for me. I am coming home."

The man took his fine feather and when he quickly blew on it, he went straight into his lodge just as the old woman asked for her spear upon her return. He lay down as if sound asleep and did not move one bit.

"At last I have beaten him," she said.

But the son said, "What are you saying? My Father came back a long time ago."

"Hmmm," said the old woman, "Has your father really come home already?"

The boy said, "Since he came home a long time ago, he is sound asleep. The old woman keeps talking and may disturb him."

Her daughter said, "Old Woman, please be quiet. He did come home a long time ago."

And so he slept.

Buffalo Calf said the next day, "O Father, she says she will play swinging with you. One cord there has been repaired in many places. The other one is quite good; it is not broken at all. When they have you examine the cord broken in many places, take that one," the boy said.

They arrived at the place, and the man took the strong cord. A high tree was standing at the edge of the cliff.

"Well," she said, "Come on, Daughter's Husband, let's go!"

He and his wife's mother swang together. As they went past the tree, his cord broke under his weight. As he came near the rocks, he remembered and took his fine feather and blew on it quickly. He went over the other side of the river and, as a feather, lay there.

They reached home, she and her daughter's husband, for she had failed again. Later they played the game *banangekide*. One young buffalo bull approached him and stood there.

"My Friend," he said, "This Buffalo Woman will go for water. When she comes in sight, she will laugh at you. Do not laugh with her. Her husband is bad."

When the woman appeared, she laughed at him. The man did not look at her. Again she came straight at him and laughed, but the man did not laugh with her. She came back ladling water out of a kettle. She would not let the man resist her. She finally made him laugh with her.

All of the buffalo calves who were playing *banangekide* ran away. Then her husband came and attacked him. He appeared, sending pieces of earth flying, thrusting his horns into the ground. He was like an angry bull, pawing the ground.

Everyone said, "Run," but the man stood there, not paying any attention at all. He stood looking at him. The bull reached him and at that moment the man threw aside the robe he was wearing and strung his bow. As the buffalo was about to gore him, the man took his fine feather and suddenly blew on it. All at once he was behind the buffalo. Again it happened this way. He jumped back and forth over the buffalo and was not hurt at all.

The man killed the buffalo bull and then went home to attack his wife's mother. He knew her ways by experience, so he approached her from behind. And he killed her.

COMMENTARY

Although the connection is distant and fragmentary, this myth is related to the preceeding one, and the hero must be Fine Feather. Dorsey observes that this myth is also fragmentary and probably has another part "which relates how the man recovered the Corn Woman and her son and then returned home with all his family."

There are several curious features to this myth that are not mentioned in Dorsey's notes. Corn Woman and Buffalo Woman appear to be powerful figures indeed, but normally corn was considered to be the Omahas' "mother," and their chief crop. The buffalo was their "grandfather," and their principal game. Therefore, as the two wives of this man, their role is peculiar. One must wonder if, perhaps in the earlier versions of this tale, there was not an outline of the origin of the Omaha people, perhaps as the children of the union described in the tale.

It is very unusual that a husband would address his mother-in-law directly as Fine Feather does here. Normally, he would speak to her through a third person.

Fletcher speaks of the Omaha sweat bath. "That kind of bath was always more or less ceremonial, indulged in for the purpose of healing, to avert disaster, or to prepare one's self for some ceremony or duty. A framework of slender poles was bent so as to make a small dome-shaped frame; this was covered tight with skins. Stones were heated over a fire and then placed in the center of the tent. Sweat baths were not usually taken alone, although this was done occasionally. The bathers entered, carrying with them a vessel of water. The coverings were then made fast and the inmates, with ritual or with song sprinkled the water on the heated stones and sat in the steam. After a sufficient sweat had been experienced, they emerged and plunged into cold water, after which they rubbed themselves dry with artemisia or grass. Both men and women took sweat baths but not together."[8]

Chief's Son, Snake Woman, and the Thundermen
Told by Cangeska

There was a chief who was a father, and he said to his son, "My Child, travel out in the world. Either hunt or work. I am a chief now, but when I sat doing nothing I was not a chief. I worked; I was at my best when walking, so I hunted. There is a reason that I am a great man, and I want the same thing for you. But if you sit and do nothing, you will never be chief."

The boy said, "All right, Father. I want to go hunting. Saddle my horse for me," and he did go hunting. He found some elk. He hobbled his horse and went after them on foot. He crept up on the elk, crawling along on his hands and knees. When he got very near them, he shot at them and wounded one slightly. He chased after it. It ran off with him right behind. It took him a long ways—a long ways from his horse, too.

Soon he became very thirsty and decided to go back for his horse. He thought, "If I don't get a drink, I will surely die." Just when his thirst was at its worst, he came upon a spring. And he prayed to God, "Ho! Wakonda, for a while I thought that I was going to die, but you have made it possible for me to live. So I shall live, Wakonda."

Well, as he was about to drink, a snake came out of the water. It scared him away and he ran off. "Wakonda, I thought for a moment that I would live, but now I am about to die!" Again he went to the water to drink, but the snake came out again, and once more he cried out and ran away. He waited until he could not see the snake anywhere and returned to drink from the spring, but the snake came back, and again he ran off.

But the fourth time he looked at the snake and he saw that it was a beautiful woman. She filled a small drinking vessel and held it toward him.

"I am very thirsty," said the youth. "I won't get enough from that. There isn't much water there," he thought. But he had plenty. There was more there than he could ever drink.

The boy looked at the woman and loved her. He thought, "What a beautiful woman!" And when he was about to go home, the woman gave him a ring.

"Wear that ring on your way home," she said, "and when you want to eat, put it on a seat and say, 'Come, let us eat.' "

So the man went home, having gone back to his horse. He got his horse and rode it home. He galloped back to his lodge.

When he got there, his father said, "Cook for him. He has come back very hungry," and they did cook for him.

"Bring me a lot of food," said the son, and they took much food to him.

He took off the ring and put it down. "Come, let us eat," he said, and instantly Snake Woman was sitting beside him. As she sat with him she swallowed food, and when she had finished, she suddenly disappeared.

The boy put the ring on again and said, "O Father, I want to see the women dance," and so his father said, "Ho! My child wants the women to dance. They shall do so." And an old man went to tell them so.

He said, "Women, the chief's son says that you are to dance," but when he saw them dancing, he could not see Snake Woman. He asked them to stop.

"Stop the dance," said the old man. And they stopped. He went home to his lodge.

"Come, O Father, have my mother cook. I am very hungry," the young man said, and she cooked. "This way. Bring it here. Bring whatever you have cooked here," he said.

They cooked a good deal of food and took it to him. When he had it, he pulled off his ring and placed it near him. He said, "Come, let us eat," and Snake Woman appeared next to him. Again she ate with him, and again they played together, for she had married the man. But once more she disappeared.

The man put on his ring again and said to his father, "I want to see the women and very young women dance," and his father said, "Ho! My child wants the women and the very young women to dance. They shall do so." And an old man went to tell them.

He said, "Women, and the very young women, too, he wants to see you dance. He says, 'You shall dance,' " and they danced.

"But when the youth looked around, he did not find Snake Woman. Since he could not find her, he said, "Father, have the women stop dancing.

"Stop dancing!" said the crier, and they stopped.

He went back home to his lodge. "Father, have Mother cook. I am hungry," he said, and she cooked. "This way. Bring it here. Bring the food over here," he said. And when it had been cooked, they took it to him.

Then he took off his ring, and said, "Come, let us eat." And Snake Woman was sitting beside him; she ate with him. They played together again, but just as before she disappeared.

The man put on the ring again. He said, "Come, Father, have the women and grown maidens dance."

"Get up, Maidens. You are to dance. Chief's Son wants to see you dance," said the crier, and they danced. He looked around for the woman, but she was not to be found. He thought, "I have not found her." He had them stop and went home.

When he got there, he told them to cook. "Come, Father, have Mother cook. I am hungry," he said, and she cooked once more. "This way. Bring it here. Bring all the food here," he said, and when it had been cooked, they took it to him.

When they took it to him, he pulled off his ring and said, "Ho! We will eat for the last time in private," and Snake Woman suddenly appeared at his side and ate with him. They talked with each other for some time.

When the father heard it, he said, "Who is he talking with? Go see."

A girl went to look and she reported, "O Father, my elder brother is sitting there with a very beautiful woman." And it was clear that Snake Woman had married him. This time Snake Woman did not disappear.

At length the young man went off. He met a very beautiful woman, to whom he said, "I want to marry you. Tell your mother and father," and the woman went home to tell about this.

She said, "Father and Mother, Chief's Son has promised to marry me." Her father said, "He is making fun of you."

Since her husband wanted another woman, Snake Woman disappeared in a very bad mood. When she had gone, the man said, "I want to eat. Have my mother cook," and she did. "This way. Bring it here. Bring me the food that you have cooked," and when it was done they took it to him. When they had taken it to him, he pulled off his ring and said, "Come, let us eat." But nothing happened. Since she did not come, he did not eat. He was very unhappy because he could not find Snake Woman.

"Take away the food. I am sad. I do not want food," he said. "Father, I want to go hunting. Please saddle my horse for me."

He put on his good clothing and mounted a fine horse with a fine saddle. He rode off and as he moved along he found the path of Snake Woman. She had returned to her spring.

He followed his wife's trail and found that it went through and even beyond the spring. He followed his wife's trail, following, following, until finally he came upon a very unsightly lodge. He thought, "She might have come here." As he approached the place, he met someone, a very old man. His clothing was torn to shreds. The young man made the old man put on his own good clothing, for the old man was sacred.

"Ho! Grandchild, you think that you have been kind to me in giving me your clothing, but I am sorry for you. I want to tell you something. The woman you have been following went that way. She crossed the great water. Ho! Put on this bad clothing and go."

The old man gave him the torn clothing and a hat and a sword, too. He gave him a bad, lame horse. And he said, "Go. The woman has reached a village which is in that direction."

"Yes," said the young man.

"When you get across," said the old man, "speak with some people who are there."

"Yes," said the young man.

"If they do not obey your words, send them away," and the young man thanked him and moved on.

When he reached the big water, it was very wide. The old man had performed a sacred rite and as he sat with closed eyes he sent the young man across the water with a single stride. When he opened his eyes, the young man was on the other side of the water.

The lodge was there; smoke arose in a straight column. "This is the lodge my grandfather was telling me about. This is it," he said. When he got to it, he went in.

He could see two old men sitting there; they were aged Thundermen. The others had gone hunting. When he pushed down on his head the old hat that the old man had given him, the old men could not see him. And behold! The Thundermen who eat, just like us.

But as they sat without seeing him, the boy was thinking, "They are acting strangely. My grandfather said I should talk with them," and so, when they lit a pipe, he made himself visible by pulling off his hat. He snatched the pipe from them. When the pipe was hot, he held it against the other old Thunderman.

"I've been burned!" said the old man, and the young man pushed on his hat again and disappeared.

"Well, someone got in here easily. Why didn't we destroy him?" asked one.

Another answered, "He was not destroyed because I was leaving him for you. The others will blame us when they come home. They will scold us because he came in so easily and escaped again."

Eventually one of them came home carrying a man he had killed. "Take it," he ordered. They took the body and put it at the side of the lodge.

"Oh, you will surely blame us for the trouble. A man walked in here and then got away again," they said.

"Oh no! What were you doing that you let him get away and didn't kill him? We always have to go so far, and now, when he comes walking right into the lodge, you foolishly let him get away. I hate you. Come here and fill my pipe, you idiots!" he cried.

They filled the pipe and gave it to the man who had brought back the dead man. When the old man had taken a whiff from the pipe, the youth snatched it away from him and pressed it up against him. "I have been burned," he shouted.

"It wasn't me," said one.

And the other said, "Nor me."

The young man pulled off his hat. And suddenly there he was, sitting among them. "What did you say?" he asked.

"We didn't say anything," they said.

"Well, you were saying something," said the young man. "Come on. Do whatever it was you were going to do."

"No, friend. We weren't talking about anything," they insisted. And as they were looking at him, he pushed the hat on his head suddenly and disappeared.

"All right, Younger Brother, you were putting the blame on us before," they scolded. "Younger Brother, why did you let that man go instead of killing him? You were putting the blame on us before. Now the others who are coming home will blame all of us," said the first ones.

Then another one came home. He brought home a child on his back. "Take that," he said, and they put it by the wall. He said, "I went a long ways and I brought this home on my back."

Then they said, "Younger Brother, a man came in here a while ago. We did not kill him and he ran off. That one over there blamed us for this, but he was just as unsuccessful. We left it up to him to kill the man, and so we didn't get him."

Then he said, "What?! I went through all the trouble of going a long ways, and when someone comes walking right into the lodge, instead of killing him, you let him go again. You really handled it wrong. If *I* see him, *I* will kill him whatever else happens."

While they were scolding each other the youth pulled off his hat and was suddenly sitting there right in the midst of them. "What did you say?" he asked.

"We didn't say anything," they replied. "Friend, we didn't say anything. Oh no." They were afraid of the boy.

"You were saying something. Say whatever it was you were talking about."

"Friend, we weren't talking about anything special," they said.

When he put his hat back on, he had suddenly disappeared.

"Younger Brother, what were you doing when you let him get away instead of killing him? You were the one who was blaming us. He keeps coming in here, and we haven't been able to do what we want to do to him. We haven't been able to kill him. It is going to be hard for the ones who are coming home not to hate us. They will be furious," they moaned.

Another one came in. He was carrying a woman and a girl.

"Ho! Younger Brother, you will hate us. A man came in here, but instead of killing him we let him go," they said.

"Oh no!" he said. "Why didn't you kill him? We always have to go so far to go hunting. It is always such trouble to go so far. Why didn't you just kill him? I hate you."

"Yes, Younger Brother, it is true. Even though we could see him, we couldn't get him. He got away every time. You are right. Perhaps he will return," they said.

"If *I* see him, *I* will kill him. Fill the pipe," said the one who had just come home, and they filled the pipe and gave it to the one who had just brought in the slain woman and girl.

As he drew a whiff on the pipe, the youth snatched it away from him and pressed it up against him. "I have been burned! You burned me," he accused.

"It wasn't us," they said.

The boy pulled off his hat, and he was suddenly sitting in their midst. He was visible again. They kept looking around at each other. "I want to talk with you, and if you do not obey, you will surely vanish. You are hurting these people. Why do you kill them?"

"We want to eat them," they said.

"And who are these people you want to eat? This is wrong. You must stop killing these people," he said.

"Yes, Friend," they said.

"Have you ever seen those that have horns?" he asked, referring to the buffalo.

"Yes. There are a great many of them," they answered.

"Wakonda made these for food for all people. You are doing great wrong when you eat these human beings. You must stop," said the young man.

"Have you ever seen these?" he asked, meaning the elk.

"Yes," they answered.

"Eat them," said the youth. "And have you seen these?" he asked, meaning deer.

"Yes, we have seen a great many of them," they replied.

"You can eat such animals. But let these human beings alone. You have no reason to make them suffer so. If you will do as I have commanded, I will tell you things."

"Yes, Friend. We will do it."

"And you will promise to stop eating people?" he asked.

"Yes, Friend, we promise."

"And you will eat only these animals I have told you to eat?"

"Yes, that is what we will eat."

"Ho! I must go. And although I must go now, I will stop here again on my way home. Those of you who do not tell the truth will surely be destroyed. And those of you who eat the animals when I return, will endure. Anyone who is violating our promise when I come back will be destroyed," said the youth, and he left.

He once more followed Snake Woman's trail as it went along, and went and went, until finally it came to a large village. Snake Woman had gone there.

When the boy got near the lodges, he decorated himself, painting his face, sticking feathers in his hair, and so forth. He performed a sacred rite, making the clothing the old man had given him very good. He made his horse very black. He wore the sword in his belt. He rode into the village. The horse ran along, making great leaps. When the people saw the youth, they were bedazzled. They said, "A man has come along and his clothing is magnificent. He is also riding a fine horse."

Because he had come looking for his wife, Snake Woman, he rode about among the lodges. He rode looking for his wife. But when he found Snake Woman, he found also that she had taken a man for her husband. He had come looking for her, but now he hated her; he was jealous. Because of his jealousy, he took out the sword the old man had given him and waved it about. And on the fourth wave, he killed everyone in the village. He killed Snake Woman too.

The youth went back home and on his way he again came to those with whom he had talked before. He found that they had not told the truth when they promised to stop eating people.

"You have been disobedient! Even though I said that you were to stop, you did not obey me. You must go. If you were to remain here I am afraid that you would treat the human race very badly. So you will go up above. When you who kill men go up above, you will make men cool again whenever the day is very hot," he said, thinking of the rain. And then he said, "Go." And he sent them up above.

Then he went homeward. He reached the big water. "Ho! Old Man, I am coming back to you," he said. And when the old man sat with closed eyes, he sent the boy across the water in one step. He got across when the old man opened his eyes. He went up to the old man again.

"Ho! Grandfather, I have come back. I talked to the people to whom you said that I was to talk. But they did not obey my words and so I sent them up above," he said.

"Ho! That is good," said the old man. "It was right for you to send them away."

"And I didn't reach the one I was looking for until she had taken another husband, and so I killed everyone in the village. I did everything just as you commanded me to do."

"Yes, that is fine. I gave you this task because I wanted you to do it," said the old man, pointing to the sword.

"Come, Grandfather, I want to go home. I want to see my father," said the young man, and he did go home. His horse was very lame, his clothes were torn, his hat was badly worn; everything was worn out. His father thought that he had died.

"He has died," he thought. The boy came home, but when he entered the village, the people there did not recognize him. "A very poor person has come," they said.

He went to the lodge of the head chief and having approached his father's lodge, he went on in. His father did not recognize him either. "Father, it is me. I have come home," he said.

"Yes. It is good. You have come home. I have been sad, for I thought that you were dead. Now you have come home, and everything is good again. When I was young, My Child, I traveled widely all the time. I always came home poor, having given away everything I had. And so I became a great man. Ho! You shall take a wife. You shall have a woman," said his father.

The young man said, "Father, I love that woman over there. Is she married?"

"No," said the father. "She is still unmarried."

"Then, Father, send someone over there for her." And the father did send someone over for her.

When they arrived they said, "The chief's son wishes to marry your daughter."

The woman's father said, "I never thought that this would happen, for I am very poor. But if he feels sorry for her, that is good," and he gave the woman to the man.

The young man married her, and so he now had a wife. They had a lodge. But some other people ran in and attacked now and again, and the young man was killed. Though there is much more to this story, I do not remember it.

Chief's Son and the Thundermen
Told by Joseph La Flesche

There was a tribe, whose chief had a son, a young man, but the young man was very lazy. He did not want to do anything at all. He lay around all the time.

His father said, "My Child, when one becomes a man, he usually travels out into the world. Go, travel about. Go with the young men and travel. Give some attention to the women. At least take one for a wife."

But the son never said anything. He was always sad. Even though his father spoke to him about such things, he never answered. But this time he said, "Father, have Mother make a tent for me," and his mother did make a tent for him. "Mother," he said, "make a bed for me, too."

And the boy entered the tent and fasted. He fasted for four seasons. He did not eat any food and he did not drink any water. Only now and then did he take a little food and drink a little of the water brought in to him by his mother. As he fasted, he thought in his heart, "Let me see. I will wear a robe of scalps."

And a deity spoke to him, saying, "You will do whatever you want to. You shall surely wear your robe made of scalps," and he ended his fast.

Then he said, "Father, have my mother cook for me. Send some one after an old man for me. I want to go traveling."

"Yes, my Child," said the chief. "When one becomes a man, he should travel. So I have always wanted you to go traveling. I do not want you to die in our lodge. I want you to go to some place that is far from our home. I have always been sad because you would not travel."

The old man arrived and the young man told him, "Old Man, go after some of the young men for me," and the old man left. He went to each of the lodges and said to the young men, "The chief's son has called for you," and a great many young men went to the chief's son.

He said to them, "Ho! I have invited you that we might go traveling. Let us go on the warpath," and the young men were very glad. He said, "Have yourself moccasins made for the next four days," and in four days they departed on the warpath. They came to an old Thunderman who was very poor. None but the leader knew that he was a Thunderman. They felt sorry for him and said, "Let's give him some of our robes and other things," and they did so.

Then the old man said, "You think that you have been kind to me. I will really be good to you. I will tell you about something." As he said this, Coyote, who was the old man's servant, standing at the door, winked to the chief's son, who followed him outside.

Coyote said, "When he tells you to choose one of the four sacred bags, take the otter-skin one. All of them are good, but the rest are not as good as the otter-skin."

These bags were, first, a hawk-skin bag; second, a martin-skin bag; third, a bag made of the skin of a bird whose name is forgotten; and, fourth, the otter-skin bag. The chief's son and Coyote came back into the lodge, and the old man said again, "You have been kind to me, and I will be kind to you. Which of these four sacred bags will you take? If you wish to return with scalps and booty in half a day, take the martin-skin one. If you take the one made of hawk-skin, you would return in two days. If you want to be gone for several days, take the third. This otter-skin one is good, but it is old and worn."

Chief's Son took the otter-skin bag and said, "Grandfather, I want to take this one even though it is old."

The old man got mad and scolded his servant. "Ha. It was probably you who told about it."

"No, Grandfather, he didn't tell me anything. I just decided that I wanted that bag."

Along with the otter-skin bag the old man gave him a wooden club. "The owner of the otter-skin bag can do whatever he wants, no matter how difficult it is. It can kill a great many people. If you want to kill everyone in a village or some other place, just wave this club around your head four times and on the last wave say, 'Kau!' There will be thunder."

The old man knew what the chief's son was thinking in his heart, and he said, "After a while say, 'I want to wear a robe made of scalps, I say.'" And in about four days four men went scouting. They arrived at a large village. When they returned to camp, they said, "Leader, we have seen a great many lodges."

"Warriors, this is it," he said, and they approached very close to the village.

When they were close to it, his followers said, "Ho! Leader, we have come to the village."

But he said, "Ho! Warriors, I am looking for something else," and they passed by three other villages in exactly the same way.

Again they went scouting. And their leader said, "Warriors, if you encounter one of your grandfathers, be careful not to kill him."

And it so happened that the scouts found a buffalo bull. They talked about killing him there.

One said, "Friends, let's kill the buffalo bull over there." But another said, "Why, Friend, the leader said that we were not to kill it."

"No, I don't think that is what the leader meant," said the first, and so they tried to kill it. But the buffalo killed one of the men.

The three returned to camp, and when they got there they said, "Leader, a buffalo bull was there, and he killed one of us."

"Warriors, I said, 'Don't kill your grandfather,'" he said.

When they reached the place where the scout lay dead, the leader said, "Just keep right on going. He apparently wanted to fall here, and we will let him lie," and so they passed on by.

At another time, four went scouting. But before they left, the chief's son said, "Ho! Warriors, if you encounter one of your grandfathers, be careful not to kill him."

And it so happened that they spied a big wolf. They talked about killing the wolf.

One said, "Friends, let's kill him."

But a second said, "Hey, my Friend! The leader said we were not to kill him."

The first said, "No, the leader didn't mean that, I think. How could he have meant a wolf?"

So they shot at the wolf, but he attacked them and killed one of the four. When they returned to camp, they said, "Leader, there was a big wolf there, and he killed one of us."

"Ho! Warriors, I said that you must not kill your grandfather," he said. And when they passed by the place where the scout lay dead, the leader said, "Ho! Warriors, pass right on by. Since he apparently wanted to lie here, we will just let him lie. Let's move on."

They did go on, and again four went scouting. As they were about to go, the leader said, "Warriors, if you should encounter one of your grandfathers, be careful not to kill him."

And it so happened that the scouts found a grizzly bear. They talked about killing him.

One said, "Friends, let's kill the grizzly bear."

But another said, "Hey! My Friend, the leader said we shouldn't kill him."

The first replied, "No, the leader didn't mean that, I think."

"No, how could he possibly mean a grizzly bear?" agreed the first.

They tried to kill the bear but he killed one of the men. And the three returned again to camp. When they got there, they said, "Leader, a grizzly bear was there, and he killed one of us."

"Ho! Warriors, I said, 'Do not kill your grandfather,'" he said, and when they arrived at the place where the scout lay dead he said, "Ho! Warriors, go right on straight ahead. Since this warrior apparently wanted to lie here, we will just let him lie."

Eventually they came to the end of the earth, where the sky went down into the ground. The leader said, "Don't be afraid of it, Warriors. Let's go across to the other side. Let's jump on over. Be careful not to be afraid of it."

The leader jumped over to the other side and the rest jumped then, too, but one failed to make it. When the youngest of them tried to jump, he failed. He fell deep down into the ground.

"Come on, Warriors. If we want to be warriors, we must expect such things. Let him lie here," said Chief's Son, referring to the one who had fallen.

They left and traveled on for some time. They reached a very high hill and a dense forest, a very dense forest of cedars. "Ho! Warriors, that is where we are going and from where we shall return. Warriors, scout around," said Chief's Son, and four went out.

They arrived at a place where they saw smoke but no lodge. They went back and said, "Leader, we reached a place where there was smoke, but we could not find a lodge."

"Ho! Warriors, that is what I am looking for," he said.

Again, four scouts went out, and they too reached the place where there was smoke but no lodge. When they returned, they said, "Leader, although there was smoke, we didn't see a lodge."

So it happened four times. The fourth time they arrived at the lodge itself. And the leader said, "Come, Warriors, let's go into the lodge," and they did so.

A very old man was living in the lodge. His head was very large, and his hair was very white. When the leader entered the lodge, he did not recognize the old man, but after sitting for a while he recognized the old man.

The old man thought, "My relatives work hard and go great distances in search of game, but here some human beings have brought themselves right into my very lodge. Right here at home I shall kill myself some men."

But the leader was thinking, "Good! I have said, 'I want to wear a robe of scalps,' and this will be a fine robe. I want it."

Then one of the old man's younger brothers came home with a black bear he had killed. The brother's head was enormous and his hair was very red.

The old man told the news to his brother who had just returned home. "You had a hard trip, but some game has brought itself right into our lodge. I shall kill them."

Another brother came home carrying a buffalo. His hair was very yellow. Eventually, all of the brothers came home. And one had very green hair and came home carrying a dead man.

The first one who had come home said, "Old Man, have these men eaten?"

"No, they have not. Cook for them," he said. "Cook slices of squash for them," but they really cooked the ears of the dead man for them.

"We don't eat such things," they said.

"If you don't eat such things, what do you eat?" asked the old man, acting as if he did not understand them. "Cook them some fine sweet corn," but he meant lice.

And again they said, "We don't eat such things."

So one of the old men said, "Let them cook the black bear and the buffalo for themselves." The men were happy about that and cooked for themselves, eating well when they were through.

Well, finally night came, and the old man said, "Grandchild, when a man travels about, he usually has many things to talk about. Tell us about yourselves."

"Yes, Grandfather. Since you are grown and an old man, you, for your part, must know a great many things. Please tell us about you first."

"Well, Grandchild, even though I am an old man, I have nothing to tell about myself. I will tell you a myth," and the old man did tell a myth.

"Once upon a time, Grandchild, there was an old man. And he dwelt in a lodge with his three younger brothers. And when his younger brothers went a very great distance hunting, they didn't come home until late at night. But once when the old man was alone watching the lodge, some people came into the lodge. And the old man sat there thinking, 'My poor brothers suffer a good deal, traveling long distances for game, but I shall kill a great many men right here in our lodge.' "

Then the old man said, "Now, Grandchild, you tell a story."

"Yes, Grandfather, let me tell a story. Once a chief had some villages. And he had a child. The boy was very lazy; even though his father ordered him to travel about, he would not travel. He didn't want to do anything at all. Finally the boy spoke of fasting and had his mother make a separate lodge for him. And the boy thought as he fasted, 'Let me see. I want to wear a robe of scalps!' And the boy went on the warpath with a great number of warriors. And there were also four men who lived together, and the war party arrived at their lodge. When they were there, the boy sat thinking, 'I said, "I want to wear a robe of scalps!" and this will be a fine robe. I want it.' One of the brothers had very white hair and one had very red hair and one had very yellow hair and one had very green hair."

The old man laughed with him, "Ha! ha! ha! My grandchild, it seems, guessed exactly what is going on."

And when night came, the leader lay with his eye fixed at a hole in his robe, for he wanted to watch the old men. He said to his followers, "Followers, be careful not to fall asleep. Just lie and rest without sleeping."

As he lay there during the night, the old man lifted his head very gently and looked now and then at the pretend-sleepers. Then the old man took his stone hammer. Just as he grabbed it, the leader jumped up and flourished his club with a terrible roar, saying "Kau!" and he killed all four Thunders.

"Ho! Warriors, stand up and take off their hair. Be careful to cut it off them in one piece. Take the whole scalp," he said.

When they had finished, they started home. On the way they again came to the end of the sky. "Ho! Warriors, let's jump to the other side. Go over and stand in a row," he said, and they did so. He sent them all home ahead of him, and he followed. He ran along very fast and made great jumps. And the boy who had fallen into the ground went homeward with him, having come alive again, as alive as the leader.

They continued on their path, coming to the place of the grizzly bear. And the same thing happened. He sent them all on ahead of him. He followed them, running and leaping great jumps. And he took homeward with him the boy who had been dead, now alive. The same thing happened at the place of the wolf and again at the place of the buffalo. He reached home with every man alive; he had not lost one.

On the way home they passed by a great many villages. As they passed them, he said, "Ho! Warriors, that will do. You too shall surely wear robes made of scalps."

And they arrived home, having killed everyone in the villages and having taken their scalps. They had killed all the people in four villages.

When they came home to their own tribe, all the villages made Chief's Son their head chief, and he governed them.

The Boy Called Badger
Told by Francis La Flesche to Franz Boaz

One summer we went on the usual buffalo hunt, following a river called *Wate*, now known as the Elkhorn. We knew nothing about white man's bridges, so we crossed the river on horseback or on foot. The women rode their horses and made an attractive display, all dressed in their gay costumes. The young men walked together, stopping now and then to gamble.

In this tribal hunt there was a man and his wife who had one son who was very troublesome to them as well as being selfish, but they never scolded or punished him. This son was always satisfied to sit around his home and eat.

When he was not at home he followed the young men and gambled away his own belongings and those of this father and mother.

The father was a medicine man and made most of his earnings at that service. It grieved the parents very much that their son should gamble when they had so little, but they said nothing of this to either the boy or to the neighbors who camped close to them.

There came a time, however, when the father grew tired and out of patience with the son's actions, and he said to him, "Listen to me, Son. You have never done one useful thing. People live around us who are busy making many useful things. But when you are at home you do nothing but eat."

Then the father began to work on a shield. The son wanted to know for whom the shield was being made, but the father worked on in silence. The mother, as usual, prepared food for the boy. But he only pretended to eat, thinking about what his father had said to him.

One day, very early in the morning, there was an excited stir in the village. The people brought up their horses and saddled them; some were carrying spears and bows and arrows. The father brought home the son's horse and put a saddle on it, and the mother stood holding the boy's spear in her hand. Soon the boy came running home.

Before he could speak, the father said, "Son, from your earliest childhood you have never done anything for your mother or me, but have always done only what pleased yourself. I am now asking you to go to battle as the other young men are doing. We are being attacked. I want your horse to be among the first to meet the enemy."

The boy's horse was anxious to go. He pawed the ground with impatience. The boy mounted him, and his mother placed the spear in his hands. He took it and quickly followed the other warriors who were just now dashing to the battlefield. He overtook them and arrived just in time to hear the battle cry. Then the battle began.

Neither side gave way as they knocked each other off their horses. The boy was the first to be struck by the enemy. A spear was thrust into his body. But he pushed his own spear into the body of his attacker and threw him from his horse.

When the battle was over, the men gathered the wounded from the ground and found the bodies of these two speared warriors. The enemy was dead, but the boy was still breathing. The boy was carried to his father's tent.

The father sent messengers for doctors, who worked over him until the fever was broken. Then, early one morning, the boy slowly opened his eyes. Looking around, he saw a shield hanging up.

The father saw his glance and said, "Yes, my son, it is your shield. We know now that you need it. You have earned it with your strong arm of valor."

COMMENTARY

Courage, eloquence, and generosity were the primary virtues of Omaha culture, and in large part still are. Omaha mothers and fathers regretted seeing their sons going into battle during the Vietnam War, for example, but far more than any other element of American society they prayed that their sons would distinguish themselves in battle, and those young Omaha who came home with decorations or with the clear evidence of courage— war wounds—enjoy even today special respect and regard in social and political activities within the tribe. The old concept of the Plains Indian warrior and of taking *coup* may have faded away well before the turn of the century, but the basic idea of a warrior class is very much alive today in Indian warrior societies like the Tiapiah Gourd Dance Society, recently transmitted to the Omaha from the Kiowa, or in equivalent white men's societies like the American Legion.

The Brothers, the Sister, and the Red Bird
Told by Joseph La Flesche

There were four brothers who lived alone. They had neither mother nor sister. One day three of them went hunting, and the youngest stayed at the lodge. He happened to hurt his foot with a splinter. He pulled the splinter out, wrapped it up in some fine buffalo hair, and put it at the side of the lodge. He wanted to show his brothers the splinter that had caused him such pain.

By and by the boy went for some water, for he was thirsty. When he came back to the lodge, he heard a child crying inside. While he was gone, the splinter which had hurt him had become a child. He wrapped it up and put it at the side of the lodge.

When his elder brothers reached home, he told them, "Elder Brothers, my foot was hurt. I took out the splinter that was hurting me, and it became a child."

They said, "Stop! Younger Brother, get it and show it to us. We must see it." When he got it, they saw that it was a girl. "Younger Brother, up to now we have had no children. Let's bring her up well," they said.

The younger brother said, "Elder Brothers, what relation should we consider her?" and one said, "Let her be our child," but they said no. "We have no sister. Let's have her for a sister." They all agreed and took her for their sister. Since she was a child and they wished to bring her up, they took very good care of her. And she became a grown woman.

Once all four went hunting. Only the woman did not go. The four men were always very kind to the woman. While they were gone a man arrived at the lodge and took the woman home. The brothers came home and, finding their sister gone, sent the youngest to search for her. He could not find her. Then the rest went to look for her, leaving the youngest brother by the lodge.

He noticed something very red shining through the lodge from the inside. When he peeped in, having wondered what it could be, he found that it was a bird. He seized his bow and shot at him, but he missed him everytime. Even though he had a great many of them, he shot all but one, which he then made sacred. He wounded the shining red bird with that sacred arrow but the bird flew off home with the arrow sticking in him.

The boy followed him, having thought, "My brothers prize the arrow very much, and I had better not lose it."

The boy came to a very populous village. When he got there, the people recognized him. "The youngest of the four men who are called brothers is here! One of those famous marksmen has come," they said, and they went to tell the chief. "The youngest of the four men who are called brothers is here! One of those famous marksmen has come," they said.

And the head-chief said, "Bring my daughter's husband to me," and they went to get him and brought him to the chief. The chief said, "My Daughter's Husband, you will marry this girl. And I will give you a lodge."

After a while they laid down. The young man lay with the girl. He questioned her, "Did you see some kind of bird passing by here on its way home?"

"Yes," she said. "Very early yesterday morning a red bird passed by with an arrow sticking in it."

And he said, "You can tell your father that though I have taken you as a wife, I must go traveling. I will come back." And the young man left.

She told her father. "Father, he has gone traveling, but has promised to return."

The youth traveled some distance until he arrived at a very large village. "One of the four men who are famous is here," they said, and the chief heard it. This chief, too, gave him a daughter for a wife, and so did the chiefs of two other villages. But he left his wives behind and continued to search for his sister and the red bird.

After leaving the fourth village, he came to a great lake. The red bird had gone into the water of a very large lake. So the boy went there, and his sister came up out of the water.

"O Elder Brother, come this way," she said, but the boy was afraid of the water. As he went closer, the water separated, leaving a passage, and that served as an entrance.

When they arrived inside, he saw that the woman and her husband were far from being poor. They had a great abundance of possessions, and the young man was very glad to see his sister. And she was very glad, too. And the sister's husband was also glad to see him.

His sister had hung up the arrow with which he had wounded the red bird which was her husband. It had been placed nicely in a horizontal position, and it was still lying in that position.

After he had been there a little while, he remembered his elder brothers. He said, "Well, my little sister, I want to go home. I am thinking of your elder brothers." And the woman told her husband, "Your wife's brother is thinking about going home." And his sister's husband made him four small boats, each one very small (about six inches in length).

"Wife's Brother, take these things home with you. Wife's Brother, whenever you want anything, say 'Such and such things I wish!' and put a boat into the water," he said, and the young man went home.

In addition to the small boats he also took home his arrow with which he had wounded the red bird. On his way home, he approached his lodge in the last village.

He put one boat in the water of a creek that was there. When he put the boat in the water, the boat became very full of different kinds of goods; the boat and goods grew very large. And when he had finished he went back to his lodge and to the woman.

And he said, "I have brought back from my sister's husband a boat which is over there. Let someone go after it for the honorable man, your father." They went after it and brought it back. And it was very full of goods.

And when it was night, they lay down. When they lay down, the man said, "I will go home tomorrow, for I want to see your husband's brothers."

And the woman said, "O Father, he says he is going home."

The chief said, "They who take men for husbands always follow them. Follow him." And the woman went home with the man.

And when they lay down for the night on the homeward way, the man lay alone; he never lay with the woman.

The woman wondered why he did this, but he was saving her for one of his brothers. He did this same thing with the daughters of the chiefs of the third and second villages. But when he reached the first village, he kept the daughter of the chief as his wife, for she was not jealous and, besides, he loved her. The other women were jealous.

When he arrived home, he gave the other women to his brothers, and so all found wives.

So it was.

COMMENTARY

The conclusion of the myth was provided by Frank La Flesche, who also offered the following variation of the first section of the tale:

When his brothers reached home, he told them what had happened. But they ridiculed his story as an impossibility. When he unwrapped the bundle, they exclaimed, "Brother, you spoke the truth. It is indeed an infant. She will grow up and be our sister. She can keep the lodge for us." She was not long in reaching womanhood, although when found, she was tiny, just the size of the splinter. When she was grown, a red bird came to see her. It was not a real bird, but a man who took the form of a bird. One day, when the brothers were absent, the red bird carried her away. When the brothers returned, they found their sister was missing. So they started in search for her. In the meantime, the red bird flew back to the lodge, his intentions being to lead them to the place where he had taken the girl. When he reached the lodge, the younger brother was there. As soon as he spied the bird, he tried to shoot him. But though he emptied his quiver, he could not hit the bird. At last he made a sacred arrow, which he shot at the bird, wounding him. But the bird flew off with the arrow sticking in him. The young man followed the bird.

All of the people heard reports about the four young men. And when the boy reached their village, they knew all about him. They said, "One of the four famous men is here, they say."

The Adventures of the Badger's Son
Told by Cangeska

Badger's Son went to visit a very populous village. "Badger has come to visit. Take him to the chief's lodge," everyone said. "Badger has come to visit," they told the chief.

The chief said, "Oho! Bring him here, first-born Sons." They brought him there and invited him to feasts.

"I have come to invite Badger's son to a feast," said one. And they kept inviting him to feast with them.

The principal war chief had a beautiful woman as his daughter. When they invited Badger's Son, the woman said, "Please bring me back a piece of the meat which is offered to you." "Yes, I will," he said, and went to the feast. The woman sat outside the door.

Badger's Son said, "I have brought you this fresh meat you asked for," and the woman said, "Bring it to me." He took it to her and gave it to her and she said, "How long will it be before you go home?"

"I will leave in about three days," said Badger's Son.

"And when the time comes for you to go home, we shall go together," the woman said, but they kept inviting him to feasts.

He said, "I am going home tomorrow. You said earlier that when I went home, *we* would go home."

"Yes, I said that. We will go home together. Wake me tonight," the woman said.

When everyone was asleep, Badger's Son awoke. He woke the woman. "Get up. You said, '*We* will go home.' I am going home," he said, and he took her home with him.

Soon her father knew that his daughter was missing. Her father said, "Badger's Son has taken my child away. Chase them for me. If you overtake them, kill Badger's Son. Bring my child back to me."

The old man said, "It is reported that Badger's Son has run off with the chief's daughter. You are to pursue them for her father. When you overtake them, kill Badger's Son. Bring the woman back to him."

"Oho! Badger's Son has run off with the chief's daughter, so he has asked us to chase them," they said, and they did pursue the two.

The woman commanded Badger's Son to go faster. "Go faster. If they overtake us, they will surely kill you. But why should they kill me after all?"

Soon the pursuers came into sight. The woman said, "Here they come. We have been caught. They will kill you. Go faster!"

But the pursuers caught them and took hold of the woman. Then they chased Badger's Son. One ran on until he overtook Badger's Son. When he finally caught him, he said, "My Friend, even though the chief said that we should kill you, I will not kill you. Run faster. I will say that I broke my bow. Run with all your might through that dense woods by those trees."

And when another arrived where the first was, he said, "You caught him. Why didn't you kill him?"

"I broke my bow so I couldn't kill him. There he runs. Hurry and catch him."

And when the second pursuer caught Badger's Son, he said, "Ho! Friend, even though the chief said that we should kill you, I will not kill you. Run faster. Run with all your might to those trees. You are nearly home. I will say that I broke my bowstring."

Another one came along. "You caught him. Why didn't you kill him? How did you let this happen?"

"He got away because I broke a bowstring. There he goes. Hurry after him."

And so the third pursuer also caught up with Badger's Son and said, "Ho! My friend, even though the head chief said that we should kill you, we aren't the ones to do that. You will live. I will say that my foot hurt me. Run faster. Run with all your might toward those trees."

And when another pursuer came up to where the third one was, he said, "Ho! You did catch him. Why didn't you kill him?"

"My foot hurt me, so I didn't kill him. There he goes now. Hurry and chase him," he said.

Again the pursuer caught Badger's Son. "Ho! My Friend, over there is a lodge. Run into it. You will stay alive. I will say that I sprained my ankle while I was running," he said.

Another chaser came along. He stopped running. "Why, you caught up with him. Why did you let him go?"

"That is true. I sprained my ankle while I was running, so I had to stop. There he goes. Hurry and catch him."

Badger's Son had run headlong into an earth lodge. He had escaped. The pursuers made a great uproar. A woman was sitting inside the lodge, and she was very cross. She was carrying her own shield. She took her spear and brandished it toward Badger's Son. "Speak. Why are you here? If you do not speak, I will kill you," she said.

Badger's Son did not look at her. Even though she was brandishing her spear at him, he didn't move. He didn't run from her.

A man was lying by the wall. And he spoke to her from there, "O Sister, let my Sister's Husband alone."

"I will let him alone," said the woman.

The woman married Badger's Son. When he married her, the boy, her brother, kept his head always covered. And so Badger's Son said, "Why does my wife's brother always do this?"

"Oh, even if I tell you, how could you do what he wants?" said the woman.

And the boy said, "O Sister, tell my sister's husband."

But the woman said, "My dear Younger Brother, if I tell your sister's husband, how could he ever do it? Even I have not been able to harm them."

Again, after sitting there a while, he questioned her again. "Tell me what it is," Badger's Son said.

"O Sister, tell it to my sister's husband, I beg," the boy said.

"O my dear Younger Brother, if I tell it to your sister's husband, how could he ever get it? Even I have not been able to hurt them," she said.

He asked her again. And the boy said, "O Sister, tell it to my sister's husband."

And she said, "I will tell it to your sister's husband. A woman who resembles me has made your wife's brother suffer. She cut off his hair and took it with her."

Badger's Son said, "How many of them are there?"

And the woman answered, "There are four women. I have gone there again and again, but I have had to come home unsuccessful."

"Well, I will still go there, even if I come home unsuccessful. Prepare some food for me."

So he left. He walked and walked and walked and walked. He slept on the way. The next day, when the sun was still low, he got there. He saw the women dancing. They were beating the drum. Since they had taken the hair of his brother-in-law, they were dancing over it. He crept up on them and watched them. He was scouting.

Then the women stopped beating the drum. They went back to their lodge. Soon they came back out. They had packstraps and axes. They were going for wood.

One woman had very white hair; one had very red; one very green; and one very yellow. As they approached, they kept scaring each other, frightening each other off.

Badger's Son had painted himself very well. He had made himself very good looking. He had also made his clothing look nice. He stood leaning against a tree.

The youngest sister among the women, a girl, came first. She found Badger's Son. "O Elder Sisters, I have found myself a husband," she said.

"O Little Sister, we will break wood and my sister's husband will stand guard," said another.

They broke wood. When they had finished tying up the wood in bundles, they said, "Help us get the wood on our backs."

"Oho! Put the straps on the bundles. I will help you carry them on your backs," he said.

When they had put on the straps, he pulled out his bow and killed all of the four women. He cut off all their hair. He went to the lodge and seized the hair of his brother-in-law, and he put it in his robe above the belt. He set the grass on fire. The smoke was black.

And the brother-in-law said, "O Sister, I think that my sister's husband is coming back. He has fired the grass."

"But even I have always failed. How could it be that your sister's husband would be coming home with them?" asked the woman.

Again he set fire to the grass. When he had fired it, the smoke was red.

"There is your sister's husband, coming home with them," said Badger's Wife.

Again when he had come very near, he set the grass on fire. The smoke was very white.

"There is your sister's husband coming with three of them," she said.

Again he fired the grass and the smoke was very green.

"There is your sister's husband, coming home with all of them," she said.

Soon he came into sight. "There is your sister's husband," she said and went out to meet him.

"I have killed them all. I have also brought back my wife's brother's hair to him," he said.

"That is good. It is good for you to bring home everything," she said. And at night Badger's Wife sang the dancing songs for the three. They had a scalp dance.

The next day her husband said, "Put stones in the fire." The two men entered a sweat lodge. Then Badger's Son took the hair of his wife's brother and scraped the scarred place on the top of his head. When it was bloody, he put the hair back in place, and the hair was as it had been before. He did a very good thing for his relation. The three danced for a long time, for Badger's Son had brought home the hair of the four women.

COMMENTARY

The form of the Plains Indian tipi is familiar to everyone, but less is known about the earth lodge, mentioned in this tale. These huge mound houses had a framework of heavy timbers, which was then covered with lighter wands and bundles of long, tough prairie grass. Sod and dirt were piled on this. The result was a very secure, permanent home.

Plains Indians frequently did fire the prairie grass to announce their approach; with dry grass and a favorable wind, the fire could race across the grass tops faster than a man could ride on horseback, and so the system was effective, yet dangerous.

"On the way home the booty is divided. . . . If they have brought back scalps or horses, they set the grass afire. On seeing this the villagers say, . . . 'I think that the warriors are coming back. They have set the grass afire.' . . . [I]f they have brought scalps, they put some of the hair in the fire, and the smoke is black. But if they put a horse's tail in the fire, the smoke is very yellow."[9]

It may seem extravagant, burning off the whole prairie simply to announce one's approach, but it was in part this very burning that maintained the integrity of the Plains. The annual burning eradicated any saplings that might have sprung up, while at the same time cutting down the dead growth so that the new grass in the spring could receive full sun.

The Youth and the Underground People
Told by Big Elk, an Omaha

There were once some very large villages. The chief's sons were unmarried and his daughter was a virgin. His two sons made a surround on some buffalo. They often killed buffalo. One of this chief's sons attacked a buffalo, quite a ways away from the others. He shot at it, and the buffalo seemed to disappear into the ground. Suddenly the man and his horse fell headlong, right after the buffalo. The father sent out criers. "He says that his child attacked the buffalo but has not come back home. He says that any of you who have seen him should tell him at once, please."

One man said that he had seen him. "I saw him very clearly. He was chasing the buffalo. Perhaps he fell into some great pit, for when he was on a very level piece of ground he suddenly disappeared completely."

The father had him help them in the search for his son. When the man who had seen him said, "It was right here," the people spread way out, looking all around for him. Everyone was looking for him. They could see that he had fallen into a pit. The buffalo had fallen in, kicking loose a piece of sod. The horse, too, had fallen in, also kicking loose a piece of sod. There was no trail beyond the pit. The people walked right up to the pit. It was very large and extended a long ways into the ground.

The father decided to move the camp there right away. They moved and camped all around the pit.

The father talked with all the young men, especially those who had been his son's friends. If there was anyone brave and stronghearted enough to go down into the pit after the young man, the father begged them to do it. Finally one young man rode around and around the village. He said that he would enter the pit and go after the missing youth. "Tell his father. He must gather the ropes," he said.

He cut buffalo hides into strips and collected the cords. "Please make a round piece of skin for me and tie the long line of cord to it," he said, and they finished it. "It doesn't matter how far I must go, I will put the body in this skin-bucket. I am now going to go after him. When I reach the bottom, I will pull suddenly on the cord. When I pull on it several times, draw it up again," he ordered.

After a while he reached the bottom of the pit. It was very dark. As he felt around in the dark, he found the buffalo, killed by the fall, but nothing else. Then he found the horse that had been killed by the fall, but it too was lying alone. Then, finally, he found the man, also killed by the fall.

He took the body of the man and put it in the skin-basket. Before he had gone down, the man had not asked any favors for himself, so when they drew up the dead man and rejoiced to have recovered him, they could think only of the dead; they forgot the living. So he sat waiting for the skin-bucket to come back, but he was not pulled up. He just sat there crying.

Now the chief had gotten him to do this deed by promising him his virgin daughter. "If you bring him back, you shall marry her," he had promised.

The young man wandered about in the darkness. Finally, while traveling along a path, he suddenly came upon an old woman. He begged the old woman, "Old Woman, though it was hard to get to this land, I have come here. I came to the hole in the ground up above. Someone had fallen through the hole down to this place. I came down to get him back. But they didn't pull me up again. And I have no way of getting back. Old Woman, please help me."

"There is nothing I can do to help you. Someone is way over there, out of sight. Go there. He is the one who can help you," she said.

They went there and, when they arrived, he knocked on the door again and again. As they stood there they could hear someone speaking, but he would not open the door. The old woman said, "Hey, someone is here. Open the door for him."

But they found that the man's child had died, and so he sat without speaking at all. He just sat there mourning. The young man went on into the lodge, the man's wife having opened the door for him. Still the husband sat without speaking.

The young man was very, very hungry. The husband asked him, "Where did you come from?"

So the young man told his story. "I come down from up above. A man headed off the herd and fell down here from a great height. I came here to take him back. But they didn't pull me up, and I have no way of getting back. Help me."

The old man told him about the death of his son. "We had a child but he died. We will treat you just like our child that has died," he said, intending to adopt this young man as his son. "Everything we have is yours."

The young man did not speak, but he wanted very much to go home. "Whatever you say, I will do it for you. Even if you want to go home, it shall be so," said the old man. So the young man spoke of going home. "If you want to go home, just say, 'I want to go home riding a horse of such-and-such color hair, O Father!' and it will happen," said the father.

"Oh no! We have just lost our son and this young man who has come along is just like him," said the wife. "Give him something of yours," she said to her husband.

"I make you my child. I want to give you something. Whenever I want something, I make it with this," said the father. That is, whenever he wanted something, he would point at it with his iron, and it would be his.

"O Father, I want to go home riding a horse with very white hair. I also want a mule with very white hair and a good saddle," said the young man.

"Go. Over there. Open the door to the stable. When you want to see us again, you will see us. When you want to go home, say 'Come, O Father, I want to go home,' " said the father.

So the young man started homeward. He made the rocks open suddenly by pointing directly at them with his iron. He went up the steps, making the ground resound under the horse's feet. And when he pushed aside a very large rock that lay as a cover over the entrance, he found himself once more on the surface of the earth.

The horse and mule were very quick in their movements. They shied at every step, as they snuffed the odor of what was, in their estimation, a very bad place.

When the young man reached the surface, he began at once to look for the land that he had left. He found that his people had only recently broken camp and moved. They had waited for some time for him to reappear, but then had broken camp and moved on. The horse and mule moved quickly, fearing the sight of the old camping ground.

The young man went along the trail left by the migrating party. Finally he found at some distance two people on a very large hill, walking in the path of the moving party. They were the head chief and his wife, who were walking along, mourning the dead. When they looked back, they said, "Here comes someone on horseback, following the trail of our move."

He rode up to them. They sat waiting for him to come up. The horse and mule were afraid of them, smelling the unfamiliar odor. "Why, where are you from?" called out the head chief.

"It is me," said the youth.

"But who is that?" asked the chief.

"Your child fell into the pit when we were surrounding the herd, and I was the one who went down to get him. You didn't pull me back up. It is me!" called the young man.

Because he had changed so much, the old man doubted his word. "Oh, tell us about yourself," said the head chief.

"When they surrounded the herd, your son went headlong into the pit, along with the buffalo, and he was killed. And when you commanded the people to get him, no one wanted to. I am the one who went to get him when you offered your daughter as a reward. I had a very hard time getting back to the surface of the earth," said the young man.

Then they recognized him. The two men stood talking on the high hill. The chief's son looked back from the camp. "Why, the old man and mother have come as far as that large hill, and a man on horseback is coming too. He is standing there talking with them. I want to go there. Let me see! I want to go see them," he said, so he mounted up and rode out to his father.

"Who are you talking with?" he asked.

"Why, this is the one who went to get your elder brother, and he has returned," said the head chief. They shook hands, and the chief gave his daughter to the young man. "Go tell everyone about this," the father told his son. "Have all the men and chiefs assemble. They can look at my daughter's husband."

They assembled, coming together to see the young man, and they brought things they intended to give to him.

The crier called, "He says that he who went to get the man killed by falling has come back. The chief says that since he has made this young man his daughter's husband, you should come to meet him. He says that you should bring whatever things you want to give him. The chief says that he will give thanks for them."

All the young men who were brave and generous went there. And they all gave him clothing and good horses. His wife's father gave him the head chieftainship.

"Make a tent for him in the center of the camp," said the old chief. They set up the tent for him in the center of camp. And when they had finished, the old chief said, "The nation did not eat. While they were waiting for you to return, they did not eat. You have returned just as they were breaking camp."

"Ho!" said the one who had just come home. "Have two men go out as criers."

"The chief's daughter's husband says that you will rest tomorrow. He says that you will not go in any direction at all," said the criers.

And the next day he commanded those who had come back on horseback to go out scouting. And the scouts returned very quickly. With the iron that he had gotten from his adopted father he had caused a great many buffalo to appear. He spoke of surrounding them.

His wife said, "I want to go watch them surround the herd. I must go see the buffalo. When they are killed, I will probably come right back." While they killed the buffalo, the man's wife stood on a nearby hill.

Her husband came up to her and said, "I killed some buffalo and they are going to cut them up."

They returned home. Again he spoke of making a surround.

"The chief's daughter's husband is talking about sending out scouts," called the criers.

The buffalo were again coming into this same place. They surrounded them. Again they shot down a great many.

But the son of the head chief was in a very bad mood. He was mad because he did not receive the chieftainship, which his father had instead given to his sister's husband, whom he envied. So when it was night, the horse told the young man about the son's actions.

"O Father, there is a man who wants very much to kill us. We are in danger every night." At night, you see, the young man used to take care of his horse and mule.

The next day they surrounded the herd on the land where they did such things. The same thing happened. A great many buffalo came and the wife's brother wanted the buffalo to trample her husband to death, so while they attacked the buffalo, the wife's brother waved his robe. He turned in his course and continued waving his robe, and when the sister's husband had gone right in among the buffalo, they closed in on him and he disappeared.

The people said, "The buffalo have trampled to death the chief's daughter's husband." And when the buffalo trampled him to death, they scattered and went away in every direction, moving in long lines. And the people could not find any trace of what had happened. They couldn't find the horse. They couldn't even find the man. When the buffalo had trampled him into the ground, the horses had gone back to the person who made such things.

COMMENTARY

Frank La Flesche told Dorsey that this tale had been borrowed from the Dakota Sioux.

From this text one might believe that going out on a buffalo surround was a fairly simple undertaking, but Dorsey and Fletcher indicate otherwise.

"Whenever scouts were sent out to survey the surrounding land, usually in a very broad circle, they would shoot all sorts of game except buffalo, which they were honorbound to report in precise numbers to the tribe. The crier would then go out in the camp and report the find and organize for a surround.

"The chiefs said to the directors [of the hunt], 'It is good to do such and such things.' The directors considered whether it would be right or not, and finally decided what course should be pursued. Then, if any accident occurred, or quarrels between men or women, dog fights, high winds, rain, etc., ensued, the director who had advised going in that direction was blamed, and his advice was disregarded from that time, so he had to resign, and let some one else take his place."[10]

"The offense of *wathihi*, that of scaring off game while the tribe was on the buffalo hunt, could take place only by a man slipping away and hunting for himself. By this act, while he might secure food for his own use, he imperiled the food supply of the entire tribe by frightening away the herd. Such a deed was punished by flogging. Soldiers were appointed by the chiefs to go to the offender's tent and administer this punishment. Should the man dare to resist their authority, he was doubly flogged because of his second offense. Such a flogging sometimes caused death. Besides this flogging, the man's tent was destroyed, his horses and other property were confiscated, and his tent poles burned; in short, he was reduced to beggary.

"This [annual buffalo] hunt was a serious occasion when all the people united in a common effort to secure a supply of meat and pelts, food and clothing, for themselves and for their children. Therefore, it was initiated and conducted with religious ceremonies. The people were placed under control of men who through elaborate and sacred rites were appointed for the direction of the hunt, and to these appointed men all persons, including the chiefs, had to render obedience. It was while on this hunt that the great tribal ceremonies took place, at which time the people camped according to their gentes [clans] in the form known as *huthuga*.

"From the detailed description of the Omaha tribal hunt . . . as it was told the writers by those who had taken part in it both as officials and ordinary hunters, it is evident that the Omaha's hunting was not a sporting adventure but a task undertaken with solemnity and with a recognition of the control of all life by Wakonda. The Indian's attitude of mind when slaying animals for food was foreign to that of the white race with which he came into contact. Perhaps no one thing has led to greater misunderstandings between the races than the slaughter of game. The bewilderment of the Indian resulting from the destruction of the buffalo [by the white man] will probably never be fully appreciated. His social and religious customs, the outgrowth of centuries, were destroyed almost as with a single blow. The past may have witnessed similar tragedies but of them we have no record."[11]

I believe that those last words of Alice Fletcher are perhaps the most powerful indictment against the conquering white culture I have encountered, and of course she is absolutely correct.

An Omaha on the hunt considered himself in concert with the game, not in combat. When he killed a buffalo, he thanked it for what it was doing for him and he assumed that this ritually complex killing enabled the buffalo to return and that the buffalo in return appreciated the favor being done for him. The Plains Indian felt that he and the buffalo were working together to enrich Plains life, which, of course, they were.

Forty Warriors
Told by Francis La Flesche to Franz Boaz

In the beginning of time, long before the land was overrun by the white people, a man called together forty young men of his people. After they had come and sat down, he said to them, "My Uncle, My Brother-in-Law, My Grandfather, all of you others who are my relatives, I want to go on a journey and wish to consult you about this. So I have called you all together. You can see that I have picked out the very best of our people for this consultation. I want to start this journey tomorrow, and I would like to know how many of you will follow me. Then I will know if I can go forward without any hesitation."

After he had said these words the young men, without exception, replied, "Ho!" All of them knew what he wanted, and all of them expressed their desire to follow him wherever he wanted to go. He had a pipe before him, which was passed around, each taking a puff as a sign of willingness to take part in the undertaking.

After the war party had been organized, the men scattered to their own homes and once there immediately prepared to go on the journey. The women were set to the task of making mocassins. The men put their bows and arrows in order, and those who had none made lances with feather banners. All of them worked this way through the night. When dawn made its appearance, the men quietly arose and went to their leader, and the journey began. They traveled quickly until noon, when they stopped. All of them knew the first of the ceremonies to be done. They formed a circle and sat down.

This time the young leader said to his warriors, "My comrades, I must ask each of you a question and it must be answered truthfully. This custom belongs to our unborn children. I hope that you will have compassion on them. I beg this of you."

He called to a young brave and had him pass the pipe from man to man. He asked the first man to whom he offered the pipe, "If your wife is about to become a mother, pass this pipe on without smoking it; if she is not, then smoke from it." Thus the pipe went from man to man until the circle was completed.

That ended the ceremonies, so they spent their time traveling. But the next morning the young leader took his pipe and again offered Wakonda tobacco with the customary ritual. And finally they came to a land that was strange to them. They had moved quickly because no hardships had slowed them.

It happened that they came to a very long creek. Here and there were towering cliffs. Late that evening they camped for the night. And early the next day, when they woke up, their leader said to them, "We have come to a land that belongs to a very strange and brave people, and from now on we shall move with great caution."

He selected three of the most reliable young braves and assigned them the task of scouting the country to be crossed by the war party. One was to follow the creek closely, the other two were to take paths on either side of him and keep within calling distance. "Now you may go!" he said.

From the beginning the three young men ran on, never changing their pace. As the sun was going down, they reached the head of the creek, which ran through a deep forest surrounded by high cliffs. The young scout decided to wait here until the sun disappeared, then he could move in closer and see what people occupied the forest. He watched the forest closely, seeing smoke but no signs of men. At last the sun went down and darkness covered the land. Then he arose and cautiously approached and entered the forest. Suddenly he heard the clapping of hands and the voices of men singing. Going further into the forest he came to an opening in the center of which he saw the outlines of a large grass house, on top of which was a light.

The song he heard he recognized as the song of a hand game. He moved quietly to the house, lifted the door flap, and peeked in. He could see shields and quivers of arrows hanging on the side of the house. The game was exciting. The stakes were quivers of arrows. Their chief was sitting in the middle of the circle watching the game. Without raising his voice, he said to the warrior who was still peeking in at the door, "Come in. I knew where you were long before you came."

The young man entered the lodge and the chief assigned him to a seat close by his side. As he sat talking with the chief, the brave watched the other warriors gambling and could see that there was not one who looked timid: they were all experienced men.

The chief asked, "How many young men are there with you?"

The warrior replied, "About as many men as I see here."

"Return to your leader and tell him that we are anxious to see him and his men. Hurry!"

It did not take long for the young scout to put on his sash and return to make his report to his own chief. When he thought he was near his band he gave a wolf cry and immediately he heard an answering cry nearby. The young man went straight to the camp of his chief. Hardly was he seated when his chief said, "Comrade, what news do you have? Speak quickly!"

The young scout answered, "Yes, Chief. I saw some people. Their speech was like ours; their clothing was like ours. When I told them about our expedition they were very glad. They are eagerly looking for our arrival. Although they spoke our language, I did not recognize a single one of them. They have a permanent camp in one large lodge. The men appeared to be very lively. They asked me to hurry."

"Good. Now let us hurry, my comrades."

Quickly they left and reached the camp. The door of the grass house was lifted for them to enter. Joyously they greeted each other, shaking hands. The gambling was put aside, and the two chiefs sat side by side talking with each other while their men listened. They did not halt the conversation until late in the night, and then each man just lay down to sleep wherever he happened to be sitting.

When day broke, one of the young men awoke and got up. He looked around and saw that there was no house over their heads. He awoke his friend and quietly told him. Both young men looked carefully at the sleepers and found the whitened bones of men scattered among them. The two awakened their friends and their chief and then told them what they had found.

When they had awakened their commander, he sat up, took his little pipe, filled it, lifted its stem upward as an offering, and said a prayer: "Wakonda, we offer you this smoke in gratitude that you have permitted us to see the light of another day. These men join me in this offering."

After this, the war party went on. After they had gone a few days, they came across a group of people in a large camp. The scouts returned to report again to their leader. "We have found a people and it seems that they are powerful. We should think this over carefully."

To this the leader replied, "My comrades, this is good. We are seeking death. We shall attack them, whatever tribe they belong to. We shall attack at dawn."

The head of the scouts said, "Ho, Chief, good. That is what we have been looking for."

Day came, whitening the sky, and the attack was made. The warriors rushed in quickly. With a great alarm the people ran out of their tents, completely forgetting their weapons. The warrior band took many horses and also took many captives and then returned home with their spoils and prizes of battle.

COMMENTARY

Many rituals and ceremonies were involved in the organization and departure of a war party of this variety, but I have been unable to find anything corresponding to the ceremony described here showing whether any man's wife might be pregnant. There was a general order of abstinence preceding a war expedition, however, and it is perhaps to this practice that La Flesche refers.

La Flesche's reference to the hand game is also curious in this context. The hand game, which now is common among all Plains Indians from Oklahoma to the Dakotas, is a fairly recent phenomenon in Omaha culture. Because it immediately became so pervasive, however, perhaps La Flesche and the other Omahas thought of it as a traditional part of the Omaha way.

It should be noted that Omaha friends and relatives of mine who are alive today recall the introduction of the hand game and recall that a similar game, the mocassin game, preceded it. The mocassin game was played with smaller numbers of participants and required close observation, while the hand game can be played by hundreds in a great arena or in a gymnasium and so provides a better social occasion than the earlier form.

The hand game is still played with enthusiasm by the Omaha today, but the gambling element has been eliminated except on the team level because in the 1920s the gambling had become so excessive. Also, by tribal decision, games are played only on weekends because when the games were being played during the week and late into the night children were missing school and workers were unable to hold to the white man's schedule and still participate in the games.

The Omaha hand game is a team game. Two sides, perhaps two social clubs, or the men against the women, vie with each other in guessing the location of hidden stones or shells, much like "Button, Button, Who's Got the Button." There is a complicated scoring system, and the entire game, which lasts between two and four hours, is accompanied by the singing of traditional Omaha songs.

The matrix of the game includes religious ceremony, feasting, oratory, gift giving, social dancing, and occasional societal ceremonies. Thus, the hand game has become the center of Omaha tribal activities and has transcended its recreational aspects to become the nucleus for the culture's economic, religious, social, and linguistic integrity. Especially in urban areas, where there is no cohesive Omaha community, the hand game has become the single most important factor in the maintenance of "Omahaness."

Two-Faces and the Twin Brothers
Told by Pathinanpaji

Once there was a man who lived in a lodge with his woman, who was pregnant. He killed plenty of deer, and they were very happy.

But then the man felt a strange fear of danger. He said, "When I go away, be careful not to look at anyone who comes. Sit with your back to him."

And one day he did go off and someone came along.

"Aha!" he thought, "She is sitting waiting all alone for me, her relative. I'm always in luck with such things."

But the woman lay at the side of the door and did not look at him. And finally her husband came home from the hunt, so the old man, the visitor, went home.

When the husband got home, he asked, "How did it go?" and she answered, "It was just as you said it would be. An old man came, but I did not look at him."

"My wife, be sure to do your best. He is certain to come again and again, but do not look at him," he said.

One day he went hunting again, and so it happened four different times. The old man arrived. "I have come again, O First Daughter of the Household," he would say, but she would not look at him. The husband would return from the hunt and the old man would leave. "How was it?" the husband asked, and she replied, "The old man came again."

"Be sure not to look at him," said her husband.

But when the fourth time came and the old man was about to leave, the woman peeked at him. And she saw that it was Two-Faces walking along.

The woman fell dead, and the old man said, "Haha! I always do that to them." He slit the woman's stomach with his knife and found that the infants were twins; both were boys. He wrapped one in a skin with hair still on it and laid it by the side of the lodge. The other he took with him. He stuck him headfirst into a crack in a log.

When the husband came home, he found the woman dead, her stomach cut open. He wrapped his wife in a robe and buried her in the ground. Then he went to the lodge, and there he found the child crying beside the lodge. "Oh, my poor child." he said and went to the baby. It was a boy, and, being a boy, he was quick to be able to sit up by himself. He was quick in learning how to run and draw the bow.

"Father, make me a small bow," and the father made him some blunt arrows, which he used to hunt birds. His father taught him when to go out hunting.

"When the fresh meat is cooked on the fire and is done, you may eat it, and then you can go to sleep. But never go far away to play," he said.

The father went out hunting, and after a while a boy came walking along. He was singing as he came up:

> Younger Brother, since you have a father,
> You stay at home and eat soup;
> But since I have no father,
> I must wander along eating turkey-peas.

Then he said, "Younger Brother, has your father gone?"

"Yes, Elder Brother, my father is gone. Come, let's eat some of this roast meat. Come on," said the younger brother.

"That there is your father, Younger Brother," said the elder.

"For shame, Elder Brother. My father has gone," said the younger.

Eventually they went into the lodge and ate pieces of meat that had been stuck on a stick to roast. Then they sat playing together.

"Younger Brother, there comes your father," he said, and he left in a sudden rush. "Let him forget everything."

The father said, "Why, I prepared many pieces of roast meat for you before I left, and you have eaten all of them!"

"O Father, I . . . " he said, and then forgot what he had wished to say.

"Ho!! I am going hunting again. I will fix these pieces of meat for you, and then I want to go," said the father.

The boy came along again. "Has your father gone?" he asked.

"Yes, Elder Brother, my father has gone. Come," said the younger brother, and again they sat eating meat.

"Younger Brother, here comes your father," said the boy, and again he left. "Let him forget everything," he said.

"Why, I prepared a great quantity of food for you before I left," said the father. "You just ate it all up."

"Oh Father, I . . . " he said and forgot what he was about to say.

"I will do it again," said the father. He fixed a great many pieces of roast meat for him.

Again the other boy came up when the father had gone off hunting. "Has your father gone?" he asked.

"Yes, Elder Brother, my father is gone. Come," said the younger brother, and again they sat, eating fresh meat.

"Younger Brother, here comes your father," he said. "Again let him forget everything," and he disappeared in a great hurry.

"Why, before I left I prepared a great deal of food for you, and you just gulped it down," said the father.

"But Father, my elder brother keeps coming by," said the boy.

"But my dear child, when your mother was pregnant with you, Two-

Faces killed her. Since you were cut out of her, you have been very weak. When your elder brother comes, you must get him to lie down, and then you pretend to hunt lice. Steal a hair out of his head and he cannot leave you. Then say, 'Father, I have caught my elder brother,' " he told the boy.

Well, when the boy came up for the fourth time and asked, "Has your father gone?" the younger brother again said, "Yes, Elder Brother, he is gone. Come."

But the father had changed himself into a buffalo neck that was dried very hard. He lay inside the door.

"Elder Brother, let's hunt lice for each other," said the younger brother.

"All right," said the elder.

As he hunted lice, the younger brother wrapped the elder's scalp lock round and round his hand. "Father, I have caught my elder brother," he shouted.

"Don't let him go," said the father, and he jumped up.

The boy tried to get away, but finally he stopped struggling and became quiet. The father said, "My child, it is me. You and this younger boy are close relations. When your mother was pregnant with you, Two-Faces killed her, and both of you grew up very weak."

"O Father and Younger Brother, make me a small bow. We must shoot birds as much as possible," said the elder brother, and they did that.

"Be careful not to go to that spring in the faraway place," the father said. But when he had gone, the elder brother said, "Younger Brother, let's go to that spring that your father was telling us about."

"For shame, Elder Brother! Our father told us not to go there," said the younger.

"Then give me back my hair," said the elder brother.

"Let's see," said the elder brother, and they both went to the spring, where they found snakes shaking their rattles like this.

"Younger Brother, we have found many pretty pets. Let's take them home."

They cut off the tails and wrapped them up and took them home. When they got there they tied the tails around the door.

When the father came home carrying a deer, he put him down so that he could open the door. But there was a slight rattling. "You have done great wrong," he said. "Take the tails back to the snakes."

So they took them back. When they got there, they stuck each tail on the proper snake.

When the father went hunting again, he said, "Be careful not to go to the deep ravine."

"Younger Brother, let's go to the gorge our father was telling about," said the elder brother.

"For shame, Elder Brother, our father commanded us not to go there," said the younger.

"Then give me my hair back," said the elder brother.

"Let's see," said the younger brother.

So both went to the gorge, and they found an old woman sitting there making pottery.

"Younger Brother, the woman sitting there is your grandmother. Grandmother, we have come for you," he said.

"Since I have been sitting here for many years, Grandchild, who can pull me loose from this I am stuck to? If I stick to you when you carry me, I will always stick to you," said the old woman.

"Come, carry your grandmother. Since your father makes us take care of the lodge, let's sit with your grandmother. Bring along some of the kettles," said the elder brother. The younger brother broke many of them. Then he carried her home to their lodge.

"Come, Grandmother, get off," he said.

"No, Grandchild, I will stick to things like this," she said.

"Tickle your grandmother's ribs," said the elder brother. But in spite of the fact that he tickled her, she stuck fast.

"Hit her on the hipbone with a stone hammer," said the elder brother. So he hit her on her lower back, and she suddenly fell off.

Finally the father came home. "O Father, we carried my grandmother and brought her home," said the younger brother.

"You have done a bad thing. Go put her back."

So they carried her back. They took her to the gorge where they found her. "All right, Grandmother, get off," said the younger brother.

"No, Grandchild, I always stick like this," said the old woman.

Finally he hit her on the lower part of her back, and she suddenly fell off.

Again they got home. The father said, "A tree stands on the headlands of the high bluffs. Be careful not to go there." And he went hunting again.

"Younger Brother, let's go to that tree your father was telling us about," said the elder brother.

"Why, Elder Brother, he commanded us not to go there," said the younger.

"Then hand the hair back to me," said the elder brother.

"Let's see. Let's go there," said the younger brother. And they found young thunderbirds hatching in the nest in the tree. There were four of them.

"Younger Brother, we have found a few new pets. We will take them home to your father. Go climb up after them," said the elder brother.

"I don't want to, Elder Brother. You go."

"All right. I'll go after them," said the Elder brother. He climbed up and finally reached them. "Younger Brother, these pets are very pretty. When I throw them down to you, kill them. You there, what is your name?" he asked.

"Lights-in-the-Lodge is my name," said the young thunderbird.

"Ho! Younger Brother, Lights-in-the-Lodge is coming down to you. Watch for him," and when he threw him down, the younger brother stunned him.

"You there, what is your name?" the elder brother asked.

"Forked-Lightning-Walking is my name," he said.

"Ho! Younger Brother, here comes Forked-Lightning-Walking. Watch out for him," and when he fell down, the younger brother stunned him.

"And you there, what is your name?" he asked.

"Sheet-Lightning-Appears-Suddenly is my name," he said.

"Ho! Younger Brother, Sheet-Lightning-Appears-Suddenly is coming down to you. Look out for him," he said, and when he threw him down, the younger brother stunned him.

"And you there, what is your name?" he asked.

"Yellow-Here-in-a-Line-Again is my name."

"Ho! Younger Brother, here comes Yellow-Here-in-a-Line-Again down to you. Take care of him," and when he threw him down, the younger brother knocked him senseless.

But as he struck at them he failed to kill them. And the tree shot up very, very high into the sky.

"O Younger Brother, try to rescue me," cried the elder brother, calling from the distance loudly.

"O Elder Brother," the younger said with tears in his eyes.

"Try, Younger Brother," shouted the elder.

Finally the younger brother got his senses together. He struck the tree with a stone hammer and sang:

Jaⁿ′ ¢é-tĕ   tcĕ′-cka-¢a ¢é, tcĕ′-cka-¢a ¢é

This tree will shorten of its own accord,
Shorten of its own accord,

and it did get shorter.

"Try, Younger Brother," shouted the elder. He did the same thing. When he sang:

Jaⁿ′ ¢é-tĕ   tcĕ′-cka-¢a ¢é, tcĕ′-cka-¢a ¢é

The tree will shorten of its own accord,
Shorten of its own accord,

the tree did it. And on the fourth time, the tree was the same size it was before. It stood as tall as it was before the accident.

"Younger Brother, that is good," the elder said, and they took the Thunderbirds and carried them home.

When they got there with them, they put them inside the lodge, and there were frequent flashes. Both boys sat laughing. "Elder Brother, when my father comes home, he cannot help but like them," said the younger.

The father came home. When he pulled back the door flap, there were flashes. "You have done great wrong," he said. "Take them back."

When they got them back, they put them in the nest again.

When they reached home, the father said, "You two be careful that you do not go to the big lake whose shore is covered with canes," and he went hunting.

"Younger Brother, let's go to the big lake your father was telling us about," said the elder brother.

"Oh no, Elder Brother, my father commanded us not to go there."

"Then hand my hair back to me," said the elder brother.

"Let's see. Let's go there," said the younger brother, and they did go there.

When they arrived, they found a very sandy beach at the water's edge. Four-footed reptiles were thick there. "Younger Brother, we have found some very pretty pets," said the elder.

The two brothers tied their tails together and made them into packs, which they carried home. They reached the lodge with them, and the lizards crawled about by the door and sides of the lodge. As the boys walked about and played, they stepped on the lizards' tails and made them cry out.

The father brought a deer home from a place quite nearby. As he threw it down by the door it pressed against the flap and made a great line of lizards cry out.

"This is very bad. Take them back to wherever you got them," he said.

They took them back. Although they wanted to keep them, they took them back and threw them into the lake where they belonged.

Then they went home.

COMMENTARY

Lion told Dorsey that the name of the fourth Thunderbird was actually Sheet-Lightning-Is-Always-Coming-Back.

The Animal World

Alice Fletcher and Francis La Flesche comment on man's relationship with the animal world.

"Nature was looked on subjectively and anthropomorphically; all life was considered as one and as related. Man's physical existence is sustained by other forms of life."

"The relation of animals to the various rites of the gentes [clans] is difficult to explain for the reason that the outlook on nature and all living creatures, of the white race is so different from that of the Indian. Accustomed as we are to classify animals as domesticated or wild and to regard them as beneath man and subservient to him, it requires an effort to bring the mind to the position in which, when contemplating nature, man is viewed as no longer the master but as one of many manifestations of life, all of which are endowed with kindred powers, physical and psychical, and animated by a life force emanating from the mysterious Wakonda."

"As has been said by the old men, 'Man lives on the fruits of the earth; this is true when he feeds on the animals, for all draw their nourishment from mother earth; our bodies are strengthened by animal food and our powers can be strengthened by the animals giving us of their peculiar gifts. . . . If a man asks help of Wakonda, Wakonda will send the asker the animal that has the gift that will help the man in his need.' This view of the interrelation of men and animals, whereby in some mysterious manner, similar to the assimilation of food, man's faculties and powers can be reinforced from the animals, may assist in explaining why animals play so large a part in Omaha rites.

"This belief concerning the interrelation of men and animals may furnish the key to a better understanding of the myths of the Omaha and their cognates, some of which appear to be survivals of a time when this belief was in an active and formative stage, a time when man was trying to explain to himself the mystery of his conscious life and of his environment. Many thoughts arising from this mental effort, while intrinsically abstract, became concrete through an imaginative, dramatic story, serious in character, with a burden that could not be shifted from symbolic to matter-of-fact speech. In some such way and at a period far back in the history of the people the myth may have had its rise. Viewed by the light of Omaha tribal rites and rituals, it seems probable that some of the myths may be survivals of very ancient ceremonies, skeletons, so to speak, from which the original ceremonial covering has disappeared."

"The Omaha did not project this dual force [the masculine and the feminine] into gods and goddesses, their imagination did not so incline to express itself; it was occupied in seeking psychical counterparts to man among birds and animals, in drawing ethical teachings from the natural phenomena of night and day, and in finding lessons in tribal unity and strength from the branching tree."[1]

It is, therefore, hard to know in many Indian tales whether the hero is indeed a beaver's son or a man whose name is Beaver's Son, nor is the distinction at all important. The animals were constant and vital participants in every Omaha's life, and every Omaha intruded himself daily into the animal world. Certainly there were times when the interactions between man and animal were more extended and central than those between men. It is not surprising, then, that the events of the animal world were of interest to the Omaha and that these occurrences are often very human, or, at least, very Omaha.

The Bird Chief
Told by Francis La Flesche

All the birds were called together. They were told, "Whichever of you can fly the farthest in the sky will be chief," and so all the birds flew to a great height. But Wren got under the thick feathers of Eagle and hid there as Eagle flew up.

When the birds became tired of flying, they came back down, but Eagle continued to soar. And when Eagle had gone as far as he could, Wren came out and went up even further. And long after the birds had reached the ground, Eagle finally landed too. They thought that they were all there, so they started to figure the winner, but Wren was still not down. So they waited for him.

After a very long time, he finally came down too. Eagle had thought pretty highly of himself. He was sure that he was the winner. But Wren was the one who was made chief.

COMMENTARY

The regal bearing and assertive personality of the wren have been recognized in other cultures and folklores too: the Germans, for example, call the wren *Zaunkoenig*, "King of the Fence."

Buffalo and Grizzly Bear
Told by George Miller

Grizzly Bear was going somewhere, following the course of a stream. At last he was headed straight for a headland. When he came in sight of it, he found a buffalo bull standing beneath it. Grizzly Bear retraced his steps, going back to the stream, following its course until he got beyond the headland. Then he came up closer and took a look. He could see that the bull was a shabby one, very thin, and standing with his head bowed, as if very tired.

So Grizzly Bear crawled up close to him, made a dash, grabbed Buffalo Bull by the hair of his head, and pulled down his head. He turned Buffalo Bull round and round, shaking him now and then, saying, "Say something. Say something. I have been around here a good deal and I have heard that you have threatened to fight me. Say something!" Then he hit Buffalo Bull on the nose with his open paw.

"Why," said Buffalo Bull, "I have never threatened to fight you. You have been in this country for a long time."

"Not so! You have been threatening to fight me," said Grizzly Bear. Then he let go of his hair and grabbed the buffalo by his tail and spun him round and round. Just as he stopped, he gave him a hard blow with his open paw right on the bull's scrotum. This made Buffalo Bull walk with his legs wide apart.

"Oh ow! Oh ow! Oh! That hurts," said Buffalo Bull, and the bobtailed grizzly walked away.

Now the buffalo was thinking, "Attack him. You can do it."

But Grizzly Bear knew what he was thinking and said, "What? What did you say?"

"I didn't say anything," said Buffalo Bull.

Then Grizzly Bear came walking back. He grabbed Buffalo Bull by the tail, pulling him round and round. Then he grabbed him by the horns, pulling his head around and round.

"Now, when I said that you were thinking of something, you denied it," said Grizzly, referring to his thoughts about attacking him. Then he grabbed Buffalo Bull by the tail and did the same thing to him again. He hit him with his open paw, and Buffalo Bull walked with his legs wide apart, crying, "Oh ow! Oh ow! Oh! That really hurts." And again Grizzly Bear went off. And again Buffalo Bull had the thoughts. Grizzly Bear knew about it and attacked him once more.

A third time Grizzly left, but when he asked Buffalo Bull what he had said, the buffalo replied, "I didn't say anything of importance. I was just saying to myself, 'Attack him! You can do it.'"

"Sure," said Grizzly Bear.

So Buffalo Bull stepped back, throwing his tail into the air. "Now don't run away," said Grizzly Bear, and Buffalo Bull threw himself down on the ground and rolled over and over. Then he kept backing up, pawing the ground.

"Now, I said don't run away," said Grizzly Bear. You see, as Buffalo Bull was backing up to attack, Grizzly Bear thought that he was frightened. But now Buffalo Bull started toward Grizzly Bear. He was snorting as he came closer, rushing down on him. He sent Grizzly Bear flying through the air. And as Grizzly Bear was coming down to the ground again, Buffalo Bull caught him with his horns and threw him into the air again.

When Grizzly Bear had fallen back down and lay on the ground, Buffalo Bull stabbed at him with his horns, just missing him but piercing the ground. Grizzly Bear crawled off, but Buffalo Bull followed him step by step, stabbing at him now and then but without piercing him.

This time, instead of attacking Buffalo Bull, Grizzly Bear fell headlong over a cliff, landing in a thicket at its foot. Buffalo Bull was running after him so fast that he could not stop right at the place where Grizzly Bear had fallen and continued running along the edge of the cliff for some distance. But finally he did stop and there he stood with his tail partly raised.

Grizzly crawled back up the bank and peeped over. "O Buffalo Bull! Let's be friends. We are so very much alike," said Grizzly Bear.

COMMENTARY

Today many of the animal participants in these stories seem geographically out of place, but the displacement is in fact historical. Grizzlies did roam the hills along the Missouri River before they were driven to sanctuaries in the Rockies by the advance of the white frontier. Great herds of elk were grazing on the Dakota and Nebraska plains, and mountain sheep roamed the Black Hills area of South Dakota.

The Lament of the Fawn for Its Mother
Told by Joseph La Flesche

There was once a doe with her fawn, and the fawn discovered the presence of enemies. "Oh, Mother, these are men," said the fawn.

"No, they are crows. They are not men."

And the fawn said again, "Oh, Mother, these are men."

"No, they are not men. They are crows," said the doe.

Then the man shot her. The fawn ran away. When he returned to the place, he found that the men had cut up his mother and put her liver on the fire. So he sang this lament:

Naⁿ-há ni-á-ciⁿ-gá-bi e-hé,   ʒa-xá-bi e-cé ¢aⁿ'-cti; ɖí ¢aⁿ ná-¢i-zi-   zí-dje.

Oh, Mother, I said that they were men,
But you said that they were crows;
Now your liver is sizzling on the fire!

COMMENTARY

Dorsey says of this tale: "I first heard of the song in this myth in 1871, when I was with the Ponkas in Dakota. But the fragment of the text was given me at the Omaha Agency."

How Big Turtle Went on the Warpath
Told by Tenugaha

There were a great many people living in a village, and Big Turtle came to live with them. And there were some people from another village who regularly attacked them. They killed one person and returned to their home. So Big Turtle cooked for the warpath. He had two people go to get the guests. He sent Red-Breasted Turtle and Gray Squirrel. He made two round bunches of grass and placed them at the bottom of the stick to which the kettle was fastened. And then the people came.

"Ho! warriors," he said. "Warriors, when men are injured, they always retaliate. I am cooking this for the warpath. I am cooking sweet corn and buffalo paunch. You will go after Corn Crusher for me. Call to him. Call Comb, Awl, Pestle, Firebrand, and Buffalo Bladder too," said Big Turtle.

So two men went to call them. And they called to Corn Crusher.

Iⁿ′-¢a-pá! wa-ská-¢iⁿ-heaú! Iⁿ′-¢a-pá! wa-ská-¢iⁿ-heaú!

Iⁿ′-¢a-pá! wa-ská-¢iⁿ-heaú! Iⁿ′-¢a-pá! wa-ská-¢iⁿ-heaú!

Corn Crusher, be sure to bring your bowl!
Corn Crusher, be sure to bring your bowl!
Corn Crusher, be sure to bring your bowl!
Corn Crusher, be sure to bring your bowl!

And they called to Comb four times.

Mí-ӿa-hé! wa-ská-¢iⁿ-heaú! Mí-ӿa-hé! wa-ská-¢iⁿ-heaú!

Mí-ӿa-hé wa-ská-¢iⁿ-heaú! Mí-ӿa-hé! wa-ská-¢iⁿ-heaú!

Comb, be sure to bring your bowl!

And they called to Awl four times:

Wá-ӿu! wa-ská-¢iⁿ-heaú! Wá-ӿu! wa-ská-¢iⁿ-heau!

Wá-ӿu! wa-ská-¢iⁿ-heaú! Wá-ӿu! wa-ská-¢iⁿ-heaú!

Awl, be sure to bring your bowl!

And they called to Pestle four times.

Wé-he! wa-ská-ȼiⁿ-heaú! Wé-he! wa-ská-ȼiⁿ-heaú!

Wé-he! wa-ská-ȼiⁿ-heaú! Wé-he! wa-ská-ȼiⁿ-heaú!

Pestle, be sure to bring your bowl!

And they called to Firebrand, too, four times.

Ná-wiⁿ-xć! wa-ská-ȼiⁿ-heaú! Ná-wiⁿ-xé! wa-ská-ȼiⁿ-heaú!

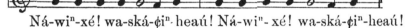

Ná-wiⁿ-xé! wa-ská-ȼiⁿ- heaú! Ná-wiⁿ- xé! wa-ská-ȼiⁿ-heaú!

Firebrand, be sure to bring your bowl!

And they also called four times to Buffalo Bladder.

Ļé-ne-xé! wa-ská-ȼiⁿ-heaú! Ļé-ne-xć! wa-ská-ȼiⁿ-heaú!

Ļé-ne-xé! wa-ská-ȼiⁿ-heaú! Ļé-ne-xé! wa-ská-ȼiⁿ-heaú!

Buffalo Bladder, be sure to bring your bowl!

When the criers got home they said, "O War Chief, they all have heard." And all those who were called arrived at the lodge of Big Turtle. Big Turtle said, "Ho! O War Chiefs, Corn Crusher, Comb, Awl, Pestle, Firebrand, and Buffalo Bladder, even though these people have been injured, they will not do anything about it. Let's go on the warpath for them. We will go in four nights."

He ordered Corn Crusher to cook. "O War Chief Corn Crusher, you will cook. And you, O Comb, will cook on the night after that. And you, O Awl, will cook and complete the number." That many war chiefs cooked, four. They were war chiefs and the rest were assistants.

And the people of the village said, "Why, of the persons who have been called, who is cooking for the warpath?"

And one said, "Why, Big Turtle cooked. Hah! Has he gathered all those who cannot move well enough, those who cannot move fast enough? Pfui! If the enemy finds them, they will destroy them. Only if a war chief has common sense can he carry on a war."

Corn Crusher cooked. He cooked turnips and he cooked a buffalo paunch with them, just as Big Turtle had cooked one with sweet corn. And Awl cooked wild rice. And Comb cooked *dethawe*.

And Big Turtle said, "Enough days have passed. Let's go tonight," and so they left.

Big Turtle made leggings with large flaps. He tied short garters around them. He rubbed earth on his face and thus reddened it. He wore grass around his head. He put fine white feathers on the top of his head. He took his gourd rattle like this. He rattled it. He sang the song of the war chief.

You say,
'Big Turtle is coming back from touching the foe.'
He is coming back from the touching.

He walked about, stepping lively in the dance. He walked around them. When they left, it was day.

At length a young buffalo bull came along.

"Warriors, wait for him," Big Turtle said. And he then said to the buffalo bull, "I am on a journey and am in a great hurry. Tell me quickly, why are you walking?"

"Well, O War Chief, it is this way. I have heard about your journey and I have come looking for you," said Buffalo Bull.

"Do your best," said Big Turtle. "I want to see your movements."

Buffalo Bull rolled himself back and forth. He jumped up suddenly. He jabbed at the ground with his horns. He tore up the ground and threw the pieces into the air. He stood with his tail in the air and the tip bent down. He charged an ash tree that was standing there. He hit it and knocked it a long distance through the air. "O War Chief, that is what I intend to do if they bother me," he said.

"Look at the people with whom I am traveling. None of them is at all fainthearted. You aren't at all like them. I am disappointed in you. Go away," said Big Turtle. And again Big Turtle sang his song:

You say,
'Big Turtle is coming back from touching the foe.'
He is coming back from the touching.

Again they began traveling. "Move on, Warriors," he said. They came to a stream that was not small. They crossed it.

Firebrand was first, moving with great effort. Finally, because he was so tired, he fell into the water and was extinguished. "O War Chief," he said, "I am not going beyond here with you."

"Warrior, stay here for a while. I will soon return," said Big Turtle.

They reached the other side and moved on. Finally a puma came along.

"Warriors, wait for him," said Big Turtle. "I am interested in what he has to say. Stand in a row. Speak quickly," he said to Puma. "What do you want?"

"Well, O War Chief," answered Puma, "I have heard lately that you were on a trip, and I wanted to go along, so I have been looking for you."

"Fine," said Big Turtle. "I want to see what you do." And Puma made his hair bristle up all over his body. He bent his tail backward and upward. He went leaping to the bottom of a hill. He caught a fawn that was about two years old by the Adam's apple and he carried it back in his teeth, making a loud cry. "That, O War Chief, is what I intend to do if anyone bothers me," he said.

"Do something else," said Big Turtle.

"No, War Chief, that is all I do," said Puma.

"You have disappointed me," said Big Turtle. "Look at these people who are traveling with me. Is there one that is less than perfect? You are very inferior. Go away. You have disappointed me."

They went on until finally they reached the foot of a hill, where they met a black bear. "O War Chief, again someone is approaching," the warriors said.

"I am interested in what he has to say, Warriors. Wait for him. Stand in a row," said Big Turtle. "Ho! Come. Speak quickly. What do you want? When I am on a journey I am in a great hurry," said Big Turtle to Black Bear.

"Yes, War Chief, it is so. I have heard about you being on a journey. I would like to join you, so I looked hard for you," said Black Bear.

"Ho! Fine," said Big Turtle. "You may have thought that you would like to do that. I want to see what you can do."

Black Bear tore the ground with his claws and threw lumps of dirt a great distance. He attacked an oak tree which had been blackened by fire. He hugged it and threw it a great distance with some force. "O War Chief, if anything threatens me, that is what I intend to do," Black Bear said.

But Big Turtle stood there and said, "Ho! Warrior, you have disappointed me. Look at these people I am with. Not one is in the least bit fainthearted. You have disappointed me. Go away. This is the way I always send away inferior ones."

They entered some dense undergrowth and Buffalo Bladder was torn open, making the sound, "Koo."

"Unfortunately I will not be going beyond this point with you," said Buffalo Bladder.

"Ho! Warrior, I will come back very soon. Stay here for a while," said Big Turtle, and again they moved on.

As they traveled along, they reached a bad path. Big logs were lying across it. Red-Breasted Turtle could not step over them.

"Ho! War Chief, I cannot go beyond here with you," he said.

"Ho! Warrior, I will come back very soon. Stay here for a while," said Big Turtle, and again they moved on.

As they moved along they encountered a big wolf. "O War Chief, again someone is coming."

"I am interested in what he has to say, Warriors. Wait for him. Stand in a row," said Big Turtle.

"Ho! Come. Speak quickly. What do you want? When I am on a trip I am in a great hurry," said Big Turtle.

"Yes, O War Chief, this is it. I have heard for some time that you are on a journey, and since I wanted to go along, I have been looking for you," said the wolf.

"Ho! Fine," said Big Turtle. "You may have thought that that is what you wanted to do. I would like to see what you can do."

Wolf decorated himself: he reddened his nose and all his feet. He tied eagle feathers to his back.

"All right. Do it. I want to see what you can do. Do it," said Big Turtle.

And Wolf turned round and round, and he launched an attack in the woods by the small creek. He killed a deer. He brought it back, holding it with his teeth. "O War Chief, that is what I intend to do if anyone bothers me," said Wolf.

"You disappoint me. See these people with whom I am traveling. There is not one that is in the least fainthearted. Go away. I am always sending off inferior ones like this," said Big Turtle. "Warrior Gray Squirrel, go out scouting," he said, and Gray Squirrel did. Soon he came back, blowing a horn.

"O War Chief, he is coming back," they said, and Big Turtle went out to meet him.

"Ho! Warrior, be honest. Tell me how it is."

"Yes, War Chief, it is this way. They did not detect me while I was there."

"Let's sit at the very edge of the camp," said Big Turtle, and he talked about going. "Warriors, I will look around and see how things are, and how many people there are there." When he came back, he said, "Warriors, let's go in that direction. This is a good place for sitting," he said. By and by, as they moved along, he said, "Ho! Warrior! O War Chief Corn Crusher, do this. Give it a try. He will go to the far end of the lodge."

"O War Chief, where shall I sit?" he asked.

"O War Chief and Warrior, you will crawl right to the door and sit on the outside," said Big Turtle.

A woman came out of the lodge to urinate. She came upon Corn Crusher crawling in a line up to her. When she saw him she said, "O, I have been wanting some mush, and I have found myself an excellent corn crusher. I will pound my corn with this excellent corn crusher. I have found it for myself."

When she pounded corn with it, she mashed her hand flat, forcing out blood with the blow. She threw it back outside again. "Bad corn crusher!" And when she threw it, it went flying back, without stopping, to Big Turtle, who was nearby.

"The one called Corn Crusher has returned, having killed one right in the lodge," he said. "O War Chief Comb, you give it a try. Sit right where Corn Crusher sat," said Big Turtle.

So Comb departed. He sat right where he was commanded to sit. Comb was very handsome. And a woman who was coming out found Comb. "I have been without a comb up to now. But I have found myself a very good one," she said. She took him back into the lodge. Soon she combed her hair with him. He pulled out all the hair on one temple by the roots. "Very bad comb, but I thought it was good," she said and threw him away quickly outside the door.

When he made her throw him away, he went all the way back without stopping. He came back with the hair. "I was called Comb and now I am back, having snatched all the hair from one person right inside the lodge," he said. He took it back to Big Turtle and gave it to him.

Big Turtle said, "You have made me very thankful. I am anxious to keep this. When we reach home we will have the women dance. I will take a wife, and you will get her for me. I will take a woman."

"O War Chief Awl, now you make a try. You will sit where the War Chief Comb sat," said Big Turtle. Now, Awl was very handsome; he was very good to look at. And he sat where he was told to. A woman came out and found Awl. "O, I have found myself a fine awl. I had no awl before, so I am very thankful to find one now," she said.

She took him back to the lodge and spoke of sewing her moccasins with him. "I will sew my moccasins with it," she said, and she did it. But she pierced her fingers with him. She missed while pushing him in, pushing him with great force. There was a great deal of blood, and she threw him out the door suddenly. "The awl is terrible. I've really hurt myself. This is a bad wound," she said. And then she threw him far from the door, sending him homeward.

"I am called Awl, and I stabbed one right in the lodge, killing her," he said. His blade was very bloody. He returned to Big Turtle.

"O War Chief," the others said, "Awl is coming back, tell his own name. He has killed one."

Big Turtle said, "Ho! War Chief, you make me very thankful. Since it is you, I will blacken my face. The village will be joyful. Ho! Pestle, now you give it a try. You will lie where War Chief Awl lay," he commanded.

Pestle was very handsome. And when he arrived there, he lay where he was commanded to lie. A woman went out and found Pestle. "O, I have found a very good pestle for myself. I didn't have a pestle before," she said.

She took him back into the lodge. She took some corn. She filled her mortar and pounded the corn. She beat it fine. But she thrust Pestle too far, right onto her knee. She missed the mark while she was pounding, and he flew with great force and hit her right on the knee. "O, what a bad pestle!" she said and threw him outside, sending him all the way to where he had come from.

He said, "It is the one you have called Pestle. He is coming back, having hit one right in the lodge. He has killed one." He returned to Big Turtle. "O War Chief, I have killed one," he said.

"You make me very grateful," said Big Turtle. "Ho! Warrior Gray Squirrel, give it a try," he commanded.

"But how can I do anything?" he asked.

The lodges were among some trees. "You will pass along the trees above the smoke holes of the lodges. If they find you, they will shoot at you. Do your best. Try hard to evade the arrows and blows. If anyone moves apart, attack him," said Big Turtle.

Eventually a boy spotted him. "There is a gray squirrel running along!" he shouted. Everyone ran out in an uproar. They shot at him with guns. They even hit at him with sticks. One boy stood to the side. He attacked the boy and bit him. When they attacked him, they failed and were trying to reach him.

"Unbelieveable! It has always been easy to get a gray squirrel, but this one time we have failed. He just bit us," they cried.

"The one whom you have called Gray Squirrel is coming back, having killed one right in the midst of them," they said to Big Turtle.

"Ho! real warrior, be honest," said Big Turtle.

"O War Chief, it is true. I did kill one," he said.

"Ho! Warrior, you too make me thankful."

"Ho! Warriors, I—even I—will give it a try. I will not return for some time. Do not go home. Be certain that you do not go home and leave me here alone," said Big Turtle.

He went to the village. Some ashes had been poured out. They had been extinguished. Finally Big Turtle pushed his way through. He went on in. He sat there with his eyes sticking out, looking around. A woman came up, just as it was morning. She stood very close to Big Turtle. Big Turtle was carrying his shield. "You will step on my shield," he said, and the woman looked around. Again he said to her, "You will step on my shield. Stand further away," and so the woman found him.

"Oh!" she said.

"Stand still. I bring you a message," Big Turtle said. "Go home and say, 'Big Turtle says that he has come for war. He says that he has come desiring the chief's daughter, whose body has been placed on the bough of a tree.' "

All of the people said, "Don't waste any time in breaking in his head."

But he asked, "How would it be possible for you to break in my head right now? If your weapons slip off of me, you will break your legs with your own blows."

"When the water is hot, we'll put him in it," they said.

"For shame! When the water is hot I will splash it with my feet, and many of you will be scalded to death," he said.

"What he says is probably true. And if it is true, it might be better to burn him," the people said.

"How stupid! If I scatter the fire by kicking it, I will cause all the land to burn. Be careful that your children don't also burn from the fire," he said.

"What he is saying is probably true," they said.

Then a child asked for some water, saying, "O Mother, some water!"

And Big Turtle said, "Oh, no!" trying to tempt them with the reference to water.

"Have the child ask for water," someone said.

"What do you mean by that?" others asked.

"When the words 'O Mother, some water' were spoken, Big Turtle here said 'Oh, no!' "

"Wonderful! He is afraid of water," they all said. They took him to the water, holding him by the tail. But Big Turtle clung to the earth with his forelegs. They held his tail and dragged him to the water. They forcibly threw him into the water. He swam through the water for a little ways, crying a little and pretending that he did not know how to swim.

He said, "Wee! wee! wee!"

"Wonderful! Throw him out in the middle of the stream," they shouted.

And again they threw him headlong into the water. He drifted about and finally he sank. And they all said, "He is dead," and they went home. The people said, "You should have done that to him right away."

After the people had gone home, some boys were standing there. Big Turtle floated up. He peeked at them. Some boys were looking at the place where it had been done. Big Turtle said, "When Big Turtle came some time ago to make war on you, you said that you had killed him. Look here at me."

The boys ran home to tell about this. "You said that you killed Big Turtle, but back there he showed himself to us and laughed at us. It was Big Turtle and he is still alive," they said.

"Ho! Let's attack him!" said the people. And so they did. They arrived there. "Where is he?" they asked.

"Right here," the boys said.

"Where are Otter and Grass Snake? They alone can find him," the people said.

Big Turtle lay under the mud at the bottom of the water. Only the tip of his nose and his eyes were sticking out. The Otter and Grass Snake looked for him under the water. They came very close to him and repeatedly stepped over his head. When Otter was about to pass over him, Big Turtle bit him in the stomach.

"Ho! Elder Brother, you have hurt me," said Otter.

Big Turtle said, "Why are you looking for me?"

"I'm not looking for you. I was looking for food and just ran into you," said Otter.

"No, you're in with those who are trying to kill me," said Big Turtle.

"O Elder Brother, O Elder Brother, O Elder Brother! I beg you. I was not looking for you," he repeated.

"You're not getting out of my mouth no matter what," said Big Turtle.

"But Elder Brother, how long will it be before you finally let me go again?" asked Otter.

"When the thunder god comes back, I will let you go."

"Hey! He will let me go when the thunder god comes back. Help! He is biting me between the legs. Hey!" he called, shouting for his people to help.

"He says that he has been bitten. He says that he is being bitten between the legs. Hit the tent skins for him," said the people, and they made the tent skins resound by hitting them.

"Ho! Elder Brother, the thunder god has come back," said Otter.

"They are just hitting the tent skins," said Big Turtle.

And the people said, "Maybe it would be a good idea to chop down those trees," and so they felled some trees. The trees went "Kwee! Kwee!" as they fell crashing to the ground.

"Ho! Elder Brother, the thunder god has returned," said Otter.

"They were just chopping down trees," said Big Turtle.

"Maybe we should fire some guns," said the people.

"Elder Brother, he has returned," said Otter.

"They are just shooting guns," said Big Turtle.

Finally the thunder god did roar very far away. "Ho! Elder Brother, he has come back," and Big Turtle let Otter go. Otter had grown very thin, and he started for home. He arrived there very haggard.

His people said, "Let two birds drink the stream dry. Bring some pelicans here."

When they came back with them, they told them, "Drink the stream dry. Someone is coming here to wage war, and although we killed him, he is alive again. He laughs hard at us whenever we catch him and try to kill him." The birds drank the stream dry. There was only a very little puddle left in which Big Turtle sat.

And Big Turtle said, "Ho! Warrior Gray Squirrel, come back, wherever you are. They have almost killed me."

Gray Squirrel came running back, crying loudly. He was coming back to attack them. He bit at their water pouches and tore them open. He bit many holes in them. Soon all of the water was back in place. The creek and lake were filled with water, just as they had been before.

But the people said, "Sew up their pouches for them," and they repaired the throats of the pelicans. When they had finished, they said, "Come. Drink it up dry again. Do your best. Be certain not to fail," and they did drink it dry again, so that once more there was very little water left.

"Ho! Warrior Gray Squirrel, wherever you are, they have nearly killed me. Come back again," shouted Big Turtle, and when he returned he again bit their throats and tore holes in many places. And again all of the water returned to its place. He made their throats very bad. In fact, he damaged them so much this time that they could not be sewed up again.

"Now it is certain that we will fail. Gray Squirrel is terrible. But I think that Gray Squirrel is the only one with Big Turtle. He is the only one on his side. We still have not defeated them," said one of the people. They rested.

When night came, Big Turtle returned. He went back to his comrades. "Ho! Warriors, when men get the better of their foes in a fight, they usually return home. I suspect that your sisters are getting tired of waiting to dance!" he said, and so they went homeward. He walked around them, rattling his gourd. "Warriors, I said that I would do this, and it has been done," he said. He set fire to the grass. He said of the people in his village, "You did nothing but laugh at Big Turtle when he went on the warpath." He set fire to the grass so that they might know that he was coming home after defeating his enemy. Finally they arrived in sight of the village, their home. They fired guns and tied scalps to a stick.

Those in the village said, "Here come the ones who went to war!" The returning warriors ran round and round. "They are coming home, having killed the people of the enemy," said the people in the village.

An old man said, "Corn Crusher says he killed one. Hooray! He says he killed her right at the lodge. Hooray! Comb says he killed one right at the lodge. Hooray! Awl says he killed one right at the lodge. Hooray! Pestle says he killed one right at the lodge. Hooray! Gray Squirrel says he killed three right in the midst of the enemy. Hooray! They say Big Turtle was held captive right in the midst of them, with a great uproar. Hooray! It is said they didn't even injure him. Hooray!"

And Big Turtle walked about very proudly, carrying his shield. He entered his lodge. He sat and told his story. People wanted to hear the story and kept stopping him. "Why did they fail against you when they were so close to you? If you crept in so close to them, why are you still alive?" asked the people.

"I pretended to be afraid of water, and so I am still alive," he said.

"If that is true, those people over there must have no eyes. How is it that they did not find you when you were alive?"

"I don't know, but I sat in the ashes and I am still alive. I have returned home after killing many people. Do you doubt me? Since you didn't go to take vengeance on the people who used to attack you, I went there myself to wage war on them. I killed them. How can you doubt me? I will tell my story no more. I am through," he said.

And so it was.

COMMENTARY

Some of Dorsey's commentary helps clarify obscure points of this myth. He says of the bundles of grass mentioned in the opening passage, for example: "The two bundles or wisps of grass are used 1) for wiping the mouths and hands of the guests; and 2) for wiping the bowls and kettles. They are then put into the fire, and the bowls are passed through the smoke which ensues."

Further: "*Dethawe*, the root of a water plant, is scarce at present. The plant has a leaf resembling a lily, but it is about two feet in diameter, and lies on the water. The stalk extends about two feet above the water, and ends in a seedpod. The seeds, which are black and very hard, are almost oval. The Indians dry the root, and cut it into pieces about six inches long, if required for a long time; but, if not, they boil it."

The words to the war chief's song are actually Iowa Indian in origin. The words translate, "The Big Turtle is coming back from touching the foe, they say, you said. / He is coming back from touching." Among Plains Indians, touching the enemy constituted an even more laudable performance of bravery than killing him.

Dorsey says that the use of the gun to simulate thunder is an innovation, that Francis La Flesche had told him that the original thunder simulations were striking skins, striking the tent walls, and beating the drum.

The turtle was a figure of bravery among the Omaha, despite this cynical view of his courage and leadership abilities. It seems unlikely to the non-Omaha that the turtle could conceivably be viewed as courageous, but Alice Fletcher offers some clarification.

" 'Boys used to be made to swallow a turtle's heart so as to make their hearts strong. I was an orphan, and tenderhearted and when any woman talked to me I would easily weep. I did not like this, but I could not help it. I swallowed a turtle's heart and since then I can control myself. He [pointing to a man in the group about him] has swallowed three. The turtle is hard to kill; even when the heart is cut out it will still quiver and the turtle's head will be able to bite after it is severed from the body. The heart is flat and about an inch long. The boy took the heart and swallowed it by himself.' "[2]

Big Turtle's preparations and ritual preparing for the warpath are of course in keeping with Omaha tradition. Dorsey describes these ritual preparations in full detail, some of which might be of interest in comparison with Big Turtle's.

"It is generally a young man who decides to undertake an expedition against the enemy. Having formed his plan, he speaks thus to his friend: 'My friend, as I wish to go on the warpath, let us go. Let us boil the food for a feast.' The friend having consented, the two are the leaders, . . . if they can induce others to follow them. So they find two young men whom they send as messengers to invite those whom they name. Each . . . messenger takes one half of the [tribal] circle . . . . These invitations are made at night, and as quietly as possible, lest others should hear of the feast and wish to join the expedition . . . .

"After the return of the messengers, the guests assemble at the lodge or tent of their host . . . . The two . . . hosts sit opposite the entrance, while the messengers have their seats next the door, so that they may pass in and out and attend to the fire, bringing in wood and water, and also wait on the guests. Each guest brings with him his bowl and spoon . . . .

"The food generally consists of dried meat and corn. Pathinanpaji said that he boiled fresh venison . . . .

"A round bundle of grass is placed on each side of the stick on which the kettle is hung. The bundles are intended for wiping the mouths and hands of the men after they have finished eating. At the proper time, each messenger takes up a bundle of grass and hands it to the [leaders] on his side of the fireplace. When the [leaders] have wiped their faces and hands, they hand the bundles to their next neighbors, and from these two they are passed in succession around to the door. Then the bundles are put together and handed again to one of the [leaders] for the purpose of wiping his bowl and spoon, passing from him and his associate to the men on the left of the fireplace, thence by the entrance to those on the right of the fireplace to [the leaders]. Then the messengers receive the bundle and use it for wiping out the kettle or kettles. Then the host says, 'Now! Enough! Take ye it.' Then the [messengers] put the grass in the fire, making a great smoke. Whereupon the host and his associate exclaim, 'Hold your bowls over the smoke.' Each one tries to anticipate the rest, so the bowls are knocked against one another, making a great noise. This confusion is increased by each man crying out for himself, addressing Wakanda [sic], or deity of thunder, who is supposed by some to be the god of war."[3]

I have in a previous context discussed the system of prairie firing to signal approaches of successful war parties to the home base.

The series of events climaxing Big Turtle's war excursion are classics of folk literature; for example, the hero escapes by being exposed to his natural element while his enemies are led to believe that it must be that thing he fears most. In this tale Turtle is thrown into the water, where, of course, he most desires to be. I have collected Danish tales of fishermen who upon catching an eel try to decide what to do with it; one says that they obviously cannot hang it because it has no neck, another points out that it is too wet to burn, and so a third suggests that they drown it. When it swims into the depths, the fishermen proudly declare their victory over the hideous beastie. In American literature, Joel Chandler Harris used this same folk theme when he had Br'er Rabbit convince the Bear to throw him into the briar patch.

Animal and Man

As I have mentioned, the Indian felt that he was one with the very buffalo he hunted. Indeed, he felt himself always in concert with the world around him, which included not only the natural but also the supernatural. Even today the American Indian honors profoundly the American flag, the flag that Custer carried into battle, because to the Indian the flag is a symbol of the land, of the mountains and forests and rivers. One of the cultural problems encountered by the Indian in the white world today is that he considers himself one of many, many elements moving within the universe, subject to a million forces and not really capable of influencing but a few of them himself—a realistic view!

The white, on the other hand, considers himself a prime mover, able to determine his own fate, to deduce the nature of god—to the Indian, an unthinkable arrogance and naivete.

To the Plains Indian, the line between man and animal was not at all distinct. He knew that god, Wakonda, could be seen all around him in nature and within himself, which implied a strong connection between himself and nature. While there were no explicit totems among the Omaha, that is, they did not explicitly trace their family or clan lines back to some animal ancestor, the fact that the clans all bear names drawn from nature and mostly from animals clearly suggests to us the close connection between the Omaha and the animal world.

The Man and the Snake Man
Told by Nudanacha

Once there were a great many lodges in one place. A young man, who was a very handsome person, left there in a bad humor. In the very dense forest he went up the hill to a large bluff. From the forest in the other direction another person was approaching, following the other creek. He too was climbing this hill. They came right toward each other, eventually coming together. They stood looking at each other. The first man came up and stood there.

"Come with me and you will eat," the second man said, and the youth went with him. But he could see the bones of many men in a great curved heap. The man with him was the one who had killed all of those dead men.

Well, an old woman was sitting there. The old woman put some food in the boy's bowl, but the food in the lodge was the flesh of the men who had been killed there. She cooked it until it was done.

"I don't eat that," the boy said.

"I have put aside some corn. Perhaps you eat that," she said.

"Yes," he said. So she put the corn in the broth from the human flesh. And so when it was done, she filled a bowl for him, and he ate it.

"This is very bad," he thought.

"Young man, I pity you," said the old woman. "Young man, you are very handsome, and I pity you. How did he tempt you to come here? When he brought you here, how could you agree to come? He is far from being good. He killed the men whose bones you see there. He will leave tomorrow, very early in the morning," she said.

The one who had brought him home, it seems, was Snake Man. He would fatten his guests and then kill them on the fourth or fifth day.

"It is always this way," the old woman told him. "Kill me. When you have done that, quickly lay my bones down and cover them with a robe. I will give you one pair of these moccasins that I have put away. Please do your best. No matter how far you go, when evening comes, Snake will overtake you. As for these moccasins I am giving you, if you take one step forward, you will reach the headland you see over there. A man is standing there. When you get there, give him this paper. Then pull off the moccasins and place them facing this direction. They will come home."

After the old woman had told him all this, the young man killed her. Early in the morning he cut her flesh into strips. When that was done, he uncoiled her entrails and went to the stream with them. He put them about a foot below the surface of the water. The entrails lay floating on the water, in tiny waves. He put her bones out and covered them with a robe. He took the mocassins, and so he left and arrived at the peak where the headland could be seen. He took one step forward and arrived at the headland. He was there almost at once.

A man was standing there. The boy gave him the paper. "Ho! Hurry," said the man.

He pulled off the moccasins the old woman had given him and faced them in her direction, thinking, "They will go home." And the man gave him some similar moccasins and another piece of paper. "When you get there, show the paper to him. When you get there, take off the moccasins and place them at the door," said the man.

"Yes," said the young man.

"Hurry," said the man.

The young man hurried along and arrived at the place. Again a man was standing there. He gave him the paper. "Ho! Hurry," said the man. He pulled off the moccasins that had been given to him and placed them at the door.

And the other man gave him a pair of moccasins and said, "Put these on and go. Another man stands in a certain place. Go there. Do your best," and again, in the same fashion, he gave him moccasins and a piece of paper.

He arrived there too. "Oho! Hurry!" said the man. The young man placed the moccasins outside. And the man said, "In that unseen place lies a stream. When you take sudden steps forward, do not look at the water."

And it was so, and he departed. He reached the other side. He pulled off the moccasins for the owner. Evening came. It was still the evening of that day when he had killed the old woman. He moved up the hill, following the course of the creek. When he reached the very middle of the path around the lake, he found Snake. He was coming back around the lake. He was following his own trail on the way home again. The young man changed himself into a red-tail fish.

Little Fish lay still, making little ripples in the water. Snake lay in sight on the hill. Snake said to him, "I am looking for someone. Since you move about on the surface, in the open, even if a bird comes flying along, you would see it."

"Yes, that is true. But I have not seen him. If I do see him I will tell you," said Fish.

So Snake moved along with the current. He followed along right at the edge of the stream. Eventually he came upon a gray toad. Snake went up to him. "You might have seen a person coming along here. Even if there was only a shadow, you might have seen him. I am looking for him," he said.

"Yes, my friend, as I was lying here during the day, a person came by here. A person walked by, shaking the ground with his walking. Where he was going and where he came from I don't know," said Toad.

"That was him. That was the one I am looking for," said Snake, and he left again, following the course of the stream. He thought that he had cut him off, but the young man did not arrive. So again Snake moved along the bank, but there was no one there. He moved on, following his own trail by the stream. Finally he came back down the middle of a path on the bank of this very large stream, and there was a very large fish lying in the shallow water along the bank.

Snake asked him, "I am looking for someone, my friend, but I have not yet found him."

"The one you were talking with back there is him," said Fish.

"Is that possible? I went through all that trouble looking for him, and even when I saw him I did not recognize him," said Snake, and so he went home.

But the large fish was the young man. And when Snake reached home, where he had first taken the young man, he met a muskrat pushing up the stream. Snake grabbed him. "I want to ask you something," he said.

"What would you want to ask me? Talk fast," said Muskrat.

"I was talking to someone and I left him here, and I think that you are the one," said Snake.

"No," said Muskrat. "But I remember the person you were talking with. As I was sitting here, a man came along, walking right over my lodge, despite all of my efforts to stop him. His weight broke a stick under the water. When he asked me to go under water with him, he broke for me whatever I carried home to sit on," said Muskrat.

And Snake said, "On what day was that?"

"Why, yesterday, when the sun was very high, he came along, passing over my lodge. And as he walked by he broke a stick by stepping on it," said Muskrat, and Snake believed him.

Again he left, moving along the bank of the stream. And along this stream bank the red willows were leaning over close to the water. A red-breasted turtle was sitting there. Snake grabbed him.

"I want to ask you something. I have been looking for someone, but I have not been able to find him," said Snake.

"I can't help you. I have just returned. I just came back from this pond. Therefore, my friend, I don't know anything at all about this," said Red-Breasted Turtle.

Snake traveled on. A very green frog was sitting there, floating by the edge of the shallow water. Snake came to him. "My friend, I have been looking for someone for some time now. Perhaps you have seen him," he said.

"Yes," said Frog.

"Tell me about it. I have been looking for someone for a long time, but I have not found him. I hope that you will tell me exactly about it if you have seen him," said Snake.

"Fine. My Friend, very late yesterday evening, as I was sitting in an eddy at this place behind us, I saw the shadow of someone," said Frog.

"Yes, my Friend, that is him. I am looking for him," said Snake, and so he went upstream on that side. Again he moved along following the course of the stream. And Big Turtle was moving along, pushing up some green scum in the lake.

Snake jumped onto his back. "My Friend, I want to ask you something. Come out of the water," he said.

"Why? What do you want to ask me? If that person is moving about here and you do not recognize him, he will kill you, so you had better give this thing up," said Big Turtle.

Snake drew himself up and coiled, with his head held high. He was thinking that Big Turtle was the one he was after. "My Friend, tell me the truth," he said.

"Well, what I have told you, I told you truly. Give it up. If that person is moving about and you do not recognize him, he will kill you," said Big Turtle, but still Snake was coiling to strike.

"This is the one," he was thinking. "Come, my friend, tell me," said Snake. "I have suffered a great deal. Tell me."

"How strange. He will not listen to his friend," thought Big Turtle. "I will tell you," he said.

"Do your best," said Snake.

"The person you are looking for is lying in that very large stream you were walking along. Do your best," said Big Turtle.

"My Friend, are you telling the truth?" asked Snake.

"He is there. Do your best. If you don't recognize him, he will kill you," said Big Turtle.

"I am going there," said Snake.

"Do your best. If you don't recognize him, he will kill you," said Big Turtle.

He went out into the middle of the stream where the person he was looking for was lying. Snake moved along. He arrived at the eddy of the stream. It moved fast and carried him under the water. It was the person who hated him; he had changed himself into water, the eddy. Although Snake tried to reach the surface of the water, the eddy held him under. So he drowned. The young man killed Snake.

Then the young man went home, and he eventually got there.

The Warriors and the Three Snakes
Told by Nudanacha

Some men who were on the warpath had reached their destination and were camping on their way home again. They found some large logs in the place where they intended to sleep. It was a good place to camp with these three big logs lying around.

Day came, and there was a very high wind. The war chief looked around, and he saw that the three logs were three immense snakes.

"Ho! Followers, this is very bad. Get up," he ordered.

All the snakes were lying with their mouths wide open. The men took hold of each other, but the high wind continued to blow the men along toward the snakes' mouths. The one at the end was crying.

He said, "Ho! I have a plan," and so they gave the snakes all their possessions, such as arrows, moccasins, and knives. The snakes then closed their mouths, and the wind stopped. The snakes had made the high wind by lying with their mouths open.

The men would have to jump over the snakes to get home, however.

"Ho! One of you jump first," said the war chief, but no one wanted to, for they were all afraid.

"Oho! Then I will be the one. Since the war chief is supposed to be one of those who try anything at all that needs to be done, without fear of death, I will be the one to give it a try," said the war chief.

The middle snake was lying right in the war chief's path, his mouth wide open. The war chief jumped right over him and said, "Oho! Be strong."

Then the other war chief jumped in the same way and went homeward too.

"Oho! Be strong. Try to do just what we did, and we'll be on our way home," they said to the others.

So one by one they tried, one after another, until thirty had jumped. Again one leaped, and yet another. Everyone who made it across shouted encouragement to the others.

But the last one hesitated. Tears ran down his face.

The war chief shouted to him, "Ho! You are a man. We are men and so we are on the move. You are wrong to cry."

But when the man tried to jump over, the snake arched its back, forming a hump, over which the man stumbled and fell. Then the snake threw the man onto his back and swallowed him whole.

"Oho!" said the war chief. "We must go without him. When a person wishes to die someplace, he simply dies," and so they went homeward.

They usually camped along the way home at regular intervals. Two scouts went out and reported,

"O War Chief, there are two lodges over there."

"Oho!" he said.

"War Chief, we are tired. We want to ride," they said.

"Oho," he answered.

They rode in that direction and stopped at the very edge of the lodges.

Both war chiefs went into the village. They found a great many horses standing in a line. The war chiefs drove them ahead of them back to their comrades. After a while they had returned with the horses.

"Go ahead and tell them," said the one war chief. And so the other one went ahead and told them.

"Your war chief has done a good thing."

"Ho! War Chief," they all called. And the war chief who had the horses came along with them.

"Oho!" he called. "Tie up these horses with your lines," and they did. They drove the horses with them on their way home. They camped as they went along the road home.

Soon they reached the lodges they had left when they ventured out against their enemies. They gave all the horses they had brought back to the women and old men.

COMMENTARY

This story provides a narrative example of a full trial of discretion and then a bold display of courage, the sequence of action most favored by the Plains Indian.

Dorsey provides another narrative display of attitudes toward courage:

"An old man had a son who reached manhood, and went into a fight, from which he returned wounded, but not dangerously so. The son asked his father saying, 'Father, what thing is hard to endure?' He expected the father to say, 'My Child, for one to be wounded in battle is hard to endure.'

"Had he said this, the son would have replied, 'Yes, Father, I shall live.'

"The father suspected this, so he made a different reply: 'Nothing, My Child. The only thing hard to bear is to put on leggings again before they have been warmed by the fire.'

"So the son became angry and said, 'My Father, I will die,' "[1]

Dorsey does not finish the story, but I suspect that the son lived and, with a father that wise, he too probably became a wise man.

The Warriors Who Were Changed into Snakes
Told by Nudanacha

Twenty men once went on the warpath. They had eaten nothing and were very troubled from their hunger. They had made a circuit and were coming back.

"That is it, Men. Keep watch as you march. Do your best at scouting about," said the war chief, and soon one came running back.

"O War Chief, I think an animal is moving around over there," he said.

"What kind of animal do you think it is?" asked the war chief.

"War Chief, I think that it is a buffalo," said the runner.

"Oho!" said the war chief. "If that is so, we just may live. Go again and look carefully at it."

One ran off and saw that the buffalo bull was walking along. "No! Let's just wait until the war chief comes along," said the rest of the scouts, and they walked along slowly waiting for him to appear.

"Sit down here," he said to them, and he walked off. "Lie down and watch me." He stood up with the idea of intercepting the buffalo, and soon the buffalo bull came toward him. He aimed at it. He brought his gun up suddenly. He aimed directly at it. But when it drew near, he could see that it was a strange kind of animal. He was very frightened by it. He brought his gun back down.

He thought, "If I don't shoot at him, he will probably kill me. But if I shoot at him and miss, he will most certainly kill me." All this time he lay in fear of the animal, which was a huge snake, with a rattle as big as a man's head. Whenever he lifted his tail, he rattled it, "Chu!"

The chief shot at the snake, which had stopped and was standing perfectly still. When he shot at it, it suddenly dropped. "Now our warchief has killed him," they all said.

The war chief went back to them, and when he got there he said, "Ah, Followers, I have killed a very dangerous animal."

"War Chief, let us examine it to see exactly what kind of animal it is," they said.

"It is a big snake," he said.

"Really," they said. They were all curious and so went over to it. "Let's split it lengthwise with knives," War Chief said, and they did so.

They found that the snake was very fat and had a good odor, just like that of the buffaloes when Indians kill them. "O Chief, the smell is very good. It is just like that of buffalo," they said.

"Test it," said the war chief.

They lit a fire and put it on to cook. The fire was very hot. They were very, very hungry.

"Come, Followers, try it," said the war chief.

The sun had almost set, and so he said, "We will be camping here." They put sticks through the spareribs, running one end of each stick into the ground close to the fire. When the spareribs were cooked, they put them in a pile. Each one was uneasy about being the first to taste it, and so they just put it all into a pile.

Finally the war chief said, "Oho! Followers, bring a piece to me," and they took a piece to him, which he ate.

Soon he said, "Friends, it is good. It is just like the buffalo we eat," so everyone ate it, except one boy, who simply didn't want to eat it.

"Comrade, it is as good as the buffalo we eat. The odor is not bad. It is very good. Eat," said the war chief.

"I don't want to," said the boy.

They were sitting in a circle around the fire they had lit, but the boy sat a ways off. Eventually it grew dark and they all fell asleep, having eaten their fill.

Then after a while, however, the war chief said, "Oho! Followers, get up. Something is wrong," but they couldn't hear him, for, strangely enough, they had all changed into snakes. Even the war chief's body had changed partly into a snake; the whole of his one side was in the form of a snake now.

The war chief said, "Oho! You over there," calling to the boy, who ran over to him. "Come here! Look at us! Friend, you are saved because you were afraid to eat."

The boy stood crying and the war chief went on, "There is nothing that can be done. You alone will live. Try to get home. You can take everything that we have accumulated in our travels." And they gave him their charms.

"You have waited this long for us," they said, "but now you should go." But the boy was afraid to leave them.

"Put us all in one of the large robes and carry us on your back then. Put us on a good piece of land, on one of those large hills," said War Chief.

Day came. All were coiled up together and so the boy took them and put them into a large robe. He left, carrying them on his back. He took them to a high hill, where he left them. It was not a small hill. It was a hill with a curved top, like the one over there, with two trees right in the middle of the top. He put them there, at the bottom of the trees. Since they knew that he was about to go home, all the snakes coiled about his body. He left them and started for home.

When he returned to the lodges, he said, "The one who was our war chief ate an animal, and his body was changed into an animal of that sort. He said that this summer he wanted to see whatever he owned—you who are his relatives, the women and children, and even his horses," for the war chief who was now partly a snake had said, "In the summer I want to see the lodges, if nothing else."

So when it was summer, they broke camp. They went to the place.

"Here it is," said the boy.

And the people said, "Let's camp right here."

So everyone went there, women and children, everyone. And when they had settled, the snakes came into sight. They had made dens there.

"There they are. Don't be afraid of them. Those are the ones. Don't run from them. Stand still," said the boy.

Soon the snakes had coiled around the boy. They moved past him to where the people were standing in a row. The people mourned and cried;

they made a great uproar. And when the snakes had gone down the line, passing over the bodies of all the people, they were satisfied. The snakes were in a row before their dens, coiled together. They lay looking at all the people.

Their horses were tied there, as well as their packs, saddles, whips, bows, and the leggings which they had abandoned when they approached the great snake to kill him, and their moccasins too. All were put there.

Winter passed, and again the people broke camp and went to the place, but the snakes were not to be seen. The horses they had left were gone, but their manure was left behind. Therefore, the people thought they had taken the horses down into their dens.

COMMENTARY

Fletcher discusses food habits, and Dorsey specifically lists those foods not eaten by the Omaha, but neither mentions snake. It would appear from this tale, however, that the Omaha had an aversion to snake meat even before the advent of the white man.

The Bear Girl
Told by Nudanacha

Once there was a camp with some lodges. In the village lived a girl who was fully grown. And her mother used to comb her hair for her. One day the girl went for some wood, and she came home with some grass sticking in her hair.

"This is bad because I have just combed her hair for her. This is really bad," said the mother. You see, the girl was in love with a grizzly bear.

A man came along looking for a horse. He came across the grizzly bear lying on the ground.

The people all said, "He says that Grizzly Bear is lying up there. He is lying sound asleep in a den. Be careful that he does not kill one of the people. Everyone take guns." And so they got on horses and surrounded the bear.

The girl said, "Father, please bring me the skin of the grizzly bear."

They killed Grizzly Bear, and the girl's father asked the people, and so the skin was given to him. He said to the girl's mother, "Fasten the skin down over there."

But the girl took it away, for she had to hurry to get it before her mother. She sat working at it. She cried continually. As she sat working, her younger sister sat with her. And when the girl worked, she mourned for Grizzly Bear. She kept saying, "Etha!"

The younger girl called to her mother to tell her about this. "O Mother, when she works on the skin of Grizzly Bear, she keeps saying 'Etha!'"

And when the girl sat working again, it was the same thing again. She would say nothing but "Etha!" Again the girl called her mother to tell her about this.

"Mother, when she is working on the skin of Grizzly Bear, she says only 'Etha!' "

The girl finished the skin. She dried it. She arranged it just so.

The children were playing games, and the girl who had loved Grizzly Bear joined in the sport.

"Little Sister, go after my grizzly bear skin," she said, and the little sister brought it to her. Then the elder sister tied it on over the whole of her body. Then, growling like a grizzly bear, she charged them. Without exception they all ran in great confusion.

"The grizzly bear will attack us," said the boys and girls.

It was that way every time. She kept charging them. Finally, the fourth time, she became a grizzly bear. She killed all the girls she was playing with. Her little sister was the only one that remained. She destroyed everyone in the lodges.

She then slept alone in the den. She dug a corner in one part of the den, near the door, and she made the younger sister sit there. "You are probably hungry. Go to the lodges," said the elder sister.

The little sister went there and walked along, following the line of lodges, whose owners had been destroyed, and she returned to the den with a very full stomach. Again the next day the elder sister told her.

"Go there. You are probably hungry. You must eat."

And she sent her there again the following day, too.

Once, however, she followed the line of lodges and found four people there. They were sitting in the lodge. She recognized them. The four elder brothers of the Bear Girl had come home.

"O Elder Brothers! My sister has completely destroyed everyone in the village," she said. She stood there crying and telling them the story. "I alone am left of my people," she cried.

"Why is that?" they asked.

"Elder Brothers, my sister has become a grizzly bear."

They said, "When did she tell you to come back? Go. You can come back when the time arrives and she tells you to come here."

"No, Elder Brothers, I always walk for some time in the morning. Therefore, I shall have to come here at a certain time in the morning. Sleep over there by those trees, then I won't have so far to come in the morning and can spend a longer time with you," she said.

So the little girl went back, and the men left too. The little girl reached the den again. When she approached it, the Bear Girl sniffed the air.

"Why are you doing that?" asked the little sister.

"You have a fresh human smell," said the Bear Girl.

"No, Elder Sister, be careful. That is enough. Stop saying such things. It is not true," said the younger sister.

But the Bear Girl did not stop talking. "Younger Sister, you have a fresh human smell, I say," said Bear Girl. But finally she did stop saying such things.

They went to sleep and morning came. The Bear Girl said, "Go. Eat," and the girl departed. She rolled up her robe and put it over her shoulders.

The men scouted and one said, "Your younger sister is coming,"

When the girl got there, they immediately left with her. On the way they crossed a creek. One pulled off his leggings and carried his sister on his back. When he reached the other side, he put on his moccasins and his leggings and ran, going straight across the country.

Finally it was noon, and the girl had not returned to the den. So her elder sister followed the trail. She came to the place where they sat kindling the fire.

"No matter where you go, how could you ever escape from me?" she demanded. So the men ran and Bear Girl followed them. They left the four peaks behind. When they had just left the fourth peak out of sight, Bear Girl came into sight.

"Oho! Your sister has just come into sight. Do your best," they cried. And they went on, she following them. She almost caught them.

But the eldest man said, "Oho! I will give it a try," and they were nearly overtaken.

They put up thorns, very thick, with no space in between, but Bear Girl got through them, although she had a good deal of pain on account of the thorns. When she came up to them again, she said, "You have made me suffer a good deal, so you shall most certainly die."

"Come, Elder Brother, let me give it a try," said the next eldest man. They crossed a very small creek. He made a dense forest, through which Bear Girl simply could not force her way. He also caused there to be small bushes over a large area of land. So Bear Girl could not reach the end of the forest for a long time.

But once more she did approach them. In fact, she nearly caught them. Again she said to them, "Since you have made me suffer not a little bit, you will most certainly die."

"Now, Elder Brother, I will give it a try," said the youngest. He made very sharp thorns, resembling awls. They would cut right through your foot.

Bear Girl walked along, leaving blood with every step. But again she overtook them. And again she said to them, "I have said, 'Because you have made me suffer not a little bit, you will most certainly die.' "

"Oho! You just might be the one to die," said the eldest brother. And he made the ground crack apart. When she tried to jump over, the ground on each side went even further apart. And she fell headlong into the chasm.

All of the brothers ran back. They brought their guns. "Your sister has made us suffer a good deal too, so we will do to her what she said she would do to us." They gathered around her, shot at her, and killed her.

The ground came together as it had been before it parted.

COMMENTARY
The discovery of grass in the girl's hair is a subtle clue that she had been sporting on the ground, a sensitive narrative motif.

Etha is an exclamation of surprise or sorrow.

Marriages between bears and human women are common in America Indian folk tales, but more often than not on the Plains the marriage is forced by the bear after the girl is abducted, later to be rescued by a brother or lover. Just north of Macy on the Omaha tribal reservation there is Big Bear Hollow, which is the subject of a legend of this theme. A bear terrorizes a nearby village, finally carrying off one of the most beautiful girls from the village. The hero, the girl's lover, like all others, fails in his rescue attempts because the big bear, a grizzly, and his retinue of smaller bears are too strong. Finally the hero goes off and adopts two grizzly cubs, which he raises to serve him. Together they regain the young woman.[2]

Adventures of Puma, the Adopted Son of a Man
Told by Pathinanpaji

A man was keeping a puma. He had no children at all, and so he regarded this puma as his child.

One day a young man came walking along. He arrived near the lodge and saw some deer grazing. He hid from them and crept along to the lodge, for he had no gun. But neither did the father of Puma.

The young man said, "O Father, some deer are out there. They would be very easy to kill. Lend me a gun."

"Oho! I don't have a gun," he said. But he spoke to Puma, the younger brother of the young man. "Go with your younger brother. Be careful not to scold him. Make a habit of being very gentle with your younger brother," said the man. Then Puma went with the young man.

"There they are, Younger Brother," said the young man, pointing to the deer. And the moment he pointed to the deer, Puma attacked them. He killed one of them right where they stood.

"I prize my younger son because he always does that," said the father to the young man. "If you want any kind of animal, just tell your younger brother."

So Puma continued to kill all manner of animals.

"Father, I want to go hunting with Younger Brother," said the young man.

The father took him and said, "There are deer just out of sight, where that forest stands on that hillside. Sit here on this hill and wait for your younger brother."

So he sat on the hill waiting for Puma. When Puma came, the young man said, "O Younger Brother, this is where my father said that you might hunt." And the young man sat on the hill while Puma ran into the dense forest.

He seized a deer and made it cry out bitterly because he had it in his claws. He came back to the hill dragging it along. He hung it up.

Then the young man said, "I want a black bear, O Younger Brother, so that I might eat the fat meat." So Puma caught one. He came back, having taken some time to kill it. Puma came back rubbing himself, for he had gotten foam on himself while fighting the bear.

Then the young man said, "Ho! Younger Brother, I want a beaver." The water was dammed up, but Puma jumped into the water and finally came back, bringing a large beaver.

"O Younger Brother, I want an otter," said the young man, and Puma killed an otter.

Their father was feeling sad, and so he went looking for them. First he came to the place where the deer had been killed. And then he came to the place where the black bear had been killed. And then he came to the place where the beaver had been killed. And then he came to the place where the otter had been killed.

"This is no good, My Child. You are killing your younger brother with work. Stop right now," he scolded. And they went home carrying those animals. The father carried all of them on his back.

When they got home, the two sons sat eating. Puma was the principal son, for he had a father, so he sat with his father, near him but not touching him. And the mother took care of her child in the same way.

After that the young man went hunting regularly with his adopted brother.

"When your younger brother has killed just one animal, carry it on your back and come home with him," said the father. The father was afraid that his son would run himself mad if he killed too many animals.

And so things went. The younger brother would have Puma kill just one animal and then they would come home. But once they went out hunting and the father said, "Go out there with your brother to that place where the trees stand very thick along the creek that comes from so far away." And they went there.

After they had been there a long time, Puma killed a male elk that was there. Then the young man said, "O Younger Brother, kill a grizzly bear," and at length Puma caught one. He fought him. The grizzly bear cried out, "Ha! ha! ha!" but soon he was dead. But Puma, too, had been wounded very badly by the bear's claws on both sides of his body, under the forelegs.

Then the young man made Puma attack a buffalo bull. He killed the bull. And again the young man said, "O Younger Brother, track down a black bear." And all this time Puma was swelling up where he had been bitten on the body under his forelegs, in fact, all over his body. But still the young man made him hunt, for he was not satisfied.

Finally the father went out to find the hunters, his sons. He followed the trail, and he came to the place where the grizzly bear had been killed, and his heart was sad. Then he came to the place where Puma was dragging along the black bear he had just killed. Puma embraced his father.

"You should not send your younger brother after such savage animals," said the father.

"Yes, Father," said the young man.

"Do not even send your brother out after one any more."

And again the father carried back all of the animals that had been killed. He carried them on his back. The mother cried bitterly and embraced Puma when she saw his blood. And the woman repeated to the young man the words that his father had spoken to him.

"Even if you see one, do not tell your younger brother about it any more. You came very close to making me mourn in sorrow," she said.

After that, they stayed home, letting Puma recover. They didn't need to go hunting for they had plenty of food. But one day Puma was missing, very early one morning.

"Father, Younger Brother is missing," said the young man.

The father said, "Your younger brother has gone hunting. He will come back soon," and when the sun was high, Puma did come home. He pushed against his father to get his attention. He went out and his father followed him. They went toward the place where they got water for the household. When they got there, a large beaver was lying there. They moved on downstream, and a large beaver was lying there too. Puma had killed just these two. The father carried them home on his back.

And about the third day the young man went with him. The puma killed two deer. He killed two black bears. He killed many animals. He killed ten: deer, black bears, and beaver. They didn't reach home until the sun was very low.

"Father, Younger Brother has killed very many animals," said the youth.

The next day they went out to carry the meat back to camp. The young man went with his father and mother. Puma did not go. Some people attacked the family. First they killed the young man. Then they killed the woman. The father barely reached home.

"They have killed your mother and elder brother. Let's go there," the father said to Puma.

Just as they got there, the men killed Puma's father. The puma attacked the men. Puma killed one and his horse. He charged them again. Puma fought one after the other. He killed another man along with the horse that he was on, and so on, right through the ranks of the enemy. He killed one hundred. He tore them with his claws, he pulled them from their horses, and he killed them.

When the sun set, only one man was left.

COMMENTARY

It has been speculated that one of the reasons so many of the Western World's fairytales deal with stepchildren and stepparents is that the hard life of the Middle Ages created so very many orphans, who, out of their insecure lives, created the themes that survive in folklore.

It would be easy and logical to propose the same rationale for the many Omaha tales that tell of the painful situation of the adopted child. The fact that this child is a puma only underlines the intense feeling of alienation of the stepchild. The puma is loved by the parents and is faithful in his devotion, but he can never really be a brother or a son.

The Vigil
Told by Francis La Flesche to Franz Boaz

A man called his people to a council one day. He was one who had the office of assembling a council of war. The men came quickly to the lodge where the council was being held. When all of the men were there, the caller said, "For a long time we have not had a good time. The tribes around us are imposing on our good nature and are closing in on us. They steal our horses and kill our women. Today I have decided that we should face them, and that is why I have called you together here. You have heard what I say. Now, will you go against them?"

There was a shout of approval. One man arose and said, "Let the keeper of the war pipe be brought before us with the pipe," and the keeper of the pipe responded to the command.

Again the man arose and said, "Have the messengers bring Little Hawk before us." When Little Hawk had been brought before them, they all sat down, but one person arose and asked him a question.

"We have selected you for the position of chief of this war party. Are you willing to go?"

To this Little Hawk replied yes, and, arising, he continued.

"As my helper I would like to have my father, Washoshe."

So the ceremonial messengers brought the father before the gathering. Before taking his seat Washoshe said, "My son wants me to be his assistant and I am willing to accept the position. On behalf of my son I beg you not to omit any of the rites that pertain to procedures like this, and avoid mistakes that can be criticized. In this respect I hope that you all will give him sympathy and keep strictly to the words of the ritual."

Washoshe then sat down beside his son and said to him, "My son, you must now undress," and when he had finished undressing as he had been instructed, he came out, wearing only a loin cloth and mocassins. His father then arose again, took the tobacco bag by its strap, put it around the young war leader's neck, and handed him the little pipe, saying, "My Son, whatever you encounter that does not bear on your purpose must be ignored. You must think only of Wakonda. Go now!"

So, fully prepared and instructed, the young war chief went out crying, as was the custom on such occasions. First he cried quietly, but when he came out of the house he cried aloud, making the forests echo. While he was crying, he offered his pipe to Wakonda.

Then the assistant ordered him to give seven days to finish his appeal and wanderings. As evening approached and darkness came and men's faces could not be easily distinguished, he went to the creek and bathed his face in the cool water. Then he went and sat down, leaning against a small tree to rest.

He was awakened by the crashing of horns. Two buffalo bulls were struggling in a fight. Toward morning they stopped. As the sun appeared and day began again, the young chief took his little pipe and filled it with fresh tobacco, offering it in prayer to Wakonda.

Having finished his prayer, he felt something very cold on his bare back. He felt it crawl over his shoulder and on down his chest until it finally reached the ground. Looking carefully he saw that it was a rattlesnake. But he had not been harmed. Slowly the snake moved on.

Continuing his wailing, the young chief walked over the hills. In the evening he again settled down to rest under a tree. As he slept he heard the sound of battle and awoke to see two bull elk who were battling and very nearly stepping on the war chief. They circled and fought until midnight, at which time they stopped the struggle.

On the sixth night he again sought a place to rest, but just as he was about to close his eyes in sleep, he felt the flap of wings, and when he opened his eyes he saw two birds chasing each other in flight. Again and again they passed right in front of him. Being very anxious to find out what kind of birds they were, he placed his head near the ground and when they returned he could plainly see that one was a hawk and the other an owl. Their movements interested him very much. They chased each other, each time coming nearer, until they almost touched his face with their wings. All night they fought, showing no apparent signs of fatigue.

By now he had changed his position and was sitting upright with his knees drawn up. It was nearly morning when he felt the hawk fluttering under his legs.

It said, "Friend, I need your protection until daylight, which will be very soon."

The owl stood a little ways off and said, "Whatever promises that person makes, I will also offer you. Perhaps he told you that he has the power to attack at night; well, he does not possess such a gift. That gift is mine. Push him over here toward me!"

The hawk won the heart of the boy because he was such a small bird.

Again the owl said, "Push him over here toward me!"

The sun was now coming up and day beginning. The hawk said to the young man, "The time has come for me to act. Reach down and pull the longest feather you can find from my left wing. This is your reward for protecting me. Whenever you go into battle, tie the feather to your scalp lock. Now I am going to attack that owl. Stay here and watch me."

With great speed he flew to the top of a nearby tree. Then, with piercing cries he attacked the owl, who fought back with great strength, for he was afraid of the hawk now. With a mighty stroke the hawk severed the head of the owl from its body, which fell to the ground. When this had been done, the hawk returned to the tree and again spoke to the young brave.

"When you go to attack your enemies, always do it in the same way as I have just done, and don't forget to think of me as you are doing it."

Now, the young leader felt that his vigil was finished and he started for home. He was very tired from fasting and from his loss of sleep. At the head of a hollow he saw a willow tree and there he sat down to rest.

Suddenly he heard a voice, like a man's voice, saying to him, "Son, your little ones shall lean on me for rest and protection. They shall have long life." The warrior found that it was the willow tree speaking to him, the tree that never dies.

The exhausted warrior finally reached his home. After a few nights of rest, he set out with his warriors on the march to the enemies' country.

They came home afterward in great triumph.

COMMENTARY

The father's insistence on absolute accuracy in the performance of the rituals leading up to the departure on the warpath is based on the common Indian belief that any mistakes or departures in the performance or recitation of a ritual detracted from its effectiveness. In other words, a wrong word, a forgotten line, an omitted gesture might mean the loss of many warriors, including his son. Indeed, his role as ritual assistant was to insure that the boy make no mistakes.

Readers of Mari Sandoz's *Crazy Horse* or John Neihardt's *Black Elk Speaks* will recognize the importance of the young man's quest for a vision which will reveal to him a bit of the divine power. Fasting and lack of sleep encouraged the onset of such visions, much the same as peyote does in the institution of the Native American Church today. The Plains Indian believes—wisely, I feel—that mere man does not possess sufficient understanding or wisdom to grasp the whole of god or even to understand those small segments that may be granted to him in such visions. The only recourse then is to be content with whatever enlightenment is granted man during his brief years here on earth, to accept the fragments, obey them, emulate them, respect them, and to wear the feather without fully grasping its meaning.

Creation and Origin

All peoples question where the things that surround them came from. Everything has a beginning. Where was that of this world? How did man, so very singular a being, come to live on this earth?

The answers are sometimes inaccurate, contradictory, or illogical, but upon entering the realm of traditional narrative, the tales are accorded the mantle of Truth. Then as they become also divine histories, myths, they gain an even higher level of undeniable truth that may transcend the understanding of mere man.

More surprising to me, however, is the remarkable historical accuracy of some of the creation myths, albeit they are often blurred as they are simplified and compacted by time.

Creation Myth

In the beginning the people were in water. They opened their eyes, but they could not see anything. From that we get the child name in the Honga Clan, Eyes-Open-in-the-Water. As the people came out of the water they saw the day, so we have the child name, Sees-the-Clear-Sky. When they came out of the water they were naked and without shame. But after many days passed, they wanted to be covered. They took the fiber of weeds and grass and wove it about their loins for covering.

The people lived near a large body of water in a wooded country where there was game. The men hunted the deer with clubs; they did not know how to use the bow. The people wandered about the shores of the great water and were poor and cold. And the people thought, "What shall we do to help ourselves?"

They began chipping stones. They found a bluish stone that was easily flaked and chipped, and they made knives and arrowheads out of it. Now they had knives and arrows, but they were still suffering from the cold, and the people thought, "Now what shall we do?"

A man found an elm root that was very dry, and he dug a hole in it and put a stick in and rubbed it. Then smoke came. He smelled it. Then the people smelled it and came near; others helped him rub. At last a spark came; they blew this into a flame, and so fire came to warm the people and to cook their food. After this the people built grass houses; they cut the grass with the shoulder blade of a deer.

Now the people had fire and ate their meat roasted, but they got tired of roast meat, and the people thought, "How could we cook our meat differently?"

A man found a bunch of clay that stuck together nicely. He brought sand to mix with it, and then he molded it into a vessel. He gathered grass and made a pile. He put the clay vessel in the middle of grass, set it on fire, and made the clay vessel hard. Then, after a time, he put water into the vessel and it held water. This was good. So he put water into the vessel and then meat into it and put the vessel over the fire, and the people had boiled meat to eat.

Their grass coverings would fuzz and drop off. It was difficult to gather and keep these coverings. The people were dissatisfied, and again the people thought, "How can we have something different to wear?" Up to now they had been throwing away the hides they had taken from the game, but now they took their stone knives and scraped down the hides, making them thin. They rubbed the hides with grass and their hands to make them soft, and then they used the hides for their clothing. Now they had clothes and were comfortable.

The women had to break the dry wood to keep up the fires. The men were concerned about the women and tried to figure a way to make life easier for them. So they made the stone ax with a groove and put a handle on the ax and fastened it with rawhide.

The women used this, but they wanted something better for splitting wood, so they made wedges of stone.

The grass shelter was also unsatisfactory, so the people thought, "How can we better ourselves?" So they substituted bark for grass as a covering for their houses.

Then the people decided to put skins on the poles of their dwellings. They tried deerskins, but they were too small. They tried elk, but both deer and elk skins got hard and unmanageable under the effects of the sun and rain. So they forgot the idea of skins and returned to covering their lodges with bark.

Until they had the buffalo, the people could not have good tents. They took one of the leg bones of the deer, splintered it, and made it sharp for an awl and with sinew sewed the buffalo skin, and made comfortable tent covers.

Then a man in wandering about found some kernels—blue, red, and white. He thought he had found something of great value, so he hid them in a mound. One day he thought he would go see if they were safe. When he came to the mound, he found it covered with stalks with ears bearing kernels of these colors. He took an ear of each kind and gave the rest to the people to experiment with. They tried it for food, found it good, and have ever since called it their life.

As soon as the people found the corn to be good, they thought about making mounds like that in which the kernels had been hid. So they took the shoulder blade of the elk and built mounds like the first and buried the corn in them. So the corn grew and the people had plenty of food.

In their wanderings the people reached the forests where the birch trees grew and where there were great lakes. Here they made birchbark canoes and traveled in them around the shores of the lakes. A man in his wanderings discovered two young animals and carried them home. He fed them and they grew large and were friendly. He discovered that these animals would carry burdens, so he put a harness on them to which poles were fastened, and they became burden bearers. Before that every burden had to be carried on the back. The people bred the dogs and they were a help to the people.

COMMENTARY

This tale probably offers a fairly accurate encapsuling of Omaha tribal history. They did once live near the Great Lakes, where their homes were probably grass or bark wickiups. The discoveries of fire, skin clothing, corn, and the work dog were significant enough events to be recorded in this simple myth.

Omaha names were arranged within clans, some names occurring in two lists. My own name, *Tenugagahi*, or "Buffalo Chief," could be in either the Buffalo Clan or the Wind Clan. Thus, a child's name in the Honga Clan could be, as mentioned in the opening passage, "Eyes-Open-in-the-Water."

Story of Creation
Told by Standing Buffalo

When I was a boy I often asked my mother where my people came from, but she would not tell me until one day she said, "I will give you the story as it has been handed down from generation to generation.

"In the real beginning Wakonda made the *Washazhe*—men, women, and children. After they were made, he said, 'Go!' So the people took all they had, carried their children, and started toward the setting sun. They traveled until they came to a great water. Seeing they could go no further, they halted. Again Wakonda said, 'Go!' and so once more they started out, wondering what would happen to them.

"As they were about to step into the water, there appeared some rocks from under the water. They were projecting just above the water, and there were others just below the surface of the water. The people walked on these stones, stepping from stone to stone, until they came to land.

"When they were again standing on the dry land, a wind came up and the water became so violent that it threw the rocks up on the dry land, and they became great cliffs. Therefore, when men enter the sweat lodge, they thank the stones for preserving their lives and ask for a continuation of their help that their lives may be long.

"The people lived here on the shore, but again Wakonda said, 'Go!' and again they started out and traveled until they came to a people whose appearance was like their own. But they did not know whether they were friends or enemies, so they charged each other as if for battle. In the midst of the confusion Wakonda said, 'Stop!' and the people obeyed him. They talked with each other and found that they spoke the same language, and they became friends.

"Wakonda gave the people a bow, a dog, and a grain of corn. The people made other bows like the one given them and learned to use them for killing wild animals for food and to make clothing out of their skins. The dogs multiplied and were used for burden-bearers and for hunting. They planted the corn and when it grew they found that it was good to eat, and they continued to plant it.

"The people traveled on and came to a lake. There the Omaha found a Sacred Tree and took it with them. The people [Ponca] went on and came

to a river now called *Nishude* [the Missouri]. They traveled along its banks
until they came to a place where they could cross the water. From there they
traveled back across the land and came to the river now called *Nibthaska*
[the Platte]. They followed the river and it led them back to the Missouri.

"Again they went up this river until they came to a river now called
Niobrara, where we live today."

COMMENTARY

This tale, also taken from Fletcher and La Flesche as was the previous
myth, emphasizes the folk memories of the years of migration and the
fundamental importance of corn, true to the present day, and again the
memories of the importance of the dog before the advent of the horse.

Fletcher also underlines the obeisance to the rock during the sweat bath.
She recorded the following text as given her by a member of the Pebble
Society; it summarizes the importance of the rock and the ritual.

At the beginning all things were in the mind of Wakonda. All
creatures, including man, were spirits. They moved about in space
between the earth and the stars, the heavens. They were seeking a place
where they could come into a bodily existence. They ascended to the
sun, but the sun was not fitted for their abode. They moved on to the
moon and found that it also was not good for their home. Then they
descended to the earth. They saw it was covered with water. They
floated through the air to the north, the east, the south, and the west,
and found no dry land. They were sorely grieved. Suddenly from the
midst of the water uprose a great rock. It burst into flames, and the
waters floated into the air in clouds. Dry land appeared. The grasses
and the trees grew. The hosts of spirits descended and became flesh
and blood. They fed on the seeds of the grasses and the fruits of the
trees, and the land vibrated with their expressions of joy and gratitude
to Wakonda, the maker of all things.

The following song was sung as the men entered the sweat lodge.

He! You, our lodge here, eska!
Our dwelling place, eska!
And you great animals, eska!
He! You who have made this covering for us, eska!
You have told these little ones,
You have told them
To remember you reverently, eska!

He! You, our lodge frame, eska!
You stand over us with bent back,
With stooped shoulders you stand over us.

There you stand.
You have said that my little ones should speak of you,
Brushing the hair from your forehead, eska!
The hair of your head,
The grass that grows about you,
Your whitened hair, eska!
These hairs grow on your head, eska!

The paths that these little ones should take, eska!
Whatever way they can escape from danger, eska!
Wherever they can escape!
Their shoulders shall be bent with age as they walk,
As they walk the well-worn path,
Shading their eyes with their hands,
As they walk in their old age, eska!

He! Old one, eska!
Old rock, eska!
Venerable one, eska!
He! I have taught these little ones
And they will obey me, eska!
Old one, eska!
He!
He! You, who have never moved through all time,
There you sit, eska!
There you sit, directly in the storm,
There in the middle of the wind, eska!
Old one, eska!
He! Small grasses grow around you, eska!
You sit there as if they were your nest, eska!
He! There you sit, covered with bird droppings, eska!
Your brow is covered with the downy feathers of birds, eska!
Venerable one, eska!

You, you stand next in power, eska!
You, you stand next in power, eska!
He! you are water, eska!
You are water,
Flowing for unknown ages, eska!
He! These little ones have drunk of you,
But your mysteries remain hidden from them!
These little ones want your touch, eska!
He! This is what my little ones want, eska!
They want to partake of your strength, eska!
So it is

That the little ones want to walk closely by your side, eska!
Old one, this is what they want.

Fletcher notes that *He!* is an exclamation involving the idea of supplication and distress and that *eska* is a refrain meaning "I desire," "I crave," and, sometimes, "I implore."

She continues. "In the ritual the primal rock, referred to in the opening ritual, that which rose from the waters, is addressed by the term 'venerable man,' whose assistance is called to the 'little ones,' the patients about to be ministered to. [The sweat lodge was primarily used for medical purposes: Welsch] . . . The small grass refers to the means of heating the stones placed in the sweat lodge as a 'dwelling place.' Again, the abiding quality of the rock is referred to: . . . Immovable the rocks have remained while the droppings of the birds and their molting feathers have fallen season after season. . . .

"The standing house, the sweat lodge, is next spoken of; the animals who have given it a covering are remembered gratefully, the bent-over boughs are mentioned and compared to the bent shoulders of the old men whose long life is like 'the well-beaten path.' The prayer for the gift of life for the 'little ones,' whose health is desired, is curiously and poetically blended with this description of the standing house, wherein the power is sought by which they, the 'little ones,' 'shall desire to walk closely' by the side of the long-lived rock, and, because of these supplications to rock and ever-flowing water, shall secure health and length of days. These rituals, naively poetic, reveal how completely man is identified with nature in the mind of the native."[1]

The Sun and the Moon
Told by Pathinanpaji

"I am out of patience with you. When I call the people together, you scatter them, and many of them are lost in this way," said the Moon.

"I," said the Sun, "have wanted the people to grow, and so I have scattered them, but you have put them into darkness and have therefore been killing many of them with hunger. Ho ye! People, many of you will grow up. I will look down on you from above. I will guide you in whatever things you attempt."

The Moon said, "And I will live in this way, too. I will bring you together, and when it is dark you will gather together and sleep. In fact, I myself will guide you in whatever you do. And we will walk in the same road, one after the other. I will walk behind him."

The Moon is just like a woman: she always walks with a kettle on her arm.

COMMENTARY

Dorsey comments: "The Sun and Moon used to reside on the earth prior to their quarrel recorded in the myth, of which this fragment is all that has been preserved."

The Shell Society

Once a long time in the past, a stranger came to the village. He was entertained by the chief and all the prominent men. There was a man living in the tribe who, while he was a good hunter, was also a quiet man who never pushed himself into notice. His modest behavior was a source of worry to his wife, who was ambitious and did not share her husband's aversion to notice. She heard about the stranger's presence and noticed how much attention was being paid to him, so she decided to have her husband entertain this man too.

She said to her husband, "You will never be an important man in our tribe if you don't push yourself forward. You must ask this stranger to our lodge. I will prepare a feast and you can entertain him, just as all the other men are doing." She called her eldest son and said, "Go to the chief's house and tell him that his guest is invited to your father's house. Mention your father's name."

Then she set about making the tent clean and putting everything in order. She cooked food, spread a robe on the seat of honor, and was ready for the guest. The boy did as his mother had told him. When he delivered the message, the chief, who knew the retiring nature of the boy's father, asked him, "Did your father send you?" The boy answered yes.

In due time the stranger came. He was wearing his hair roached, his leggings were yellow and embroidered, his mocassins were black, and, while he had no shirt, he wore his robe with the hair outside. He had a fine bow and at his back a quiver of otter skin filled with arrows. The man, his wife, and the four children were all dressed in their best and were waiting to greet the stranger.

The eldest two of the children were boys, the third was a girl, and the youngest was a boy. All of them were healthy and well formed. The wife set before their guest deer meat and beans cooked with raccoon fat. He ate and talked with the family, and then he thanked them and left.

Soon he left the village and was not heard of again that summer or the following winter. When spring came, the stranger again appeared and was treated with honor by the chiefs and leading men. And, again, the woman took the initiative in inviting the stranger to her lodge, and, again, the chief asked the son who brought the invitation, "Did your father send you?" and the boy again answered yes.

He thanked them again, but he told them nothing about himself, and he left their lodge. Another year passed and spring came and so did the stranger. Once more the son carried the invitation and the chief asked him the same question and got the same answer. The stranger came, enjoyed their hospitality, and left, leaving the man and his wife in ignorance as to who and what he was. Nor did anyone know anything about the stranger.

The fourth spring came, and so did the stranger, and the same invitation was extended, to be questioned by the chief and answered by the boy in the same way as before. The stranger was received as he had been for three years, but this time, as he was thanking them, he said, "I am a being of the Mysteries. I have been looking for the proper people to instruct in the knowledge of these Mysteries. You have shown that you are interested in what I have to bring, for this knowledge can only be given to those who seek it. You have entertained me four times at the proper season. I have observed you and I am satisfied that you are the ones to receive knowledge of the Mysteries. Everything is ready now for me to fulfill my purpose. Now is the time for the people to go away on the hunt. I want you to stay where you are. When the people have gone, then we will travel for a season. During that time I shall teach you these Mysteries. I shall expect a return from you. I will tell you what it must be at the appropriate time."

The tribe moved off to hunt, but the man, his wife, their children, and the stranger remained behind. At night, as they all lay down to sleep, the father kept wondering about the stranger and lay awake watching him. The stranger pretended to be asleep, but he too was watching. When morning came, the stranger got up, went for water, returned with it, and gave it to the children to drink, and also to the father and mother. Then he combed the children's hair and washed them. These actions puzzled the parents, but the stranger remained silent about his motives.

The next day the stranger told the father and mother to get ready to move, and they all did so, going where the stranger directed them. As they traveled, the stranger pointed out the different trees, told about their fruits, and also about the herbs and roots that were good for food and those that were good for medicinal purposes, and he told the couple to observe and remember them.

The stranger said to the man, "You must go to a certain place on the other side of that stream where there are elm trees scattered about, thickets and vines of wild beans, and look around and see if there are any animals."

The man started off as he was told to, and when he got to the place he saw a deer. He took aim and shot it. It was a young buck about four years old. He looked around and saw other deer. He killed twelve, making thirteen in all. He pulled the carcasses to a place where he could camp, and then he went back for his family.

On the way he met his wife and three of the children and the stranger, who was carrying the youngest on his back. When they reached the camp, the stranger told the man to roast four shoulders. When this had been done, he gave a shoulder to each child and another cut to the father and mother and told them to dry the rest of the meat in front of the fire and then cache it. In the morning the stranger went for water, as before, and gave them all some to drink. Then he combed the children's hair and washed them, to the great perplexity of the father and mother.

The stranger told the man to go to a place where there were sand hills and scattered cottonwood trees and see if there were animals there. The man went, and as he drew near he saw an elk feeding. He shot it. It had forked horns and was four years old. As he looked around, he saw deer and killed several of them. He dragged the carcasses to a camping place and started back to his family. He met them as before, the stranger carrying the youngest child. The stranger told the man to take the heart and tongue of the elk and lay them aside, for that night they would have a ceremony and sing. The father did so, putting the heart and tongue where the children could not meddle with them.

After sundown the stranger told the woman to get some water and cook the heart and tongue of the elk. The stranger cleared the fireplace and took a seat at the south side of it. Next on his left sat the father, on his left the mother, and the children on her left, beginning with the eldest, down to the youngest. The stranger sang twenty-two songs and taught them to the father and mother. During the pauses between the songs, the cries of the different animals with which the stranger was associated could be heard, showing their satisfaction at the progress the stranger was making. They sang all night. The two little children went to sleep, but the two older ones kept awake. When they were through singing they sang a song by which to go out, and the stranger told them to remember this song.

After about four days, when the meat had dried, the stranger told the man to go on to a creek that ran through ravines where there were great elms and knolls with stumps and see if there were any animals there. The man did as directed and was peering from behind a stump when he saw a buffalo cow. He drew his bow and shot it through the heart. It was about four years old. The man was greatly astonished at the sight of the animal, for he had never seen a buffalo around there before. He saw several deer and killed them too. He dragged the carcasses to a camping place and started back to his family. On the way he met them. The stranger was carrying the youngest child.

"What have you killed?" he asked. The man told about the buffalo. The stranger told the man to take the heart and tongue and put them aside. When they reached camp and the sun was down, the stranger told the woman to go for water and to cook the heart and tongue of the buffalo.

When the tongue and heart were cooked, the stranger took his seat at the south side of the fireplace; the father sat on his left, the mother at the father's left, and on her left the children, from the eldest down to the youngest. They ate of the heart and tongue. That night they sang other songs. All night they sang. The little children fell asleep. The two older boys joined in the singing. Between the songs, the cries of the animals were again heard. At the end they sang the song to accompany their going out. The stranger told the father and mother never to forget to sing that song before going out.

The next day, as usual, the stranger got up early, got water, gave them all some to drink, and then combed the children's hair and washed them. By this time the stranger had won the confidence and the affection of the children, but the father was getting worried. He was puzzled about the stranger's behavior, and he and his wife talked together and wondered about the man. They came to the conclusion that he must be thinking of his own children and that was why he was so attentive to their little ones. He had already brought them great fortune in hunting, and they not only wanted to show gratitude and appreciation for what he had done, but they wanted to test him, to see if he was really human.

They didn't have much to offer him, for they were not very wealthy when the stranger had become their guest, but they were determined to offer him whatever they had. So they said to him, "We do not have much, but we have these things," showing him their stores, "and we have our children. Take your choice, for we are offering you everything." They felt sure that he would never choose their children, but to their surprise he handed back all their goods and said, "Since you have offered them, I will take the children."

Then the stranger went on to say, "I am an animal and have been sent by all the animals that live near the great lake to get your children and to make you great in your tribe. All the animals living near this great lake have had a council and I am their messenger." Then he went on to tell the man that there were seven leaders in this council: the black bear, the buffalo, the elk, the deer, the cougar, the gray wolf, and the skunk. These were especially connected with man. There were seven other animals that would be connected with woman; these were the otter, the raccoon, the mink, the swan, the silver fox, the squirrel, and the owl. Of these animals, the black bear, the buffalo, the elk, and the deer are for food; the cougar has strength and courage, for it rises with the sun and goes out to get food for its young; the gray wolf does the same; the skunk is a hunter and lives in a snug house and is clean. The otter hunts in the water. The raccoon hunts along the streams and takes the fruit growing there; the mink does the same. The swan provides clothing that gives comfort and also beauty. The silver fox is a hunter. Squirrels live on food from trees, and the owl hunts at night.

At this council the first seven counseled with the second seven, and all agreed to help man. Then the sun was appealed to, and the sun agreed that the animals should help man, giving him some of their powers, so that by their powers he could have the power to become like them and share their qualities. The sun said, "I shall stay up above and look down on my children."

They appealed to the moon, and the moon also agreed, saying, "I shall stay up above and look down on my children."

Lightning agreed to make paths, the small paths for the elk, the deer, the buffalo, and the bear, and a wide path for all the other animals.

All then said, "Go find the right person to give this power." This was the explanation that the stranger gave the father and mother when he accepted the gift of their children.

After the meat that had been secured by the father had dried and had been hidden away, the family moved on and came to the edge of a great lake. Willows were growing on its banks, and it was a beautiful sight to see. In the lake was a high rock, and there was also an island with trees growing on it. There was a smooth beach where the water was lapping the shore and the fish were jumping in the sunlight. The stranger told the father to look for animals. He went off and finally spied a black bear. He took aim, shot, and killed it.

Just then he saw something coming down. It was an eagle that dropped and landed on a cottonwood tree. Then the eagle spoke to the man and asked if he might share the food, and then he would come and be one of them.

The man's family had stopped on the second bench above the lake. The man cut up the bear and carried it all up to his family; he left nothing, not even the blood. The stranger told the man to put aside the heart and tongue of the bear. Then the father went out and killed a deer. At sunset the wife brought water and cooked the heart and tongue, and again the stranger sat at the south of the fireplace, the father on his left, the mother on the father's left, and the children at her left, from the eldest to the youngest. And all ate.

The stranger sang songs and taught them to the father and mother. They sang all night, and the youngest children fell asleep. The two older boys joined in the singing. At the close they all sang the song they had been told to sing.

On the evening of the third day, the stranger told the father and mother that he had been looking for a family like theirs for a long time, a family to whom he might be able to give his magic gifts, so that they could find plenty of game, accumulate wealth, and become chiefs in the tribe.

He said, "I am going away and shall take your children that you have given me. But I shall come again. You will find me on the lake shore. I will be in what you find there."

The morning of the fourth day the stranger got up early. There was no wind, and the water of the lake was perfectly still. He got some water and gave them all some to drink. Then he combed the hair of the children and washed them. He told the mother to put on the children's best clothes, to make the tent tidy and in order, and to spread a skin at the back of the fire with its head to the west. He told the mother to sit on the south side of the fireplace near the door, and on her left her husband; and on his left the stranger took his seat. He told the children to all go out and play, but to stay within sound, so they could hear when they were called.

Then he talked to the father and mother. He told them to remember everything that he had taught them and to tell no one. After a while the man could choose seven men and the woman could choose seven women and initiate them. Then they must wait four years, when another seven could be chosen. They would have power, when they initiated the others, to impart the power given them. When he had finished his instructions, he sang a song, and all the animals living by the high rock beat on the drum and sang the same song. Four songs were sung by the stranger in this way, and with each one the animals on the rock beat the drum and sang. They were joined by all those that lived on the island.

When the songs were finished, the stranger ordered the mother to call her eldest child to the tent. She circled the lodge, went out, and called her son. Then she came in and took her seat. Soon his springing steps were heard approaching the tent. He lifted the door flap to enter. The stranger shouted, "Hah!" and the boy fell forward, striking the pole standing by the fireplace; he was dead. The stranger told the father and mother to lift the boy and lay him on the south side of the skin, his head to the west. Then the stranger got up and painted the boy. He made a red line across the mouth from the right ear to the left, then drew a red line from the left ear down the left arm to the thumb, then a similar line from the right ear down the right arm to the thumb, then a red line over the chin down to the heart, where a red circle was made, then a red band across the forehead to the ear. Then he painted the body blue from the waist up to the neck and the elbow up to the neck.

When the painting had been finished he took his seat and ordered the mother to call her second child. Again she circled the lodge and went out. She called her second son to come to the tent and returned to her seat. Soon he was heard coming rapidly along. As he stooped to enter, the stranger shouted, "Hah!" and the boy fell as his brother had. The stranger told the father and mother to carry the boy and lay him on the skin to the left of his brother. Then the stranger got up and painted the second child, making the same red lines, but when he came to paint the body, he put the blue paint on in spots. When he had finished, the stranger resumed his seat.

Then he told the mother to call her third child, and she got up as before, circled the tent, went out, and called her daughter to come to the lodge. Then she reentered and took her seat. Soon she heard the little girl skipping toward the tent, singing as she came. As she put her head in, the stranger shouted, "Hah!" and the little girl fell dead, as had her two older brothers.

Again the father and mother at the bidding of the stranger lifted the child and laid her on the skin at the left side of her brothers. The stranger then got up and painted the red lines across the face and on the arms and from the chin down to the heart, as on her brothers, but put blue in spots on her body and cheeks and tied a sash across her heart and returned to his seat.

Then he told the mother to call her youngest child. She got up, as ordered, circled the tent, went out, and called the little boy. Then she returned to her seat. She had hardly reached her place when she heard the little boy running to answer the call. He poked his head into the tent, the stranger shouted, "Hah!" and the boy fell down and died. Again, as the stranger directed, the parents carried the little boy and laid him on the skin at the left of his sister. Then the stranger got up and painted the child as he had all the others, except that the body and arms above the elbow were made the color of the earth.

The stranger told them that the red lines were the rays of the sun that give life. The blue on the body of the eldest boy was the clear sky. The blue spots on the body of the second son were the night sky, the blue spots on the girl, the moon and the night. The brown spots on the youngest child were the earth. The stranger further explained that the painting on the body of the eldest son, which represented the day, the clear blue sky, was related to the painting on the girl's body above the sash and on her cheeks, which stood for the moon, the power at night. The painting on the body of the second son, which represented the night sky, spotted with stars, was related to the painting on the body of the youngest child, which was the color of the earth, for the earth and the stars were brothers. He told them to look at the circle of stars near the handle of the Big Dipper; this circle of stars were all brothers. Moreover, he told them that the shells were like the stars. He said there was a holy bird which was the leader of all the animals around the lake. This holy bird was the white swan, and the birds flocked in sevens and fives. He said that the down near the left wing should be worn on the head. The left wing of the bird would be a symbol of its power. He told them to notice that the water of the lake was still, so the mind of man, he said, must be quiet like the lake, where dwell the mysterious animals, so that they could give man their powers and by means of this magic gift he would be able to perform strange and mysterious acts. He told the father and mother that they were to remain where they were for four days. When the stranger had finished his instructions he sang two songs, and all the animals around the lake joined in the singing, and those on the rock struck up the drumming.

When the singing was over, the stranger told the father and mother to pick up the eldest son, carry him out of the lodge, and lay him on the beach, face down, his head toward the water. When they had done so, he told them to bring the second son and lay him down so that his head would be at the feet of his elder brother. When they had done so, he told them to bring the girl and lay her like the others, face down, her head to the feet of the second son. When they had done so, he told them to bring out the youngest child and place him face down, with his head at the feet of his sister.

Then the stranger entered the tent and left his robe there and came back out, walking on the water to the place where the sky and water meet, and then he disappeared. Soon a great wave arose and rolled over the quiet waters until it reached the shore where the children lay. It covered the body of the eldest boy and drew it in. The parents stood silently watching, and as they looked on, in the far distance they could see the stranger loom up and disappear again.

Then a second wave rolled up in the east and swept over the lake, which had become tranquil again. On it rolled until it came to the beach, where it lapped over the body of the second child and drew it in. As the wave receded and the lake became still, the stranger arose and looked at the parents and then disappeared again.

Then another wave came. It rolled on and on until it reached the body of the girl, covered it, and drew it in, and once more the lake became quiet, as it had been at first, while in the distance arose the form of the stranger. As he disappeared, a mighty wave came up and rolled over the lake, finally reaching the beach and sweeping away the body of the youngest child from the beach where it lay, and again the lake became still.

The father and mother had watched these proceedings with a bewildered state of mind. They did not make a sound nor did they speak. The silence of the lake and all sounds, the absence of the stranger, the empty place where the children had lain, brought an overpowering sense of desolation to the parents, and they finally gave way to violent demonstrations of grief. They cut their hair, threw away their clothing, and wailed as they walked beside the placid, silent lake.

Night came on, but still the man and woman wailed, until they slept, totally exhausted. Before the sun was up, the woman got up and began to wail anew. Her husband joined her, wailing as he came along. The lake lay quiet but covered with a mist. As the woman walked she remembered the words of the stranger and began to search, hoping that she might find something as he had said she would. Her eye caught sight of a gleam in the water. She stooped and took from the water a white shell, saying as she did this, "I have found it! I have found it!"

Her husband heard her cry of joy, and he began to search too. By and by he saw a dark object in the water; he stooped and took from the water a dark shell. Then he said, "I have found it!"

Just then, as they stood holding their shells, the mist parted, making an opening down the lake like a path, and in the path stood the four children, well and happy.

As the parents stood gazing in wonder, the children spoke, saying, "Don't grieve for us. We are happy. Death is not a thing to fear. It is not what you think it is. In time you will come too, and you will know this for yourselves."

And as their voices died away, the mist closed the path; they could no longer be seen except through the mist. As if through a veil, they saw the outline of a strange animal. It seemed to be as large as the large lake itself. Its skin was covered with hair. It had branching horns and hoofs like the deer and a slender tail with a tuft at the end, which swept toward the sky at the farthest end of the lake. At last this mysteriously shadowy figure melted away and the lake lay quiet before the astonished couple.

Then the man said to the woman, "We have found the mystery. Let's go home." His wife agreed; she was now content. She had seen the children, and what they had said stayed in her mind. So they returned to their tent to live there as the stranger had told them. The man went out to hunt. He knew where the game could be found, and they had a large store of meat and many pelts.

While they were still camped alongside the lake, a messenger from their tribe came to their camp. He said that he had been sent by their people to look for them. They had stayed behind the others with a stranger, and their relatives were afraid that they might have been lured into danger and that something bad might have happened to them.

"Where are your children?" the messenger asked.

"They are dead."

"Where is the stranger?"

"He has gone away, but he has given us all that you see, and he has promised to give us more when this supply is gone. Go back and tell the people what the stranger has done for us."

When the messenger saw the great store of meat and the many caches filled with dried meat, the pelts, and all the wealth given to the man and his wife, he was astonished, and he returned to the tribe to tell what he had seen and heard.

Then the man and his wife left their camp, and, taking all they could with them and caching the rest until they could return for it, they started back to rejoin their tribe. When they were with their people again, they decided to organize a society, as the stranger had told them to do, so that they might give the members some of the magic power they had received.

The first lodge was made up of seven people; the man and his wife and four children under the leadership of the mysterious stranger with the magic power. The man and woman each initiated seven others. Then they waited four years, as they had been told to. They made packs in which to keep the articles they had to wear when the society met, as well as the medicinal roots the stranger had pointed out to them. Some of these roots were for curing disease; others were poisons that were to be used to punish offenders by death. A knowledge of all these roots and herbs was given to the man and his wife as secrets by the stranger, never to be revealed to anyone other than members of the society. The man and his wife could not only teach this knowledge to others, but they were also able to give the initiates a share of the magic power given them by the stranger, who had been the messenger of the council of animals that lived in and around the great lake.

COMMENTARY

Alice Fletcher does not list an informant for this myth, but it was probably given her by her coauthor Francis La Flesche. The tale is recorded in *The Omaha Tribe*.

The Shell Society no longer exists, but many minor societies, primarily social organizations, remain as evidence of the Omaha subculture that was once so rich in such societies.

"Roached" hair means that a strip of hair running from the forehead back over the head to the nape of the neck has been left long and "teased" to stand up, like a crest. Now roached hair is almost always simulated with deer tails.

Lodges were always arranged with the opening to the east, toward the rising sun. In the center of the lodge was the fireplace, and the seat of special honor was directly opposite the opening, on the west side of the lodge. Singing sacred songs all night long is still, incidentally, a part of Omaha culture, being a feature of the ceremonies of the Native American Church, currently the predominant faith among the Omahas.

The Peace Pipes
Told by "chiefs and other prominent Ponca"

The people came across a great water on rafts—logs tied together—and pitched their tents on the shore. While there they thought that they would make themselves *ushkon*—limits or bounds within which they could move about—and regulations by which their actions were to be governed. They cleared a space of grass and weeds so that they could see each other's faces, and they sat down with no obstructions between them.

While they were deliberating, they heard the hooting of an owl in the timber nearby, and the leader, who had called the people together, said, "That bird is to take part in our action. He is calling us, offering us his aid."

Immediately after that they heard the cry of the woodpecker and his knocking against the trees, and the leader said, "That bird is calling and offering us his aid. He, too, wants to take a part in our actions."

The leader then spoke to the man he had appointed to serve as assistant. "Go to the woods and get an ash sapling." His assistant went out and returned with a sapling with rough bark.

"This is not what we want," said the leader. "Go again and get a sapling that has a smooth bark, bluish in color at the joint, where the branch comes out." The assistant went out and returned with a sapling of the kind described.

As the leader took up the ash sapling, an eagle came and soared above the place where the council was sitting. He dropped a downy feather. It fell and balanced itself in the center of the cleared space. This was the white eagle. The leader said, "This is not what we want," and the white eagle passed on.

Then the bald eagle came swooping down as though making an attack on its prey, and balanced itself on its wings directly over the cleared space. It screamed fiercely and dropped one of its downy feathers, which stood on the ground as the other eagle's feather had done. The leader said, "This is not what we want," and the bald eagle moved on.

Then came the spotted eagle and soared over the council and dropped its feather, which stood as the others had done. The leader said, "This is not what we want," and the spotted eagle flew on.

The fantail eagle (imperial eagle, *Aquila heliaca*) then came and soared over the people. It dropped a downy feather which stood upright in the center of the cleared space. The leader said, "This is what we want."

The feathers of this eagle were those used in making the peace pipes, together with the other birds (the owl and the woodpecker) and the animals, making in all nine kinds of articles. These pipes were to be used in establishing friendly relations with other tribes.

COMMENTARY

This tale is also taken from Fletcher and La Flesche. The shafts of such pipes were usually of wood, beaded, decorated with woven porcupine quills, and even sheathed in beaver fur. While some late pipes employed commercial heads, usually made of steel with a light axe blade opposite the pipe bowl, the earlier and most important pipes had pipestone heads made of materials brought the short distance from the pipestone quarries in southwestern Minnesota.

Corn Comes to the Omaha

The Arikara were the first to find the maize. A young man went out hunting. He came to a high hill and, looking down on a valley, he saw a buffalo bull standing in the middle of a bottom land lying between two rivers where they came together. As the young men looked over the country, looking for a safe way to approach the buffalo, he noticed the beauty of the landscape. The banks of the two rivers were low and well timbered. He observed that the buffalo was standing facing the north; he could see that he could not approach the animal from any side within bow shot. He thought that the only way to get a chance to shoot the buffalo would be to wait until the animal moved close to the banks of one of the rivers or to the hills where there were ravines and shrubs. So the young man waited.

The sun went down before the buffalo moved, so the young man went home disappointed. Nearly all night the hunter lay awake, brooding about his disappointment, for food had become scarce and the buffalo would have given a good supply. Before dawn the young man got up and hurried back to where the buffalo had been to see if he could find the animal somewhere near the place, to see if it had moved.

Just as he reached the summit of the hill, where he had been the day before, the sun came up and he saw that the buffalo was still in the same spot. But he noticed that it was now facing the east. Again the young man waited for the animal to move, but again the sun went down and the buffalo remained standing in the same spot. The hunter went home and passed another night of unrest.

He started out again before dawn and came to the top of the hill just as the sun rose and saw the buffalo still standing in the same place, but it had turned around to face the south. The young man waited until dark for the buffalo to move, and once more had to go home disappointed, to pass another sleepless night.

Now the hunter's desire to get food was not unmixed with some curiosity to know why the buffalo should so persistently remain in that one spot without eating or drinking or lying down to rest. With this curiosity working in his mind, he got up for the fourth time before dawn and hurried to the hill to see if the buffalo was still standing in the same place. It was again daylight when he came to the hill, and there stood the buffalo, exactly in the same place, but it had turned around to face the west.

The young man was now determined to know what the animal would do, so he settled down to watch as he had done the three days before. He thought that the animal was acting like this under the influence of an unseen power for some mysterious purpose and that he, as well as the buffalo, was controlled by the same influence.

Darkness came on him again with the animal still standing in the same position. The hunter returned to his home and lay awake all night, wondering what would come of this strange experience. He got up before dawn and again hurried to the mysterious scene. As he reached the summit of the hill, the light of day spread over the land. The buffalo had gone, but in the spot where it had been standing there stood something like a small bush.

The young man approached the place with a feeling of curiosity and disappointment. He came to the object that from the distance looked like a small bush and saw that it was a strange plant. He looked at the ground and saw the tracks of the buffalo and he followed them as they turned from the north to the east and to the south and to the west, and in the center there was only one buffalo track, and from that had sprung this strange plant.

He examined the ground near this plant to find where the buffalo had left the place, but there were no other footprints besides those near the plant. The hunter hurried home and told of his strange experience to the chiefs and prominent men of his people. The men, led by the hunter, went to the place of the buffalo and examined the ground and found that what he had told them was true. They saw the tracks of the buffalo, where he had turned and stood, but they could not find any tracks of his coming to this place or leaving it.

While all the men believed that this plant had been given to the people in this mysterious way by Wakonda, they were not sure how it was to be used. The people knew of other plants that were used for food, and the season for their ripening, and, believing that the fruit of this strange plant would also ripen at its own proper time, they arranged to guard and protect it carefully, awaiting the time of its ripening.

The plant blossomed, but from their knowledge of other plants they knew that the blossom of the plant was only the flower and not the fruit. When they were watching for the blossom to develop into fruit, as they expected it would a new growth blossomed from this growth. It grew larger and larger, until there appeared at the top something that looked like hair. This, in the course of time, turned from pale green to a dark brown. After much discussion, the people decided that this growth must be the fruit of the plant and that it had ripened.

Up to this time no one had dared approach the plant to touch it. Although they were anxious to know the use to which the plant could be put or for which it was intended, no one dared touch it. As the people gathered around the plant, undecided about how to examine it, a youth stepped forward and said, "Everyone knows how my life from my childhood has been worse than worthless, that my life among you has been more for evil than good. Since no one would regret it if anything bad should happen to me, let me be the first to touch this plant and taste of its fruit, so that you will know about it, whether it is good or bad."

The people agreed, and the boy stepped boldly forward and put his right hand on the blossoms of the plant and brought his hand down the plant, down to the roots, as though blessing it. He then grasped the fruit and, turning to the people, said, "It is solid. It is ripe." Then he parted the husks at the top very gently, and, again turning to the people, he said, "The fruit is red."

He took a few of the grains, showed them to the people, and then ate some of them, and then replaced the husks. The youth showed no ill effects, and so the people were convinced that this plant had been given to them for food.

In the fall, when the prairie grass had turned brown, the stalk and the leaves of this plant turned brown too. The fruit was picked and carefully put away.

The following spring, the kernels were divided among the people, four to each family. The people moved their camp to the place where the strange apparition had taken place and there built their bark huts along the banks of the two rivers. As the hills began to take on a green tinge from the new prairie grass, the people planted the kernels of the strange plant, having first built little mounds like the one from which the first stalk had grown.

To the people's great joy the kernels sprouted and grew into strong and healthy plants. They grew through the summer and developed and the fruit ripened as had that of the first stalk. The fruit was gathered and eaten and was found to be good. As they gathered the fruit, the people discovered that there were various colors; some ears were white and others were blue and some were yellow.

The next season the people reaped a rich harvest of this new plant. In the fall of the year these people, the Arikara, sent invitations to a number of different tribes to come and spent the winter with them. Six tribes came, and among them were the Omaha. The Arikara were very generous in the distribution of the fruit of the new plant among their guests, and in this way a knowledge of the plant spread to the Omaha.

COMMENTARY

Fletcher and La Flesche comment on the Omaha's contacts with the Arikara tribe:

"Traditions are more explicit concerning contact with the Arikara than with any other tribe. Both Omaha and Ponca legends give evidence of the influence exerted on the people by this tribe. When the Missouri river was reached by the Omaha, they found the Arikara there, cultivating the maize and living in villages composed of earth lodges, evidently a peaceful, sedentary folk. Omaha war parties from the east side of the river harassed the Arikara, who were living on the west side. The Arikara sought to obtain peace through the influence of the Wawan ceremony, . . . but Omaha war parties seem finally to have driven them from their homes and to have forced them northward up the Missouri river. . . .

"Both Omaha and Ponca traditions say that the tribes were together when they met and drove the Arikara northward. It was from the Arikara that the Omaha and Ponca learned to make and use earth lodges. According to the Omaha legend, 'It was the women who saved the life of the people. They built the sod houses; they made them by their labor. The work was divided. Men cut the poles and fixed the frame and tied the opening for the smoke hole; the women brought the willows and sod and finished the building.' "[2]

And Other Tales*

The Indian view of the world, which I have always considered to be consummately accurate, is a series of circles, of things blending one into the other, like prairie hills—who can say with any kind of certainty where one hill ends and the next begins? But it is the white man's way to carve the hills into square blocks, with square and straight streets, upon which sit square houses. Every Indian knew, for example, where the center of his territory lay, and that somewhere out there on the other side of some river that territory began to fade into another tribe's territory. The white man, on the other hand, drew great, straight rectangles across the rounded hills and rivers, with no real regard for the realities of the earth, and called them South Dakota or Wyoming. Now, who is wise and who is stupid?

So it is also with the white folklorist. I have taken a great body of tales that in their original context blended together and were told together without any kinds of artificial distinctions being drawn. And now, as a result of that kind of arbitrary categorizing, I am stuck with a few extra tales that belong to this collection but are outside of all the categories I have so neatly carved out. And so, with apologies to my Omaha friends and relatives, I will close the collection with these "miscellaneous" tales!

The Story of Blackbird Hill
Retold by Eunice Stabler in *How Beautiful the Land of My Forefathers*

It is said an Omaha chieftain had among his many wives a beautiful young Omaha maiden. Being the ruling chief, he had bought her with wealth gained through his position. The young maiden did not love him, for she had given her heart to another. According to custom, she yielded to the wishes of her parents and went to live at the home of the chief. As time went on she became restless and dissatisfied. She made tryst with the man she loved and in time made a bold admission by going away with her lover. The chief was outraged, and in his jealous frenzy he ordered that she be brought back to him. When she was brought back, he took her into his tent and whipped her so severely she died. Realizing the horrible deed he had committed, in remorse he refused to eat or drink for many days. Drawing his blanket over his head, he sat motionless, deaf to all words of comfort and entreaties by friends and kinsmen. After all efforts had failed, a little child was sent to him with a cup of water. At the insistence of the little child, he drank water. It is said the chief lived the remainder of his days a remorseful, unhappy man. His memory haunted him; he would hear the cries of his beautiful young wife.

Omaha tradition says this incident took place on the present site of Blackbird Hill.

In 1941 the author and her husband talked with two members of the Omaha, who are among the oldest surviving members today, and who have lived in the vicinity of Blackbird Hill for many years. Both agreed that for many, many years before the white man became interested, this phenomenon took place once every year on a certain night (October 17). Both stated that the sound of the cry of the Omaha maiden does not come from one standing on the ground, but that it comes from above in space.

COMMENTARY

This is the only story in this collection taken from Eunice Stabler's little book of reservation reminiscences. But I am delighted to have this one story, for it is an interesting and very Indian version of a legend that has been prominent in Nebraska white folklore and which has been consistently attributed to Omaha folklore while not in character resembling Omaha tales.

In the more widespread white version (see, for example, the version in Welsch, *Treasury of Nebraska Pioneer Folklore*), a white man is found raving and nearly starved on the Plains. He is nursed to health by the Indians who learn from him that he had spent five years seeking his fortune, believing his true love was waiting faithfully for him in the East. But she had in reality been untrue and married a trader. The man, who was slowly making his way back home, happened to stop at the foot of Blackbird Hill and followed a trail to its top, where he found the trader's cabin and his old love.

The girl promised to ask release from her new husband, but the enraged husband decapitated her and threw her body and his own over the cliff into the turbulent river below. This tale also has the bloody trail to the top of the peak remaining grassless for all time.

A Dakota Story
Told by Francis La Flesche

Long ago a Dakota died, and his parents made a lodge for him on the bluff. In the lodge they erected a scaffold on which they laid his body.

Now in this village there was a young married man whose father lived with him. And two old men visited the father and smoked with him, talking about various things.

Then the young man's father said, "My Friends, let's go to the corpse and cut off summer robes for ourselves from the tent skins."

But the young man was against this, saying, "No! Don't do this! The young man's death was a very sad thing, and since they had nothing else to give him, they put up that tent there and placed him in it so that he could rest there. Let him rest undisturbed!"

But in spite of his son's words, the father said, "Since he is already dead, what possible benefit can he get from that tent? We don't have any robes, so all we want to do is cut off parts of the tent skins for ourselves."

Then the young man said, "Well, it is clear that you are determined to have your own way. Then go, do what you want, and we shall see what comes of this." He spoke in harsh tone.

The old man arose without saying anything and went to the place where the corpse lay.

After they had gone, the young man said to his wife, "O Wife, get my piece of white clay. I want to scare one of those old men nearly to death."

But the woman did not want to, saying, "Let them alone! They have no robes. Let them cut robes for themselves."

But the husband would not let it go that way, so she got the white clay for him. The husband took it and used it to whiten his whole body, even his head and face. When he had finished he went on a route parallel to that taken by the old men and reached the corpse before they arrived. He climbed the scaffold and lay on it, thrusting his head out through the tent skins just above the doorway.

Finally the old men approached, climbing the hill and talking together in low voices. The young man lay listening to them.

Finally, when they reached the lodge, the old men sat down, and the leader said, "Friends, fill your pipe. We must smoke this last time with our friend up there."

And one of them said, "Yes, your friend has spoken well. That must be done." So he filled the pipe. He drew a whiff, and when the fire glowed, he turned the pipe stem toward the seam of the skins above the doorway. He looked upward to the sky and said, "Ho! Friend, here is the pipe. We must smoke with you this last time. And then we must separate. Here is the pipe." And as he said this he looked up above the doorway and saw the head extending from the tent.

"O my Friends," he cried, "Look behind you!" and when the two looked up they said, "O Friend, it is really him," and they all ran away. The young man jumped down and attacked them. Two fell to the ground in terror, but he did not stop with them. He was after his father. When the old man was overtaken, he fell to the ground terrified.

The young man sat astride of him and said, "You have been very evil. Fill the pipe for me!"

The old man said, "O My Grandchild! O My Grandchild!" hoping that the ghost would pity him.

Then he filled the pipe as he lay stretched out on the ground and gave it to the son. And when the young man stopped smoking, the father said, "O My Grandchild! O My Grandchild! Grandchild, pity me and let me go. We thought that we must smoke with you this last time, so we went to the place where you were. Grandchild, pity me!"

"If that is true, then get up and beg forgiveness," said the young man. And the old man did so, saying all the time, "O My Grandchild! O My Grandchild!"

It was all the young man could do to keep from laughing. Finally he said, "All right. Go. Be careful not to come around my resting place again. Don't ever come here again!" Then he let he old man go.

Upon returning to the burial lodge, he found that the two old men were still lying where they had fallen. When he approached them, they slipped off, covering their heads, for they were absolutely terrified, so he let them go undisturbed.

And when they had gone, the young man went home too. He was the first to get there, and he washed himself all off. He said to his wife, "When they get back, be sure not to laugh. Try to control yourself. I nearly caused them to die of fright."

And when the old men returned, the husband and wife lay as if they were asleep. But the old men did not lie down; they sat in silence, smoking together until daylight. And when the young man arose in the morning, the old men appeared to be very sad. Then he said, "Give me one of those robes that you and your friends cut off and brought back. I too have no robe."

But his father said, "Why, we went there but we didn't get anything at all, for we were attacked. We came very near being killed."

To this the son said, "Why, I didn't want this to happen, so I said, 'Don't go,' but you paid no attention at all to me and went anyway. But now you know differently and you weep."

And when night came, the young man said, "Go again and give it another try. Bring back a piece for me, for I have no robe at all," but the old men didn't want to go again. Finally they became very mad because he teased them so often.

COMMENTARY

In regard to the Omaha attitudes and beliefs about ghosts, Fletcher and La Flesche reported:

"It was believed that the spirit of a murdered man was inclined to come back to his village to punish the people. To prevent a murdered man from haunting his village he was turned face downward, and to impede his steps the soles of his feet were slit lengthwise. The return of a spirit to haunt the people was called *wathihide*, 'disturbance.' Such a haunting spirit was supposed to bring famine. To avert this disaster, when a murdered man was buried, besides the precautions already mentioned, a piece of fat was put in his right hand, so that if he should come to the village he would bring plenty rather than famine, fat being the symbol of plenty. Even the relatives of the murdered man would treat the body of their kinsman in the manner described."

"Many tales are told concerning ghosts. Those who have camped on old battlefields have heard the sounds of fighting, and persons becoming separated on hunting expeditions have told of hearing the coming of strange people, who made camp, set up their tents, and went about their usual avocations. A narrator of one of these stories declared that all of the members of his family heard these sounds—even the dogs barked; but on looking out of the tent nothing was to be seen. These ghostly visitants did not always come at night; sometimes they stayed during the day and continued talking and moving about their unseen camp. Similar stories have been told by persons who have been left behind in the village when the tribe moved off on the annual hunt, tales of how the ghosts came and took possession of the earth lodges and held dances and feasts. In only one instance was it claimed that these visitors became partially visible. In that case the narrator said, 'Only the feet and the legs as high as the knees could be seen'; and then added, 'If I had been alone a little longer I think I should have finally been able to see the entire figure and recognize the people, for at first I could see only their feet.' Ghosts bent on mischief, as tampering with food after it was prepared for eating, could be thwarted by placing a knife across the open vessel containing the food. A ghost would not meddle with a knife. Nor would ghosts ever cross a stream; so, if a person was followed or chased by a ghost, he would make for a stream, wade it, or even jump across it. No matter how small the stream, it made an impassable barrier between himself and his ghostly pursuer."[1]

A Ponca Ghost Story
Told by Francis La Flesche

A great number of people once went on the warpath. They were Ponca. As they approached the enemy, they camped one night. They lit up a fire, for it was dark. They sat down around the bright fire and, rejoicing, sat down to eat. Suddenly they heard someone singing.

"Be quiet. Push the ashes over the fire. Grab your bows quietly," said their leader.

They took their bows and went out to capture him. They made the circle around him smaller and smaller, and then closed in, but still they heard the singing. The person wasn't moving at all. Soon they were narrowing down to a tree, and when they got close to it, the singer stopped his song.

When they gathered around the tree, they could see bones lying there in a pile. There were human bones lying there in a pile at the foot of the tree.

When people die, the Dakota usually suspend the bodies in trees, in a horizontal position.

A Dakota Ghost Story
Told by Francis La Flesche

The Dakota were on the warpath. As they moved along, two went out as scouts. They heard someone singing.

He-a-hetha-he-a! He-a-hetha-he-a!
He-thehe-e-he!
A-he-the-he-a!
He-the-he-e-he
E-ha-huthu-u he-the-a!
Ya-a-hu!
E-the ha-a-e-a!

They crawled up on him, but when they got very close and looked, they found that he was a big wolf.

The Invisible People
Told by Francis La Flesche to Franz Boaz

The Omaha lived in a village of earth lodges near a place called "The Hill of the Little Graves" when I was a young man. They lived in that village during the summer time, and in the winter they packed up their buffalo skin tipis and moved to the high hills near the Missouri River. At the foot of these high hills the forests were heavy and offered great protection during the winter season.

We ate a lot of hominy all through the winter. Then, when the trees began to show their blossoms, we would move back to our earth lodges to await the time for planting the corn. When this time came, about four old men who were priests would go from house to house, dressed for the occasion in sacred costume, with soft feathers on their heads, and they would distribute red corn to the people as notice that corn planting time was at hand.

When the distribution of the corn was finished, the women would race out in groups, carrying the seeds and their hoes. They worked hard to put the ground in shape for the planting.

Following this was the time to plant the squash and beans. As soon as the corn began to show its leaves, which resembled rabbits' ears, cultivation would be started, digging up the earth to make the corn grow.

When the cultivation was finished, the Honga, a clan which had control of the buffalo hunt, would call for the chiefs to do their part in organizing a hunt. When the meeting came to order, the spokesman, in a well-planned speech, told them the reason for calling the meeting.

Then the meeting was turned over to the tribal chief. Officers were chosen to conduct the hunt and then the village crier, who was sitting near the door, was brought before the chiefs. He was told to go before the people and tell them what had been done for their comfort and protection during the hunt. Then careful thought was given the proposed route of the hunt. Many things must be considered in addition to the game. The enemy they would encounter had to be considered, and it was important that the route take them where there were plenty of wild turnips.

Again the crier was sent out with instructions to tell the people what had been decided. A day was set to pack up and move out for the Sandhills, the land of the big game. Then the council adjourned.

At last the day for the move came. The women rode horses—their best ones—and were dressed in their gayest clothing. They looked beautiful.

I, being one of the people, followed along. When evening came, we camped in the bend of a creek. Campfires burned for the latecomers and the outdoor cooking. The first day was uneventful, but the people were satisfied because nothing bad had happened to mar the first day.

As we traveled, a large body of men was sent to the front of the band to protect the women and children; an equal number was instructed to protect the rear. When camp was moved again, the men and boys worked quickly. The ones who had horses were busy with them. Suddenly loud talking broke the stillness. A man was scolding his wife.

Another man who was working close to the man said to him, "Be gentle with her no matter what kind of mistakes she makes."

Just as the woman was leaving the scene, four sons came up to the father and asked, "What is the matter?"

To this the father replied, "I scolded your mother and she walked off in anger."

Running quickly, the boys tried to overtake their mother, but she kept looking back and when she saw the boys were following her she hid. Just as the sun was setting she saw the boys turn to go back. She waited quietly until they were out of sight and then she came out of her hiding place.

After two days and much walking, she reached the village and as she approached her home she saw that there was no change in it. The day was bright and calm and the woman was very glad to be back in the village and in her own home. After sweeping and setting her house in order, she sat down to mend her moccasins that had been torn in her long travels. Without any warning she heard a child's voice coming through the door.

"Mother, they are coming to this house."

The mother said, "Gather up those things lying scattered about." They hurriedly put the things in order. Then footsteps approached and the sounds of men talking. The guests came in and took their seats, and the presiding chief prayed and gave a smoke offering.

The woman sat sewing and heard all of this, but she could see nothing.

When the chief had stopped talking, a voice started singing and then there were the sounds of dancing. There seemed to be a very joyous mood. As the dancing continued, the woman tried very hard to see something of the festivities. Finally she could see dust arise from the ground, and then the feet of the dancers. She was very happy about this.

More songs were sung, and the woman became less content. The dancing stopped and the dancers went away.

Four times this same thing happened. On the second day when the dancers were heard she could see them up to their knees. On the third day she could see them up to their waists. And on the fourth day she could see them up to the shoulders, but never a face appeared.

Early one morning as she lay awake in bed she heard footsteps, as though someone were climbing the roof of her house, and then a loud voice called to the people that an order had been issued to move the camp. Besides these voices she could hear the clatter of tent poles outside. She hurried out to the entrance of the earth lodge and looked about. She cried quietly, wishing that she could go with these invisible people. Then everything became quiet, and later the band of hunters returned.

COMMENTARY

This tale was sent in Omaha, interlinear translation, and free translation to Franz Boaz by Francis La Flesche on May 21, 1928.

The lines between the dead and the living, between animal and man, between man and the earth are not so distinctly clear to the Omaha as they seem to be for the white man. Indeed, for the Omaha the living fade in and out of the world of the dead and the spirit world fades in and out of the vision of living people with little apparent discomfort for either.

The reference to someone climbing on the roof, followed by a loud voice, might be obscure to the casual white reader, but this is the village crier climbing to the top of an earth lodge so that his announcement of breaking camp can be heard by everyone in the camp.

A Yankton Legend
Told by John Springer, an Omaha

A man and his wife had only one child, whom they prized very much. He used to go playing, but once he fell into the water. His mother and father and all his relations mourned very much. His father was especially distressed. He would not sleep in the lodge. He lay outside without any pillow at all. And when he lay with his cheek in the palm of his hand, he could hear his child crying. He seemed to hear him as if he lay under the ground.

He had all of his relations come together and told them that he wanted them to dig. He told them to dig down into the ground. His relatives gathered up horses to give as payment for the digging. They gathered goods and horses.

Two men said that they were sacred. They promised to look for the child. An old man went to tell the father. He brought these two men to the lodge. The father filled his pipe with tobacco and gave it to the sacred men. "If you bring my child back, I will give you everything as a reward."

The two painted themselves. The one made his body very black and the other made his body very yellow. Both went down into the deep water. The two men went down into this place and talked with the Water God. And the child was not dead; he was sitting there still alive.

The men said, "The father wants his child. He said that we were to bring him back with us."

"If you try to take him back with you, when you reach the surface of the water, he will die. If you had taken him back before he had eaten anything, he might have lived. But he will want to eat the kind of food that I eat, and because of that he will die. Go and tell his father that."

The two men went back. When they arrived at the lodge, they said, "We have seen your child. The wife of the water god has him. Though we saw him still alive, he had eaten part of the food that the Water God eats. Therefore, the Water God says that if we bring the child back with us out of the water, he will die."

But the father still wanted to see him.

"If the Water God's wife gives you back your child, she wants a very white dog as payment."

The father said, "I will give her the white dog."

Again the two men painted themselves: the one made himself very black and the other made himself very yellow. And again they went beneath the water. They reached the place again.

"The father said that we were to take the child back no matter what. He wants to see his child."

The Water God gave the child back to them, and they took him homeward. When they arrived up above with him, the child was dead. They gave him back to his father. All the people cried when they saw the dead child, their relative. They threw the white dog into the water. When they had looked at the child, they buried him and gave the reward to the two men.

Soon the parents lost a girl in the same way. But she did not eat any of the food of the Water God, and therefore they brought her back home alive. But it was another Water God who had her, and he promised to give her back to them if they gave him four white dogs.

COMMENTARY

Dorsey says that "the Indians think that there are water deities or *wakandagi* under the water. A wakanda loved the child and had taken it, as his wife had no children, and wished to keep this one."

A Yankton Story
Told by George Miller

There was once a Yankton village in which a young man lived, just waiting for the chance to marry. The chief of the village had two daughters, full sisters, who were unmarried, and one son, the youngest child. And this man, as I said, wanted to get married; he wanted to court these sisters and he was waiting for them.

One night he went to their tent, which was a whitened one, and lay down outside the rear of the tent in order to listen to what the sisters might say. Finally the sisters struck up a conversation.

"Younger Sister, we should marry whoever takes our younger brother and makes it possible for him to insult our enemies."

"Oho!" thought the eavesdropper, and as he lay listening he formed a plan.

When he returned home, he asked his female relatives to sew some moccasins for him, and they did so. The next evening when it was too dark for people to recognize each other's faces, he started to look for the boy. The boy was playing and the man found him. He said, "Come here,

Younger Brother," and the boy went with him. The young man carried him on his back all night long, going across the prairie in a straight line. He was carrying him on the warpath.

He killed a buffalo bull and cut up the carcass and cooked the fresh meat so that it might serve as rations for the journey. He carried the provisions on his back, along with the boy. When he reached a stream, he set the boy down among the undergrowth and gave him some dried meat to eat.

Then he said, "Don't go anywhere. Stay right here. Don't look out from the brush. I will return."

And then he went out scouting. He didn't see anyone, so he returned to the boy and spoke to him as if he were a full-grown man.

"O War Captain, no one is there. I didn't find anything at all." Then he put him on his back again and resumed the march.

Late that evening he set the boy down in the undergrowth again and went off scouting. He heard someone shooting. It was a man who had killed an elk. The young man wanted to fetch the boy, but that would have been difficult, so he sat down to think about what he should do. He crept up on the man carefully and killed him before he knew what had happened. Then he got the boy. "O War Captain, I have killed a man. Hurry!"

He carried the boy on his back, running up to the place. When they got there, he had the boy walk on the corpse of the dead man. Then the two started home, having taken the scalp of the dead man.

As they traveled back, the man was thinking of the woman, "I want to take a wife." He was feeling good. But when they got back to the place where he had first met the boy and overheard the two sisters, he found that nothing was left but a single tent and the deserted village site. Everyone had gone, leaving only the one tent standing behind. When he approached it, he found that small pieces of sod had been piled up at the doorway and that only a short time had passed since the inhabitants had gone away.

He began following the trail of the villagers and finally came upon two people sitting on a hill. Nearing them, he could see that they were the parents of the boy he was carrying. They came up to him and kissed their son and the young man too.

"You have done very well, but you have been hurt," they said.

It seems that when the young man carried off the boy he did not tell anyone about what he planned to do. And when the sisters did not find the boy, their brother, they killed themselves.

The boy's father said to the young man, "You should have told us about it when you carried him off. You have done a good thing, but his sisters had only him as their real brother, so they loved him very much. When they thought that he had been either lost or killed, they killed themselves."

Then the young man told the boy's father everything that had happened to them and how he had killed the man.

The father said, "Come! Let's go. That is enough. You must eat something."

The young man said, "Go ahead. I'll join you later."

So he sat there and they departed. When they had gone out of sight, he retraced his steps until he reached the place where the sisters had killed themselves. He pulled down the blocks of sod that had been piled up against the entrance and went into the tent.

There were the two women, side by side, just as they had been put there. He went to them, forced his way in between them, and lay down. Then he killed himself.

A Story of the Skull

A woman was walking along. She was proud because she had on her finest clothes, and she met another woman, who asked, "Where are you going, Sister-in-law?"

"I am going off a long ways."

"Let us go together then," said the second woman.

They walked on and met a third woman, who asked, "Where are you going?"

When they answered her she said, "I am going also; let us go together." And they walked along one after the other.

They met a fourth woman, who asked, "Where are you going, Sister-in-law?" and she also joined them. Walking in single file, the women came to a pile of bones where people had died.

The first woman kicked them with her foot and, turning to the second woman, said, "These belong to you. Carry them."

The second woman kicked the bones with her foot and said contemptuously to the third woman, "These are the bones of your relatives. Carry them."

The third woman kicked them with her foot and, turning to the fourth woman, said, "These bones belong to you. Carry them."

And the fourth woman answered, "This is the skull of my sister-in-law. You should not be disrespectful. I will carry it along so that you shall respect it."

The woman wore a skin belted in at the waist, making a skirt of one part and leaving the other long enough to cover the back and to draw over the head. She put it between her back and the blanket, saying, "I shall carry it."

But after a time she wearied of carrying it and she put it down by the roadside in a place where no one would molest it. But the skull followed them, singing.

There were four women passing along here.
One of them is my sister-in-law.

The women heard the singing and ran. When they camped for the night, the skull came up and destroyed the first woman. It bit her and she died.

When the three women awoke and found one dead, they fled from the skull, but it followed singing,

There were four women passing along here.
One of them is my sister-in-law.

They ran away from it and camped for the night, but when they awoke in the morning they found another woman had been killed by the skull; so again they fled, but, again, they heard it singing.

There were four women passing along here.
One of them is my sister-in-law.

Next morning only one woman awoke, and the skull came up to her and said, "Sister-in-law, carry me again."

She dared not refuse, and after they had gone a short distance, the skull said, "Look among the trees until you find one where the raccoons have their nest. Then if you are hungry you shall have something to eat. Look for a certain tree, find the hollow place where the raccoon goes in to its nest, and drop me in after it."

The woman did as she was told, and she dropped the skull in. It somehow killed the raccoon. After it had got to the bottom of the tree, it called, "Cut a hole in this tree and let me out."

The woman cut the hole. First she took the raccoon out from the tree, and then she took the skull out. She cooked the raccoon; then she took the stomach of the raccoon for a bag and melted down the raccoon fat, put it in the stomach bag, and sewed it up. She hid it from the skull. She had a purpose in doing this, and the skull did not know that she had done it, and she carried the bag with her. They stopped twice more during their journey. Each time the woman did as the skull directed, and each time she made the bag and filled it and sewed it up, and the skull did not see her.

The fourth time the woman hunted for a very large tree, and when she had found it she dropped the skull into the hole and then ran off by herself. The skull called, "I have killed the raccoon. Now let me out." No answer. Then the skull knew the woman had left and said, "Wherever you go, I shall find you and have my revenge."

It commenced to gnaw a place in the tree to let itself out, and it took a day and a half to make a hole large enough to get through. When it came out, it went along saying, "Wherever you go, I shall find you and have my revenge."

By and by the woman heard the skull saying that, and she took the bag of raccoon grease and threw it at the skull; it went all over it and it could not go on, and while it stopped to clean itself the woman ran on ahead.

But the skull caught up to her, and she heard it say, "Wherever you go, I shall find you and have my revenge."

Then the woman stopped and threw another bag at the skull, and it had to stop and clean itself.

The third time it caught up to her, and she threw another bag of grease at it. But the fourth time the woman went on till she came to a woods, and the skull could not reach the woods until the next morning for it had to cross a creek. So it went back on the side of the hill and had to roll down and so cross the creek. The woman found an old man in the forest making bows and arrows and she asked him to protect her from the skull, but he paid no attention.

"Brother, help me! Protect me!" But he took no notice of her.

"Uncle, protect me!" He paid no attention.

"Father, protect me from the skull!" He did not notice.

"Grandfather," she called, "help me! Protect me!"

"That is the relationship," he said. He was an immense man, and his long hair was done up in a big knot on the back of his head. He told her to untie it and get in there, so she did so. And he told her to sit there and wait until he was ready. After a while he went on making bows and arrows.

Presently the skull came up and went round and round the old man, saying, "Old man, give me my woman."

But the old man was silent.

Then said the skull, "Give me the woman I was running after." But the old man would not answer.

When the skull asked for the woman the fourth time, the old man said, "I am tired of you." So he took a bow and broke the skull in pieces. He said to the woman, "Get down and gather up these pieces. Pile them up and set them on fire. After you set them on fire, whatever you see, don't touch it. You will be punished if you do."

When the woman saw the fire going down, she noticed a comb. She picked it up and hid it in her blanket, but it burned her side so badly that she died.

The old man said, "I told you not to pick up anything, but you did so. I punish you. Disobedience brings its own punishment."

COMMENTARY

This tale was first published in 1893.[2] George Truman Kercheval "obtained [it] in Nebraska, from an informant of Otoe extraction, married to an Omaha." He appends a conversation with the informant:

Kercheval: "Is that all?"

Informant: "Yes."

Kercheval: "When Carey [sic: La Flesche?] told it to me, he said the old man hit the skull and it went into the air; when it came down it turned into knives, forks, thimbles, threads, awls, wax, needles, and scissors. The man told the woman to come down from his hair but not to pick up anything that was on the ground; if she did he would punish her. And the old man went off and sat down under a tree. She tried to pick a pair of scissors; when she did so her hands dropped off. That is the way Carey told it."

Informant: "Carey did not get it right. This is a very old story, and at the time it was first told we never knew of such things as knives, forks, awls, or scissors. Carey has added that, or some of the younger people have told it that way because they now use these things. But I have told it to you the old way, and that is the right way."

Kercheval also added a note regarding the form of the Indian comb mentioned in his informant's version:

"The old Indian comb; it was made of wild oats, long grasses like thistles, sharp and black at the end. The Indians work these sharp ends through wool or cotton and cut off the sharp points, leaving the grass about two inches long, like bristles; then they take a piece of animal bladder, because it is soft, and tie the bundle of cloth together for a handle. This old mode of making a comb has gone; with the Indians' present opportunity of buying combs, such as we use, it is an impossibility, almost, to procure a specimen of these old combs."

The Hunter

On the Missouri River there stands a town now known as Sioux City. On its weedy banks the Omaha, a Siouan tribe, dwelt. Deer and other game were plentiful, so the people did not suffer for want of food and clothing. Here I was born, raised, and married.

My wife, though young, was an industrious woman. She roused me from sleep one morning very early and asked me to go and hunt for deer. Being young and anxious to please her, I did not object. I got up and quickly prepared myself for the hunt, not forgetting to put on my belt nor to take my gun, which I had nearby. Soon I stood before my wife, ready to hunt.

She said, "Are you going on foot?"

And I answered, "Yes."

But she wanted me to ride a very gentle horse that we had. It made me happy to think that she would want me to be comfortable, so I went after the horse, bringing it then to the house. I placed the saddle on it and started out.

As the sun rose high into the sky, about noon, I came to a large swamp. I saw some footprints, so I got off my horse and began to follow them. They did not follow a straight path, and soon I came upon a large female deer. It was very much startled. It stopped and turned its head, looking at me over its back as it stood there.

Raising my gun but without taking good aim, I fired and shot the deer in the leg, crippling it. I took a rope from my horse's back and tied his feet so that he could not run away; then on foot I chased the deer. Toward the middle of the afternoon the deer ran toward the Missouri River, making a very crooked trail. Just as the sun was setting I overtook the deer and killed it.

After I had finished butchering it, I hurriedly tried to find some good place to sleep. Near the edge of the river I found a soft willow tree covered with clinging vines, resembling a house. I took shelter there.

I put the meat in a safe place and started to build a fire, for I was very hungry, not having eaten all day. I was able to build a good fire quickly because there was plenty of hard willow kindling lying around. It burned brightly, producing a fine heat that permitted me to prepare the meat for broiling.

When the meat was nearly done, I heard a man's voice shouting with joy. I stepped to the back of my little shelter and stood waiting, my gun in my hand.

The man did not seem to see me as I stood there, for he came right up to the fire. He looked around in all directions, turning to the right and then to the left. When I looked at him, I could see that half of his face had no skin at all; his eyes were also gone, and nothing was left but empty sockets.

The forests and hills echoed from my shot, and the fire suddenly died out.

When I looked for the man, I could find nothing. The meat I had been cooking was gone too. Then the wind began to blow very hard, so I returned to my shelter. I was still very, very hungry, but I was afraid to go to sleep.

The next day I started the fire up again. Now, I was not afraid any more so I broiled more meat and finally ate. When I had finished eating, I tied up the remainder of the meat and got ready to start home.

The meat was a heavy load, and I was bent over as I carried it along, but I did not want to throw a single piece of it away. As I labored along the path, I suddenly saw a man standing on a ridge by a spreading oak tree. I approached him, lifted my head, and stopped. The skin of his face was all shrivelled up and, standing there, I recognized him.

When he died, some of his friends had laid his body in the tree tops. During a hard wind he had been blown out of the trees and had fallen in a standing position, leaning against the tree.

At that I decided to go home, so I went after my horse and found him where I left him. He seemed very glad to see me, for he came hobbling toward me, whinnying.

About noon the second day I reached home. My wife quickly ran out to meet me and helped me with my burden.

"I know that you could do this for me, my loved one," she said.

That evening she invited her friends and gave them a big feast of deer meat and sweet corn.

And the story is finished.

COMMENTARY

This tale of a revenant spirit was sent to Franz Boaz by Francis La Flesche in 1928.

Plains Indians were "buried" by being laid in state and then abandoned in a tipi or tied in a tree, as recounted in this story. Many trees in Nebraska and South Dakota can still be recognized as "burying trees" because of their twisted branches, stunted by their burdens.

Tales like this, though told in the first person as historical truth, can nonetheless be counted as legends. Legends of this type are very common within non-Indian cultures, but it is generally a friend of a cousin who has purloined the Waldorf-Astoria's recipe for Red Velvet Cake, a cousin of a friend who encountered the hook-handed terrorizer of lovers' lane, a friend of a friend who has seen the low-priced death car, or a cousin of a cousin who has actually held the treasure maps. It is difficult, sometimes painful, to inform the tale teller that, for example, stories about cats being accidentally broiled in a microwave oven are even more common these days than microwave ovens! It is this element of belief, of historically couched narrative, that makes the legend so difficult to study—and so interesting.

Notes

Introduction

1. James C. Olson, *History of Nebraska, 25.*
2. Alice C. Fletcher and Francis La Flesche, "The Omaha Tribe," 81. Hudson Bay Company is Fletcher's spelling.
3. Ibid., 80–81.
4. Ibid., 81–82.
5. Ibid., 611.
6. Olson, *History of Nebraska*, 24.
7. Fletcher and La Flesche, "The Omaha Tribe," 87.
8. J. Sterling Morton, *Illustrated History of Nebraska*, vol. II, 194–95.
9. James Owen Dorsey, "Omaha Sociology," 366.
10. Morton, *History of Nebraska*, vol. II, 223.
11. Norma Kidd Green, *Iron Eye's Family: The Children of Joseph La Flesche*, 25. La Flesche is also spelled LaFlesche, La Fleche, etc., but I have chosen to follow Green's usage in her history of the family.
12. Virginia Irving Armstrong, *I Have Spoken: American History through the Voices of the Indians*, 194–97.
13. Francis La Flesche, *The Middle Five: Indian Schoolboys of the Omaha Tribe*, xvii.
14. In some names Dorsey uses hyphens to separate units of meaning and in some others he does not; the same is true of his translations of Omaha names. Hyphenization of American Indian names has long been a practice of the whites and was perhaps justified initially as an aid to pronunciation when the problem of rendering Indian sounds into the English language was first encountered. But that time is past (just as I would not write Nel-son Rock-e-fel-ler). Except when quoting other authors, the spelling of Indian names in this book is without hyphens.
15. There is no Reptile Clan among the Omaha; Dorsey probably means Turtle Clan.
16. Margaret Mead, *The Changing Culture of an Indian Tribe*, 82, 83.
17. Fletcher and La Flesche, "The Omaha Tribe," 370.
18. Ibid., 369.
19. Larry J. Evers, "Native American Oral Literature in the College English Classroom: An Omaha Example"; discusses the relevance of traditional tales for the modern reader. Evers also (in yet unpublished work) has explored contemporary legends; e.g., the Deer Woman cycle.

The Trickster

1. Stith Thompson, *The Folktale*, 319.
2. Ibid.
3. John Greenway, *Literature among the Primitives*, 72.
4. Paul Radin, *The Trickster: A Study in American Indian Mythology*, 125.
5. Greenway, *Literature among the Primitives*, 87–88.

6. Thompson, *The Folktale*, 320.

7. Ibid., 336.

8. James Owen Dorsey, "Omaha Sociology," 267.

9. Ibid., 334.

10. Ibid.

11. Alan Dundes, *The Morphology of American Indian Folktales*, 70.

12. Margaret Mead, *The Changing Culture of an Indian Tribe*, 48.

13. Thompson, *The Folktale*, 353.

14. Alice C. Fletcher and Francis La Flesche, "The Omaha Tribe," 366.

15. Dorsey, "Omaha Sociology," 337–38

Adventurers and Culture Heroes

1. Alice C. Fletcher and Francis La Flesche, "The Omaha Tribe," 617.

2. Ibid., 331–33.

3. James Owen Dorsey, "Omaha Sociology," 317, 335–36.

4. Fletcher and La Flesche, "The Omaha Tribe," 325. The saying is equivalent to the English language "Salt the cow to win the calf."

5. Ibid., 366–67.

6. Dorsey, "Omaha Sociology," 261.

7. Fletcher and La Flesche, "The Omaha Tribe," 326.

8. Ibid., 585.

9. Dorsey, "Omaha Sociology," 328.

10. Ibid., 286.

11. Fletcher and La Flesche, "The Omaha Tribe," 215, 137, 309.

The Animal World

1. Alice C. Fletcher and Francis La Flesche, "The Omaha Tribe," 357, 599, 600, 601.

2. Ibid., 332.

3. James Owen Dorsey, "Omaha Sociology," 315–16.

Animal and Man

1. James Owen Dorsey, "Omaha Sociology," 332–33.

2. Roger L. Welsch, *Treasury of Nebraska Pioneer Folklore*, 182–85.

Creation and Origin

1. Alice C. Fletcher and Francis La Flesche, "The Omaha Tribe," 572–73.

2. Ibid., 75.

And Other Tales

1. Alice C. Fletcher and Francis La Flesche, "The Omaha Tribe," 215, 590–91.

2. George Truman Kercheval, "An Otoe and an Omaha Tale," 201–04.

Bibliography

Armstrong, Virginia Irving. *I Have Spoken: American History through the Voices of the Indians.* Chicago: Swallow Press, 1971.

Birket-Smith, Kay. *Primitive Man and His Ways.* NY: Mentor Books, 1957.

Dorsey, James Owen. "Abstracts of Omaha and Ponka Myths." *Journal of American Folk-Lore* I (April-June and July-September 1888), 74–78 and 204–08.

———. *The Ȼegiha Language U.S. Geographical and Geological Survey of the Rocky Mountain Region: Contributions to North American Ethnology,* Vol. VI. Washington: GPO, 1890.

———. "Omaha and Ponka Letters." *Bulletin No. 11* of the Bureau of Ethnology. Washington: GPO, 1891.

———. "Omaha Folk-lore Notes." *Journal of American Folk-Lore* II (July-September 1889), 190.

———. "Omaha Sociology." *Third Annual Report* of the Bureau of Ethnology, 1881–82. Washington: GPO, 1884, 211–370.

———. "Ponka and Omaha Songs." *Journal of American Folk-Lore* II (October-December 1889), 271–76.

Dundes, Alan. *The Morphology of American Indian Folktales.* Folklore Fellows Communications No. 195. Helsinki, 1964.

Evers, Lawrence J. "Native American Oral Literatures in the College English Classroom: An Omaha Example." *College English* 36 (February 1975), 649–62.

Farb, Peter. *Man's Rise to Civilization as Shown by the Indians of North America from Primeval Times to the Coming of the Industrial State.* NY: Dutton, 1968.

Fletcher, Alice C. *Indian Story and Song.* Boston: Small, Maynard and Co., 1900.

———, and La Flesche, Francis. "The Omaha Tribe." *Twenty-Seventh Annual Report* of the Bureau of American Ethnology, 1905–1906. Washington: GPO, 1911, 17–672.

Green, Norma Kidd. *Iron Eye's Family: The Children of Joseph La Flesche.* Lincoln: Johnson Publishing Co., 1969.

Greenway, John. *Literature among the Primitives.* Hatboro, PA: Folklore Associates, 1964.

Griffen, Fannie Reed. *Oo-Mah-Ha Ta-Wa-Tha (Omaha City).* Lincoln: Privately published, 1898.

Grinnell, George Bird. *Pawnee Hero Stories and Folk-Tales.* Lincoln: University of Nebraska Press, 1961.

Kercheval, George Truman. "An Otoe and an Omaha Tale." *Journal of American Folk-Lore* VI (July-September 1893), 199–204.

La Flesche, Francis. *The Middle Five: Indian Schoolboys of the Omaha Tribe.* Madison: University of Wisconsin Press, 1963.

Marriott, Alice, and Rachlin, Carol K. *American Indian Mythology.* NY: Cromwell Co., 1968.

Mead, Margaret. *The Changing Culture of an Indian Tribe.* NY: Columbia University Press, 1932.

Morton, J. Sterling. *Illustrated History of Nebraska*, Vol. II. Lincoln: Jacob North and Co., 1906.

Olson, James C. *History of Nebraska*, New Edition. Lincoln: University of Nebraska Press, 1966.

Olson, Paul A. *The Book of the Omaha.* Lincoln: Nebraska Curriculum Development Center, 1980.

Radin, Paul. *The Trickster: A Study in American Indian Mythology.* NY: Philosophical Library, 1956.

Stabler, Eunice. *How Beautiful the Land of My Forefathers.* n.p., 1943 (?).

Standingwater, Steven. "People of the Smokey Waters: The Omahas." Mimeographed. Macy (?), Nebraska: c. 1970.

Swetland, Mark J. *Umonhoniye of Elizabeth Stabler.* Winnebago, Nebraska: Nebraska Indian Press, 1977.

Thompson, Stith. *The Folktale.* NY: Holt, Rinehart and Winston, 1946.

———. *Tales of the North American Indians.* Bloomington: Indiana University Press, 1929.

Welsch, Roger L. "American Plains Indian Ethnogastronomy." *Ethnologische Nahrungsforschung.* Helsinki, 1975, 319–25.

———. "Traditional Omaha Foodways." *Keystone Folklore Quarterly* (Winter 1971–72), 165–70.

———. *Treasury of Nebraska Pioneer Folklore.* Lincoln: University of Nebraska Press, 1966.

Wilson, Dorothy C. *Bright Eyes: The Story of Susette La Flesche, an Omaha Indian.* NY: McGraw-Hill, 1974.